Propaganda in
an Open Society

Recent Titles in
Contributions in American History
Series Editor: Jon L. Wakelyn

PROPAGANDA IN AN OPEN SOCIETY:
The Roosevelt Administration and the Media, 1933–1941

RICHARD W. STEELE

Contributions in American History, Number 111

Greenwood Press
Westport, Connecticut • London, England

Library of Congress Cataloging in Publication Data

Steele, Richard W.
  Propaganda in an open society.

  (Contributions in American history, ISSN 0084-9219 ;
no. 111)
  Bibliography: p.
  Includes index.
  1. Government and the press—United States—History
—20th century. 2. United States—Politics and
government—1933-1945. I. Title. II. Series.
PN4738.S8 1985   071'.3   84-27931
ISBN 0-313-24830-3 (lib. bdg.)

Library of Congress Catalog Card Number: 84-27931
ISBN: 0-313-24830-3
ISSN: 0084-9219

First published in 1985

Greenwood Press
A division of Congressional Information Service, Inc.
88 Post Road West
Westport, Connecticut 06881

Printed in the United States of America

10 9 8 7 6 5 4 3 2 1

To my mother

Contents

Introduction

Franklin D. Roosevelt was determined to utilize his office to the fullest to meet the challenges of economic collapse and Axis expansionism. He was, however, far less certain in each instance as to what precisely he would do. He was by nature and experience disposed to flexibility, and the absence of pat solutions to problems that were at once complex and evolving reinforced his penchant for improvisation. One thing that was certain, however, was that experiment and innovation would test the public's patience and his capacity to ensure it. When Roosevelt characterized the nation's problem at his first inaugural as "fear itself," he was giving initial expression to a major theme of his entire presidency. The cooperation and political support upon which national achievement depended would rest on public faith. When FDR asked skeptical investors to redeposit their money in a discredited banking system or defense workers hungering for higher wages to forgo strikes, he drew mainly on the good will his government commanded. Moreover, the President realized that his enormous undertakings would inevitably give rise to serious mistakes and setbacks which, in the absence of public confidence, would generate the fears and skepticism upon which political opposition would fatten. In short, successful experimentation required the time and the relatively free hand that made an effective public relations program a necessary part of government.

The task was not to be taken lightly. A faulty approach could increase rather than alleviate the administration's problems. Americans were wary of the palpable manipulation they commonly associated with "propaganda," and any effort so identified was likely to produce disbelief and hostility. Roosevelt had to mount an educational effort that was believable, but not unnecessarily candid; unobtrusive, yet pervasive.

Content presented few problems. FDR believed that popular approval required only a public fully and sympathetically informed of his efforts, and this fundamental idea formed the basis of his administration's informational strategy. It was not the message, however, but the command of the media that constituted the real propaganda challenge confronting the President. It was the extent and the manner in which what the President said and his administration did was made known that would shape the public's image of government. These were decisions that rested ultimately with the privately owned media. Those who determined newspaper, radio, and movie policy were beyond the President's authority to command. They were moved by a whole range of circumstances, prejudices, and hopes susceptible only in part to the influences the White House could bring to bear. It was FDR's task to extend and use the leverage he had in what would be, like so many other aspects of the exercise of power, a test of his political skills.

Results were not always satisfactory, and from time to time Roosevelt would consider alternatives to the informational strategy and the voluntarist approach. But such ideas, born of frustration, never materialized, and ultimately the government's image was shaped by neither a centralized propaganda bureau nor by government operated communications outlets (both of which were suggested), but by the President and his staff skillfully managing the tenuous and largely informal set of "alliances" and understandings he cultivated. The process by which these White House–media relationships were formed, tested, altered, and used are the substance of the following account.

I should like at this point to acknowledge the help of those who have contributed most to this work. The archivists at the several research institutions mentioned in the bibliography rendered uniformly courteous and helpful service. I benefitted also from several San Diego State University Foundation grants, and from a timely academic leave from the university. My colleagues Joyce Appleby, Howard Kushner, and Richard Ruetten encouraged me in the project and were the source of many useful suggestions.

My chief debt is to my wife Elaine. In this, as in similar endeavors of mine, she supplied moral support, critical judgment, and her considerable skills as a professional editor.

1

A New Deal in Government Public Relations

Political leaders have always been concerned to one degree or another with reaching the public with positive images of themselves and convincing accounts of their intentions and exploits. But in the United States, as Robert Hilderbrand has recently shown, systematic and continuous efforts to influence public opinion by conscious use of the press did not begin until William McKinley instituted a series of innovations which would ultimately become standard White House practice.[1] These reflected the important role the press had come to play in the formation of public opinion. The emergence of the national wire services and other developments speeding the distribution of news meant that a single version of events in Washington could quickly be made known to millions of readers throughout the nation, and the potential for shaping public opinion made efforts to manage the press likely. McKinley, confronted with the public relations problems arising out of his foreign policies, seized the opportunity to launch the presidency into what would become its dominant mode in relations with the mass media.

Press manipulation begins with knowledge of what the newspapers are writing on issues of interest to the government, and one of the practices initiated by the McKinley White House was the collection of information on press attitudes. Monitoring the press was, of course, but a prelude to influencing the way in which reporters covered national affairs. McKinley moved toward assuring that he would have constant access to the press, and possibly the sympathy of reporters, by making certain that the White House correspondents were comfortably situated and kept supplied with timely news. When news might have its best effect by appearing unconnected with its White House origins, Mc-Kinley often employed the calculated news "leak."

Under Theodore Roosevelt, news management took on an added dimension. His outgoing personality encouraged direct and friendly press–White House relations, thus potentially expanding the president's influence. Moreover, "T. R." was what might now be termed a "media personality" and this, along with his insistence on dealing with the press directly, helped keep him in the public eye. His reformist temper inevitably meant that techniques confined by his predecessor to foreign policy issues were used by Roosevelt to ensure a favorable hearing for his domestic programs. The stepped up manipulation of the press was also encouraged by the reformer's need to offset the power of the "interests" with that of an aroused public. Nevertheless, Roosevelt's contributions, according to Hilderbrand, remained essentially extensions of the techniques pioneered by McKinley. William Howard Taft, to whom Roosevelt turned over the presidency, had neither T. R.'s ebullience nor his commitment to an activist, "progressive" government. His refusal to utilize the practices he inherited produced strained relations with the now neglected press, and his administration suffered as a consequence.

The foundations of executive management of public opinion were completed during the administration of Woodrow Wilson. Wilson presided over a government that was active in both foreign and domestic affairs, and he shared the progressive's sense of the power of public opinion and the danger from such opinion if left uninstructed. Moreover, while he did not have a personality that endeared him to reporters, he was comfortable and practiced in the persuasive arts and he at least commanded the attention and respect of journalists. Wilson's successors are indebted to him for the precedent of regularly scheduled press conferences and for the various rules and restrictions that attended this practice. He also initiated government use of motion pictures. The Committee on Public Information, created by Wilson immediately after American involvement in the World War, was critically important. Under the direction of George Creel, this agency expanded upon and centralized existing techniques of public relations and news management. The precedents of the Wilson era, important in themselves, were particularly significant in their contribution to the education of Franklin D. Roosevelt, who, together with his chief media advisors, served in Wilson's administration and drew many ideas from the experience.

By the 1920s there was a corps of Washington correspondents accustomed to "gathering" news in the nation's capital (usually from official briefings or "handouts"), and a variety of techniques for taking full advantage of press dependence had been firmly established. The potential of government news management was not reached, however, until the combination of personality and circumstances made Franklin D. Roosevelt the natural heir to the tradition established by McKinley, Theodore Roosevelt, and Wilson.

The Harding and Coolidge administrations added little to the development of news management techniques and did not fully utilize those already available to them. An important exception to this generalization was provided by Herbert Hoover. As Secretary of Commerce under the two Republican administrations, he had demonstrated familiarity and receptivity to the public relations practices of his mentor, Woodrow Wilson. Ironically, while Hoover proved himself adept in dealing with the press, the facility eluded him at precisely the time it might have been of the most service to him and the nation. Catapulted into the presidency in 1929 at least partly as a result of his skillful use of the media, Hoover was soon confronted with one of the greatest crises to befall the nation. But faced with the seemingly intractable problems of economic collapse, Hoover became uncommunicative, hostile, and ultimately all but totally estranged from the press. He had correctly identified public faith in the economic system and the people who ran it as the critical key to recovery, but his isolation contributed to the public's loss of confidence and to the deepening gloom and economic depression that enveloped the nation. His performance made reporters eager for change, and they welcomed FDR's promise of a new deal in White House press relations akin to the one he pledged the nation. They were not disappointed.

The attitudes and skills required to utilize the media effectively came easily to the new President. As perhaps no other political leader of his time, FDR was concerned with public opinion and confident of his ability to reach and mold it. Propaganda—that is, the more or less systematic effort to shape mass attitudes on controversial issues—was not something that had to be sold to FDR or imposed on him by wily or cynical media advisors. The disposition to form public opinion and a keen sense of how this might be done were integral parts of his political outlook. At the most basic level his sensitivity grew from his extraordinary interest in people. Meeting Americans from all strata of society, listening to their concerns, and comparing notes with other politicians on the state of the public mind was a passion he exhibited from the outset of his political career. During his campaigns for the presidency and while in office, his frequent trips to various parts of the country, under security restrictions much less stringent than have since become the rule, gave him ample opportunity to see the people and be seen by them. He supplemented the impressions gained from these contacts with reports from his wife, Eleanor, and from other "agents," official and unofficial, who continuously supplied him with tales of their own travels. Other accounts came to him in the flood of White House mail which he regularly and systematically sampled. With good reason, Roosevelt was proud of his masterly grasp of public attitudes, telling a group of newspaper editors that he was "more closely in touch with public opinion in the United States that any individual in this room."[2] Roosevelt's remarks were meant to humble those who occasionally sought to substitute their judgement for his, but on reflection his audience could hardly have disputed his claim—one which, with equal justice, he could have addressed to any group.

Roosevelt's efforts to reach out to the public reflected an ideological commitment as well. As Graham J. White has recently observed, Roosevelt saw himself as a latter-day Jefferson battling for the rights of the "people" against a Hamiltonian minority of wealth and privilege.[3] FDR felt impelled to run the government on behalf of the broad mass of Americans and this, in turn, encouraged him to seek the public's perception of its needs. Nevertheless, for all his populist sympathies and the inspiration and justification he found in public support, FDR was not content merely to mirror popular opinion. He was confident of his own judgements and, where public attitudes departed from his own, he was ill disposed to follow the voice of the people passively. Although he might retreat before a strong expression of public interest that he could not immediately change, his instinct was to educate—to lead.[4] He believed that most Americans were sensible and rational and disposed to support his programs if they understood them. Convinced that the public wanted what he did, he attributed opposition to ignorance or the negative propaganda sponsored by the minority that stood to lose from his policies. The "real" people need not be harangued or propagandized, merely informed. His ideal was an exchange of ideas among citizens and their elected officials from which all would gain. The size of the nation made this difficult, but he joined other New Dealers in the hope that by actively sounding out opinion and keeping the public well informed the administration would be able to create what Secretary of Labor Francis Perkins called a "modern substitute for the old town meeting, and the talk around the stove."[5]

The practical value of this new political intimacy was not lost on the President or his associates. To an extent unprecedented in American politics, the administration, and the Democratic party, had an opportunity to build voter loyalty by what government did. If this was to happen, however, the people would have to be made fully aware of administration goals and achievements. A large volume of information concerning the government's titanic struggle against economic collapse was likely to impress the mass of American voters with the new regime's concern for the "forgotten man" and its willingness and capacity to act.[6] Ultimately, of course, the fate of the New Deal would rest on the extent of the relief, recovery, and reform it achieved. No public relations effort could sell Americans on a record of failure. What it could do was provide the time and tolerance that would allow the administration to carry out its plans.

Roosevelt made every effort to start with a clean slate—to disassociate himself from his predecessor. Inherent in the idea of a new deal was both the chance to take a different tack in dealing with the depression and the promise of a better result. But until the pledge implicit in the slogan was redeemed, the administration would have to command the public's patience and cooperation. To this end FDR sought to impress upon Americans both the difficulty of the task they faced together and the scope and promise of his efforts.

A vigorous educational effort was also implicit in the new government's outlook. Herbert Hoover had stressed the limited and self-correcting nature of the depression, partly at least to explain his own restrained response. In the same way Roosevelt's decision to tackle the depression head-on made it essential to impress upon the American people the gravity of their situation and the need for extraordinary government measures. Moreover, Roosevelt's initial recovery program required voluntary public cooperation which could be elicited only from a people impressed by the collective responsibility for political and economic change. "It is your problem, no less than it is mine," he told the American people in regard to the banking crisis in March 1933, and so it was for a whole range of issues confronting the nation during the depression and the international crisis that followed.[7]

Roosevelt believed public education had to be closely attuned to the specific and immediate needs of those to whom it was addressed. He thought of the depression in terms of the personal tragedies it brought and he wished to identify his programs with the practical relief they offered. The depression to him, he told his associates, was the mother and nine children confined to bed while the tenth wore the family clothing in search of food.[8] He urged officials to picture their constituents and their problems in the same down-to-earth way. Use information, he said, "that appeals to the audience you are going to address. There is no use telling audiences in Worcester, Massachusetts, about what is being done . . . on a reclamation job in Utah. They are not just [*sic*] interested."[9] Americans, he believed, would not easily be moved by ideology or altruism alone, and although his remarks often carried such appeals they tended more often toward the practical.

While FDR believed he could successfully tap the good sense of the American people, he was conscious of certain difficulties he would face. Just as he anticipated that most people were inclined by self-interest to follow his lead, he also knew that there were those who would fight to defend their privilege or to further their radical ambitions. Not only were these people beyond reach and reason, they would do their best to distort the truth and keep it from reaching the vast majority. Establishing the bond he sought with the public was thus never simply a task of education, but of education combined with active opposition to the smaller number of people at each political extreme whom he counted upon to oppose him under almost any circumstances. The anti-democratic or un-American character of the people who made up the opposition to his programs would provide the President with a major rationale for his policies. These "enemies of the people" were put to use by Roosevelt, who often defined his program by those who stood to lose by it. During the New Deal the reform shoe pinched the selfish, privileged, wealthy elite. During the pre-war years it was the Nazi-inspired and connected American fifth column. With enemies like these, he implied, he must be doing something right.

The task of informing the public would rest primarily with the President, but it could not be accomplished by him alone. Public appearances reached relatively few; radio broadcasts, while an apparent solution, were limited by Roosevelt's fear that calling on citizens in this manner too frequently would erode his welcome and diminish the effect of his words. The public's political education, whether FDR conducted it or not, would be carried primarily in the form of news, not by public speeches. The continuous chronicle of public affairs provided by newspapers was still the public's chief source of political information in the early 1930s, and the press, through familiarity if nothing else, dominated White House thinking on public relations. It was, however, a medium that entailed certain dangers which FDR would have to offset if it was to fulfill its propaganda potential. Unlike meeting the people on the stump or reaching them over the air waves, newspapers might neglect what the President had to say, disclose what he wished hidden, emphasize or deemphasize news in ways that might hurt him. FDR's task was to make and provide news in a way that, so far as possible, encouraged journalists to report administration affairs as he saw them.

I

Roosevelt's sensitivity to the needs of the press was reflected in and enhanced by the men he chose to advise him on public relations policy. Each had come to his attention early in his political career and had participated in one or more of his pre-presidential election campaigns. The earliest of these advisors, and FDR's closest friend and confidant, was Louis Howe. A reporter for the New York *Herald* covering Albany, Howe was chosen by FDR to handle publicity in his 1912 campaign for the New York State senate. Thus began a long association which ended with Howe's death in 1936. The contrast between Howe, frequently described as an "ugly little man," and the handsome young Roosevelt belied the strong personal attachment that developed between them. When their combined efforts ultimately brought Roosevelt the presidency it was natural that Howe would come to the White House too. Serving with the impressive title of Secretary to the President, he acted as FDR's advisor on public relations and other political matters.[10]

Joining Howe on Roosevelt's original White House staff was Marvin McIntyre. A city editor for the Washington *Times* before World War I, "Mac," as he was commonly known, had gone to work for the wartime propaganda organization, the Creel Committee, and had been assigned to serve as publicity director for the Department of the Navy. It was in this capacity that he met Roosevelt, then Assistant Secretary. When the Democrats nominated FDR as their vice-presidential candidate in 1920, he chose Howe to run the campaign and McIntyre to direct publicity. After Roosevelt's defeat, McIntyre took a position in the rapidly growing newsreel industry but rejoined Roosevelt as his publicity director when the latter launched his campaign for the presidency in 1932. Success led to Mac's appointment as one of two presidential Assistant Secretaries. His primary responsibility was White House appointments, but from that post he continued to contribute the value of his wide acquaintanceship among journalists and newsreel men, and the public relations savvy he had acquired during many years of newspaper work.[11]

Although McIntyre may have expected to be assigned the task of handling White House press relations, that post went to the younger, more vigorous, and more able Stephen T. Early.[12] His experience was remarkably similar to that of his colleagues, but he was temperamentally better suited to the job. First a reporter for a Washington newspaper and later for the Associated Press, Early had encountered Roosevelt while covering the Navy Department during the Wilson administration. The relationship ripened and in 1920 FDR asked him to serve as "advance man" in his campaign for the vice presidency. He proved exceptionally effective, assuring that the candidate was briefed on local affairs and that his appearances were well covered by the press. Following the Democratic defeat, Early embarked on a successful career as an executive for Paramount Newsreels, serving in Washington. He kept in close contact with FDR who, after the 1932 election, invited him to serve as White House press secretary. Although Early had anticipated short-term employment and frequently expressed hopes of resuming a career outside of government, he stayed with Roosevelt to the end. During that time he played a role second only to the President's in managing relations with the press. He was by all accounts extraordinarily able, perhaps the most effective press secretary ever to serve in the White House.

The success of Early and, to a lesser extent, of Howe and McIntyre, derived from their knowledge of the news business and public relations, the press's confidence in their integrity, and the close professional rapport they enjoyed with the President. They knew reporting well enough to translate events and information into news and to cater to the peculiar needs of the newsmen covering the President. Early, in particular, got on well with reporters and knew many of them personally. They sensed his honesty and believed, with considerable justice, that he had their interests in mind as he carried out his White House functions. Early was apolitical and able to view government activities with rather more detachment than other members of the administration. He would often act as the newsman's friend at court, advising Roosevelt of press sensitivities and tempering FDR's inclination to strike out at offending journalists. The result was that the White House staff was able to overcome, at least for a time, those forces in the nature of government-press intercourse that tended toward adversity and to construct a relationship which served the interests of both sides.[13]

By design and happenstance the Roosevelt regime was a constant source of news. The pace of New Deal activity was frenetic and when the political tempo flagged, FDR, one of his five children, his peripatetic wife, or one of his many controversial subordinates was apt to do something that made headlines. Nevertheless, as inherently event filled as the Roosevelt regime was, and as skillful as the President and his staff were in maximizing its news value, reporters' hunger for material was never quite satisfied. They demanded not only a large volume of news, but a steady supply. This appetite for information on national affairs created an opportunity for the administration to keep itself and its activities constantly before the public. If little "hard news" was available (or even if it was) the administration could at least make certain that journalists were never at a loss for material illuminating the government's activities. Never had the Washington press corps found the task of gathering news easier or more pleasant, and for the first time since the onset of the depression, informed, timely, and sympathetic stories on national affairs flowed from Washington in great number.

Reporters began each day with a briefing from Early, during which the press secretary described FDR's schedule and suggested the stories that might develop during the day. If questions arose for which Early did not have answers, he would ferret them out. If nothing newsworthy was developing, Early was still prepared. With FDR's help he customarily set aside announcements of no immediacy for use on "slow news days." Forthcoming events might be announced well in advance so that they did not go unnoticed. Following a presidential speech, Early was ready with statistical reports on the telegram and mail responses—invariably positive—and the estimated size of the President's radio audience (very high). If in spite of Early's best efforts reporters came away with erroneous or otherwise undesirable reports, he was ready with a response. A wire service teletype machine which he had installed in his office enabled him to monitor the earliest press service reports and offer timely corrections or rebuttals if need be.

News from the White House was not only ample and timely, it was also creditable. Reporters could use it with the assurance that those responsible would stand by what they said. It had not always been so. In the past, officials had hidden behind unnamed "White House sources," thus remaining free to repudiate stories should an adverse reaction make this expedient. Early did away with these anonymous sources, permitting reporters to name him or the President as the origin of statements made for publication. Reporters appreciated both the candor reflected in this policy and the protection they now enjoyed from what had been a source of irritation and embarrassment.[14]

The administration's greatest asset in dealing with the press was Roosevelt. FDR enjoyed the press game. He was generally tolerant of reporters' persistent quests for a story, and he liked being the source of news and in a position to call on his experience as editor of the Harvard *Crimson* to advise journalists on their craft. Few in the Washington press corps had seen the likes of him, and only his uncle Teddy stood comparison. Press conferences since Theodore Roosevelt's time had been sometime affairs, often stilted, formal, and uninformative. Under FDR's predecessors, reporters were obliged to submit their questions in advance, and the president had responded only to those he selected. Such encounters naturally lacked spontaneity, interest, and, usually, news.

Roosevelt, by contrast, conferred with reporters regularly and frequently (generally twice weekly). Their meetings were pleasant, open and informal, usually taking place in the intimacy (some would say, the cramped confines) of the President's office. As reporters entered they would find Roosevelt seated behind his cluttered desk. As they crowded around him, the regulars and his favorites up front, he would chat with several he had come to know. On the signal "all in," FDR would typically begin with a formal announcement on some current issue and then for the next half hour or so he would lean back and field questions with responses that ranged from subtle avoidance to extended exposition, all delivered in a friendly bantering manner that frequently brought laughter from the assemblage.[15] Roosevelt was acutely conscious of the news value of his public statements and often would provide reporters with suggestions as to possible headlines or leads. His characterization of the Supreme Court's invalidation of the National Recovery Administration codes as based on a "horse and buggy" interpretation of the Constitution was a classic example of the kind of presidential headline-making reporters would become accustomed to. Reporters were delighted by his awareness of their craft and its needs, pleased by his eagerness to generate news, and charmed by his manner. As a result, when the President spoke, his remarks were usually fairly and accurately reported, often with the "slant" he had suggested.[16] Most reporters, like most Americans, were sympathetic to the New Deal program. But ideological affinity and personal sympathy for the President did not solely account for the administration's popularity with the press. Rather, it was the ability of the White House to provide a steady supply of readily available news and information. Even the conservatively biased business journals found it expedient to cultivate close and continuing ties with the White House and to print the column-filling copy delivered by the nation's preeminent newsmaker and his staff.[17]

Although much of the news of national affairs was inspired by the White House, the administration's education of the American public only began there. While accounts of the President's speeches and press conferences might dominate the front page of the daily newspapers, there was also much to be learned about the Roosevelt "revolution" in the inside pages. There readers could find factual accounts of various aspects of the administration's program, supplied by one or another of the many federal public relations offices. Their objective was to inform the public as to their agency's work, but in the process they unavoidably helped to sell the New Deal. To what degree this, or indeed any, propaganda shaped public attitudes is uncertain, but some residual, even subliminal message helpful to the administration was unavoidable.

Just as some government agencies had led the way in providing public services and in regulating the economy before the advent of the New Deal, so a few government departments, particularly Agriculture and Commerce, had pioneered in government public relations.[18] But the New Deal, in vastly expanding government activity, also brought a full flowering of federal informational activities. The emergency agencies in particular had a special need to explain their services to would-be beneficiaries and to justify their existence to a somewhat bewildered general public. Soon a torrent of information poured forth from agencies like the Civilian Conservation Corps, the Public Works Administration, and the Social Security Administration, including statistics on the number of youths employed in outdoor projects, glowing reports of the schools, hospitals, and other worthwhile projects under construction, and descriptions of the benefits to be made available to the elderly.

Most of this was not "news" in the sense of discrete current events, but it readily found its way into a press eager for material to fill the space between advertisements. The White House took a keen interest in these activities. When Early assumed office he personally reviewed practices in departmental press offices, selected personnel for the new agencies, and reviewed operating procedures to bring them into conformity with his own ideas on effective publicity. With encouragement and advice from the top, Early's protégés helped the press to bring the administration's story to the public.[19]

A major aspect of New Deal public relations involved demonstrating to various regional constituencies the local application of national programs. FDR insisted that Americans in the nation's widely varied communities know how government policies affected them—how they related to their immediate concerns. His educational efforts reached out in this direction as never before. The program was conducted largely through a unique system of local opinion monitoring and public relations. In the summer of 1933 the President created the National Emergency Council, composed of the heads of various emergency New Deal agencies and executive departments concerned with the recovery program. This "super cabinet" met every other week with Roosevelt and an Executive Director to discuss the progress of New Deal programs. The operating element of the organization was a corps of State Directors charged with coordinating the activities of the federal relief and recovery agencies operating in their states and with keeping the Council informed of any problems that arose. To these ends, the State Directors continuously sounded out local officials and community leaders and monitored editorial opinion in their states for evidence of popular dissatisfaction. Should it surface, the State Director was responsible for initiating corrective action. Where this was either impossible or undesirable, he might arrange for a suitable state-wide educational campaign.[20]

Information tailored specifically for the small town and rural newspaper reader was an important aspect of the local propaganda effort. In 1933, more than 17.5 million Americans received all or most of their printed news from about 6,700 weekly or less frequently appearing newspapers. Large numbers of others depended on small city dailies. Most of the news in these papers was local by editorial choice or necessity. Although some papers subscribed to lesser news services which catered to rural and weekly publications, few could afford national correspondents. This meant that some rural communities were, if not isolated, at least somewhat more detached from national affairs than the bulk of the nation's urban populace. Here were people, many of whom were out of the mainstream of American political life, possibly indifferent or even suspicious of centralized government, who could be more closely integrated into a national society and given a sympathetic portrait of the New Deal. Early took up the challenge. Having assessed rural news needs, he offered the small journals news of government in a format that many found too tempting to pass up. Thus, he supplied subscribers with special feature stories on government activities either on "clip sheets" or on mats from which a subscribing newspaper could cast a stereotype plate. These articles, written mostly by public relations officers, might be datelined Washington, but in most instances no source was indicated. Where a byline was included it would frequently name some senior administration official. Many papers ran these "canned articles"; a small number also subscribed regularly to a question-and-answer column on government activities. Some even ran administration-made political cartoons.[21]

On both the local and national level, publicity was often developed in response to the changing views and attitudes of opinion leaders. A Division of Press Intelligence attached to the Executive Council provided the administration with an elaborate clipping service supervised by Louis Howe and patterned after one he had used to keep Roosevelt informed of "public opinion" during his several election campaigns. The Division drew clippings from at least one newspaper in every American city of 50,000 or more, divided them into categories representing news and editorial coverage of various issues, tabulated the results, and issued these as a daily "intelligence report."[22] These, along with the reports from the State Directors, were available to Early who, in cooperation with the Executive Council's Committee on Publicity, recommended national publicity campaigns to be carried out by the public relations offices of the appropriate federal agencies.[23]

By the end of 1933, government publicists were producing approximately a thousand public releases per month. Usually written by former newspapermen, they were in a style and format requiring minimum rewriting or editing. At first all that one of the 300 or so reporters covering the nation's capital needed to do to turn up "news" was to make the rounds of the public relations offices and pick up the latest "handout." This he might file as he found it, or interlard with information readily obtainable from administration officials who had been encouraged by the White House to make themselves accessible. The process was made more convenient when Early arranged to have these government stories deposited at the National Press Club where reporters could shop without a trek around town. Material obtained in this manner was distributed by the wire services and printed in hundreds of newspapers across the nation, often with no indication of their actual source.[24] These releases, together with daily briefings by Early and twice weekly meetings with the President, were enough to ensure the major daily newspapers their fill of news from Washington.

Such procedures fit the needs of reporters who were expected to turn up news but were generally not encouraged to do the kind of investigative journalism that serious news gathering required. Early did not invent the practice of massive spoon feeding of the press. Conceived by the public relations industry before World War I, the process matured under the Creel Committee during the war and thrived in the 1920s as both private enterprise (most notoriously the public utilities industry) and government (especially Hoover's Department of Commerce) made extensive use of the press handout. Changes in reporting accompanied and reinforced the growth of the new government-press relationship.[25] The competition for "scoops" and the hot pursuit of new angles and exposés, the kind of reporting for which Early himself had earned a measure of fame, gave way in the 1920s to the less dramatic, more productive routine of attending news conferences and collecting official releases. Early was not enamored of the system and made a point of denying that his office had ever given out a prepared story. He was, however, responsible for perfecting procedures that had developed in the years since he had been a cub reporter.[26]

The goal of the Early/Roosevelt propaganda approach was to raise public consciousness of New Deal goals and achievements by supplying news and information in copious quantities.[27] The strategy was not new but the skill and thoroughness with which it was applied made it "revolutionary" in the same limited sense that the New Deal itself was revolutionary. This informational propaganda was not especially tendentious, but relied instead on the expectation that Americans in viewing the administration's real accomplishments through the prism of the selected facts it provided would convince themselves that the New Deal was on the right track. The strength of this educational effort was its credibility, its factualness, and its dissemination through the medium from which Americans customarily received their political instruction—

the daily press. Its weakness was that the "facts" did not always suggest the government's competence, or confidence, or that recovery lay just around the corner. Moreover, the press upon which the administration depended could not be counted upon to accentuate the positive and overlook the negative in portraying current events.

Early realized that the newspaper cooperation upon which New Deal public relations depended was uncertain, and he made every effort to cultivate a bond between the White House and journalists. For a short time good relations thrived under his careful cultivation, the novelty of the New Deal, and the integrity with which the White House handled the news and newsmen. But during 1934, as the administration was increasingly, and probably inevitably, subject to press criticism for its mistakes, FDR and other New Dealers challenged the objectivity of the press, as well as its value to the nation. Under these circumstances, Early could do no more than slow the process by which the earlier affinity based on mutuality of interest gave way to the adversary relationship more typical of government-press dealings. As it did, White House interest turned to the more stable and fruitful relationship that had been established with the nation's radio broadcasters.

II

From the outset, the New Dealers had recognized the educational potential of radio and had sought to put the medium to maximum political use. While newspapers had been encouraged to serve government informational needs by their hunger for news, radio's cooperation stemmed mainly from the broadcasters' acute awareness of their vulnerability to government regulation. Radio's sensitivity to political pressure rested in large part on its unique subjection to federal regulation. Although the First Amendment had been interpreted by the courts as guaranteeing a press free of official control, the airways enjoyed no such immunity from governmental intervention. A system of federal licensing of radio stations had grown out of the need to assign broadcasters separate transmitting frequencies. Without it, broadcasting would have rapidly descended into the chaotic babble of overlapping and interloping competition that appeared at first to be its fate. As a result, since 1927 when Congress created the Federal Radio Commission (FRC), radio stations operated at the sufferance of federal regulators.

In 1934 the Radio Commission was replaced by the Federal Communications Commission (FCC) which combined in a single agency the regulation of interstate radio, telephone, and telegraph communication. The new Commission, which was almost identical to its predecessor in regard to radio, was specifically charged with assuring that the issuance of licenses was consistent with "the public interest, convenience, or necessity." This gave the Commission authority to choose between applicants for broadcasting rights and to prescribe rules and regulations, mostly technical in nature, designed to ensure the orderly use of the ether. Licenses were granted for only six months, at which time they were subject to review and possible revocation for flagrant violation of federal regulations. Moreover, increases in station broadcasting power and the adoption of new broadcasting modes such as frequency modulation (FM) or television also required FCC approval.

These powers, although great, were at first exercised with considerable restraint. Rejections of renewal applications were rare and, as with most regulatory commissions, a cooperative relationship developed between the agency and the industry. Nevertheless, broadcasters recognized that the potential for political trouble was always present. Adverse rulings on license renewal or applications for changes in operations were possible and the industry was always fearful of unfavorable publicity and additional regulations. The threat of government mischief haunted the industry, as one network executive wrote, like a "death penalty." Another claimed that industry fear of government disapproval acted as an unwanted conscience that could "blue pencil a dozen programs for every one that an official censor might object to."[28]

Broadcasters had reason to fear for their independence. The value of the broadcast license and the propaganda potential of the medium ensured that it would be the object of constant political pressures. Although the Radio Commission and the Federal Communications Commission were by statute independent of executive control, the President appointed their members and influenced their decisions. FDR's appointment of Herbert L. Pettey as Executive Secretary to the Radio Commission put the industry on notice from the outset of his administration that he was not overly concerned with the political independence of the regulatory agency. Pettey was not only a Democrat, as might be expected, but a partisan politician who had previously served as Director of Radio Publicity for the Democratic National Committee.[29] If any doubt remained as to the administration's willingness to influence what was broadcast, it was soon dispelled. In July 1933, the Commission, acting on a recommendation by the President's Secretary, Louis Howe, adopted a procedure by which stations were to supply the regulators with copies of "all addresses on public affairs."[30] With this request came a warning from one Commissioner to broadcasters that should they permit the airing of statements critical of the administration they ran the risk of license revocation.[31] Broadcasters, claiming no right to political independence and unwilling to provoke the administration or the Commission on the issue, accepted the government's intrusive interest.[32]

In succeeding months, but particularly in election years, radio executives were reminded of the politics of broadcasting. In 1936, in separate instances, the White House supported both Massachusetts Democratic leader James Curley and the Chicago Federation of Labor in their efforts to secure additional broadcasting power for politically friendly stations.[33] On other occasions the President, through his secretaries, contacted the FCC Chairman with the object of securing the denial of petitions from applicants he viewed as political enemies.[34] The FCC was not the first or the only regulatory agency to be so used by the executive branch. What is significant is that insofar as incidents of this kind were known to the industry, they indicated FDR's willingness to play politics with the regulation of broadcasting.

Broadcasters sought safety from potentially harmful intervention by proving their value to those in power. The lead in this enterprise was assumed by the large networks, which actively lobbied for their interests among Washington politicians and sought to curry favor at the White House. Three companies operated the four largest "chains" of affiliated stations. The largest of these, the National Broadcasting Company (NBC), owned by the Radio Corporation of America, operated two chains ("Red" and "Blue"); Columbia Broadcasting System (CBS), a third; and after 1935 they were joined by the much smaller Mutual Broadcasting System (MBS). Each of the networks offered programming (usually originating in New York) to locally owned radio stations in exchange for access to that station's broadcasting facilities. The stations received popular, professional productions; the networks a national audience. Provision was also made for the allocation of revenues.

The network corporations, although not directly regulated by the FCC, were deeply concerned by the possibility of further federal regulation of local stations, some of which they owned. Their success depended on the health of the industry as a whole and federal action affecting the profitability of local stations inevitably affected the networks. Moreover, they were themselves vulnerable to investigation, regulation, and possible anti-trust action. NBC's operation of two networks, and various other aspects of network broadcasting arrangements, were the subject of reform interest. Should the forces for change gain the upper hand in Congress, the FCC, the Anti-trust Division of the Department of Justice or at the White House, the networks could be in for serious difficulties.

Each of the two major companies maintained close and friendly relations with the White House. NBC's political affairs were looked after by Vice President Frank M. Russell; CBS's by Henry Bellows, a Democrat, former FRC Commissioner, and a Harvard classmate of the President. Soon after Roosevelt's inauguration both men promised him their network's support. Bellows told Early that ''the close contact between you and the broadcasters has tremendous possibilities of value to the administration, and as a life-long Democrat, I want to pledge my best efforts in making this cooperation successful.'' Over the next several years, Bellows and his successor were to demonstrate repeatedly the genuineness of this commitment. NBC's relations, while also friendly, were not quite as close, and Columbia gained a reputation as the White House favorite.[35]

Friendship included gestures like arranging for a summer job for one of the President's sons and an offer to Early of employment on his retirement from government service.[36] But it also meant providing free and extensive government programming and ultimately a tacit commitment to keep the air relatively free of anti-administration commentary. Cooperation flowed from simple expedience. The broadcasters realized they were vulnerable. Their voluntarism provided a powerful argument against sanctions or additional regulations. In October 1934, the FCC entertained a proposal which would have obliged broadcasters to donate a specific amount of airtime for ''educational programming.'' Frank Russell of NBC protested that radio was already fulfilling its public service function and needed no government mandate. Using the administration's categorization of government speeches as ''educational,'' Russell pointed out that in the year ending September 1934 his network alone had carried 871 such broadcasts totalling 250 hours, without charge. The issue was dropped.[37]

The President's idea of responsible journalism and the broadcasters' idea of sensible news and public affairs programming dovetailed nicely.

Roosevelt once told the Society of Newspaper Editors that an ideal newspaper was one which carried no editorials and covered controversial stories "in [short] parallel columns on the front page, . . . so that the reading public will get both sides at the same time."[38] Roosevelt did not say it, but he also expected his model newspaper would carry large amounts of mostly neutral information concerning the operations of government. While the newspapers never matched the President's ideal, radio would exceed his most extravagant expectations. Everything the administration had to say went over the airwaves without the intercession of reporters, editors, or publishers. Not only did radio carry the government's message without adulteration, it carried it farther, more immediately, and more effectively than newspapers. A nationwide "hookup" simultaneously reached millions, including many never touched by newspapers. And, given the proper speaker, it reached them in a form more readily understood than the printed statement.[39]

During the 1932 campaign, Herbert Pettey, then Director of Radio Publicity for the Democratic National Committee, and other party officials began thinking about exploiting this medium to promote "greater national consciousness of Democratic Party interests." Two years later, with its plans complete and the Democrats in office, the Committee's Executive Secretary, Richard Roper, described radio's role in government and party propaganda. "The average American's mind works very simply," he wrote, "and it is not hard to keep him behind the President if we can properly inform him as to what is going on in Washington, what the President is trying to do and the *specific objectives* the President is seeking." This could best be accomplished, Roper suggested, if citizens were provided with "facts" from sources in which they had confidence—the President, members of his Cabinet, and other public officials and community leaders. By 1934, it had become clear that newspapers could not be depended upon to do the job, and Roper saw radio as "a means of reaching the public that is independent of the newspapers"; a way to "make absolutely sure that the public gets all the facts we wish to present."[40]

Although the Democrats could not afford the airtime they wanted, over the next several years the party was to realize its radio objectives as network executives extended to the administration nearly as much "public service" airtime as it could use. Although the messages were not quite as tendentious as Democrats might have wished, they nonetheless served to establish the link between government programs and citizen welfare. This, as Democratic leaders realized, was the key to the party's fortunes.

FDR and his associates were especially able to capitalize on radio's generosity. Unlike their Republican predecessors, the New Dealers had a story to tell in their efforts to combat the economic difficulties that confronted the nation. The Republicans would have found relatively little value in unlimited airtime given their circumscribed philosophy of governmental power. Herbert Hoover, in particular, had much to explain, but, alas, little to say that would satisfy the public. Moreover, while the publicly morose and muttering Hoover could not do justice to what he did do, in Roosevelt the New Deal had a master dramatist— a radio performer of "star" quality. His delivery was the envy of professionals. His speeches were well paced, his voice clear, natural, and convincing. Those moved by his eloquence to write letters to the White House testified to the compassionate fatherly image he conveyed and the confidence his voice inspired.[41] The quality of his broadcasts may be judged by the large audiences they attracted and the volume of letters they generated. So many people tuned in to listen to the President that unaffiliated stations carrying other programming at the same time found themselves without audiences. Their complaints and the White House's interest in remedying them led the administration to arrange for such stations to obtain the President's addresses from the networks free of charge so that they could participate in these popular events.[42]

Although Roosevelt had an instinctive understanding and flair for the use of radio, his success was also the product of careful White House planning and attention to technique. FDR, for example, deliberately limited his radio appearances to preserve their impact, averaging only about 25 network broadcasts per year, including two or three fireside chats. Working with a staff of speech writers, FDR crafted his comments with considerable care. Each address was heralded by pre-broadcast publicity and scheduled at a time, usually between nine and eleven in the evening, that ensured the greatest number of listeners. To sustain audience attention and to avoid imposing on the hospitality of the networks, the President would generally speak for no more than a half hour.[43]

The networks, which carried Presidential addresses as a matter of course, also generously extended the privilege to lesser administration lights. During the first ten months of the New Deal the nation was to hear twenty talks by the President, seventeen more by Mrs. Roosevelt, and 107 by members of the Cabinet.[44] In addition, the networks voluntarily produced large numbers of special political education programs, often featuring administration figures. Louis Howe, the President's Secretary, was the "star" of one such show. Howe's deep and cultured voice was heard weekly on NBC for the first nine months of the new administration; a performance for which he was generously remunerated. His fifteen-minute discussions of administration happenings took the form of an "interview"; however, both questions and answers were prepared in advance, often in consultation with FDR.[45]

The networks carried hundreds of hours of informational programming like this. Some were no more than one-minute "spot" announcements, but others included lengthy "specials" or weekly series similar to Howe's. Among the programs produced and provided by the networks themselves was "Of the People, By the People, For the People," created by CBS in 1935 to celebrate the New Deal's second anniversary. In this production, after professional actors recreated great moments in the administration's brief history, the "actual participants" discussed the events depicted. CBS arranged through the Office of Education to have civics and government classes listen to the two-hour program and even provided supplementary reading materials. Military bands supplied the proper musical setting for what was obviously intended as a patriotic extravaganza. About the same time, NBC put on a more modest program in which New Dealer Donald Richberg discussed the administration's accomplishments during 1934.[46]

By 1936 the Roosevelt regime had far outstripped its predecessor in its use of the medium and was rapidly expanding its already impressive radio presence. In March, at least three government agencies had dramatic radio programs currently on the air, and many others were soliciting the networks for time. The apparent imminent saturation of the medium led Early to seek ways to screen the flood of official requests to ensure the best use of broadcast time.[47] Early was also concerned that government agencies not embarrass the networks or the administration with overtly tendentious requests. As both he and the broadcasting executives recognized, the continuation of virtually unlimited programming depended on the plausible claim that it was a non-controversial public service.

From the administration's perspective what radio did *not* air was as important as what it did. The newspapers continued to carry large quantities of government-originated information throughout the 1930s, but the fact that they were often critical or skeptical on one page of what they had faithfully described on another would eventually lead to a break with the White House. The broadcasters sought to avoid this "problem" by adopting a stance of political neutrality. By this they meant that while they would carry administration information as a public service, they would discourage significant criticism of government policies.

The practice began for the Roosevelt administration hours after the President had taken the oath of office when he ordered the closure of the nation's banks, setting in motion a plan to end the nation's banking crisis. NBC did its part by putting into effect a policy which limited discussion of the banking situation on its networks to statements by the President and his official family. In the week beginning with inauguration day, an NBC official would later inform the President, the network would air twelve-and-a-half hours of such material while critics were provided no time at all.[48]

Other early examples of self-censorship include a 1933 decision by NBC officials to warn the Massachusetts American Legion that they would not permit Legion broadcasts to undermine public confidence in the President. That same year, CBS refused broadcast time to speakers who intended to criticize administration recognition of the Soviet Union, and in 1934 it denied time for an attack on the National Recovery Administration.[49] "Objectivity" of this kind was of particular value to the incumbents during an election year, especially in contrast to the hostile coverage the administration often found in the press. Following FDR's stunning victory in the 1936 election, Harry Butcher, a close friend of Early's who represented CBS, wrote congratulating the President on his triumph and—not incidentally—pointing to the contrast between the benevolent neutrality of radio and the "80 to 85 percent" of the press which supposedly opposed the President.[50]

The networks did what they could to ensure the neutral medium that both they and the administration wanted—but they could not do everything. Their greatest problem was the Reverend Charles Coughlin. In January 1931, concerned by the radio priest's attacks on the Hoover administration, CBS tactfully suggested that he tone down his criticism. Coughlin openly defied the attempt at censorship and some months later CBS sought to end its embarrassment by refusing to renew his contract. The transparent excuse was that the network was no longer selling time to religious groups.[51] Rather than accept this partial muzzling, the popular and controversial Coughlin formed a network of independent stations which picked up his speeches over telephone lines and rebroadcast them. In this way, after a short honeymoon with the Roosevelt administration, he was able to circumvent network censorship and continue his assault on government and the ''eastern establishment.'' Although it was not until 1939 that the industry, at network urging, was able to get Coughlin off the air, it was done, thus perfecting radio's role as the informational propaganda medium *par excellence.*[52]

III

Motion pictures offered a promising complement to the informational outlets provided the administration by newspapers and radio. In 1935 nearly 43 million Americans went to the movies at least once each week.[53] Seeking entertainment, they inevitably came away with powerful images of themselves, the life of the nation, and of people far beyond their ken. Indeed, as some have suggested, motion pictures may be the most compelling of all the media, and film propaganda, skillfully done, the most effective.[54] This potential was not immediately or easily exploited by the New Dealers. Unlike the press and broadcasting, the interests of the motion picture industry, except for the newsreel segment, did not draw them into the close natural relationship that developed between the White House and the others. Not until 1936, long after Roosevelt's honeymoon with the press had ended and his solid relationship with the radio had been established, did the administration launch serious efforts to exploit the value of film. Even then success would have to await the advent of the very different political circumstances that would make cooperation with the government attractive to industry leaders.

Effective political use of motion pictures depended on such cooperation. Without it, government film messages were unlikely to have the entertainment value Americans had come to expect from commercially produced movies and were certain to reach no more than a small portion of the movie-going public. Moreover, the didactic value of film, like that of the other media, rested in part on its integration into existing entertainment or informational formats. Messages which stood out were messages likely to be disregarded, and for this reason, too, Washington needed Hollywood.

Ideally, from the administration's perspective, the industry on its own initiative or with minimal guidance and encouragement from government, would make feature films which exposed economic and social problems and suggested that the government's actions promised effective solutions. A significant number of films dealing with contemporary social and political issues were produced in the 1930s, but only a handful came close to fitting this formula. Moreover, productions of this kind were offset by movies which, for example, depicted the plight of the unemployed but contrived to have them rescued by the benevolence of some conscientious rich person; painted unionism as radical rowdyism; overlooked the plight of the rural poor in favor of romanticizing the pastoral life; and suggested that the public's interests were best left to the hardworking, public spirited businessmen and bankers upon whom society's well-being ultimately depended. All in all, although Hollywood in the 1930s moved away from the escapist trivia of the past, its feature films provided the New Dealers with little comfort. Their treatment of reality, according to one distinguished critic, was "for the major part, so inadequate as to render it at times meaningless."[55]

Administration public relations needs were served better by the newsreels, in which the movie-going public found consistent if shallow reminders of New Deal programs and personalities. Five companies produced separate movie versions of the news and distributed them twice weekly to local theaters. Each edition consisted of about ten minutes of dramatically edited and narrated film footage which sampled the world's happenings, emphasizing the visual. Their style was breezy and sensational; their purpose unashamedly entertainment. Nevertheless, they were a major source of America's impressions of contemporary affairs, especially important for those citizens whose low level of literacy put them beyond the reach of newspapers and magazines.[56] The newsreels gave official events a more dramatic and interesting form than did either the newspapers or radio. The film version of politics emphasized the "human side" of the President as no other medium could. Shots of the President playing water polo with fellow polio sufferers at Warm Springs, placidly entertaining and enjoying his grandchildren at Hyde Park, hauling in a fish on a vacation cruise in the Caribbean—all portraits of a vigorous, down-to-earth man, full of confidence and enthusiasm for life—helped perfect his image as the happy warrior.

The administration enjoyed a special advantage in helping to shape the images cast by the newsreels. Like journalists, the newsreel makers were dependent upon government and particularly the White House for a significant portion of their material. Official affairs and particularly the events touching on the President and the "first family" were of enormous public interest. FDR was the nation's premier celebrity and his appearances on film were as attractive to theatergoers as his broadcasts were to radio audiences.[57] Inevitably, newsreel companies in pursuit of their own interests were eager to publicize the President and his works.

Such coverage was in itself of propaganda value, but the nature of the relationship between the White House and the newsreels also ensured that the administration's film image would be generally positive, and never embarrassing to the White House. Those who wished to film the President, or indeed most government activities, needed the cooperation of administration officials and there was no tendency to ignore this fact in editing the newsreel stories. Cameras were bulky, noisy, and required considerable lighting for indoor shots. Access to FDR was a valued privilege granted by the White House so long as the product served the President's interests. Those who accommodated the cameramen dictated the ground rules for coverage.

The White House was peculiarly able to take advantage of the situation. Both Marvin McIntyre and Stephen Early had worked for newsreel companies before joining the White House staff and this earlier association now secured the natural ties that bound industry and White House.[58]

The administration was, of course, not content simply to wait passively for the newsreels to cover its activities. Instead, the New Dealers were moved to create their own documentary film versions of government operations and current events. At first, this effort consisted of the production by New Deal agencies of the kinds of educational films the Department of Agriculture and other agencies had been making for 25 years. By 1937, various administration agencies had available for public use about 200 films, usually one reel in length, which sought in one way or another to describe the work of the sponsoring agency, enlist public support for its activities, or publicize the services it had made available. Although their intent was at least in part to publicize some aspect of the New Deal, their style was invariably cast in the cramped instructional mode employed in "educational" films. Early New Deal films were informative, dull, and hardly suitable for showing outside the small, quasi-captive audiences provided by schools and civic organizations. While a great deal of experimentation with documentary films was under way elsewhere, government ventures into film making during the first half of the 1930s remained narrowly conceived, with little artistic merit or other entertainment value, and consequently had minor political impact.[59]

In 1936 the forthcoming presidential election campaign encouraged administration officials to seek better ways of capitalizing on the potential of film. Harry Hopkins, Director of the Works Progress Administration (WPA), had been inspired by a positive newsreel account of an Indiana WPA project to use this medium to offset the rather poor public image from which he and his relief agency currently suffered. Hopkins turned to the WPA's Motion Picture Record Division to see if it could produce newsreel-like films on the agency's work. Not satisfied with the answer, Hopkins put out bids for a series of 30 such productions and in August 1936 Pathe News was awarded the contract. The scripts proposed by WPA reveal its purposes. One was to show a mother of four on the dole, her children hungry. She is assigned a WPA job as a weaver, is able to sell her products, and become self-supporting. Her children's hunger is satisfied, the mother is happy, and presumably the audience sees the value of the WPA and the New Deal.

The key element of Hopkins' project was his demand for a film product "of such high entertainment standard as to be acceptable for exhibition" in commercial theaters. Indeed, the contract awarded Pathe called upon the company to distribute the film nationally along with its regular newsreel productions. The arrangement drew considerable criticism, not only from the New Deal's political opponents, but from those within the motion picture industry who objected to Hollywood's involvement in the production of government propaganda.[60]

Hopkins' film venture was not repeated, but a vastly more important alternative was in the making. It emerged from the Resettlement Administration (RA), which FDR had created in 1935 to administer the several government programs currently addressing the problem of rural poverty. The Director of the new agency was Rexford Tugwell, a young and enthusiastic New Dealer, who, though he had no personal flair for public relations, understood the importance of educating the public and the Congress to the need for the "revolutionary" schemes being hatched in his agency. His concern led to the creation of one of the largest and most active information operations in government. It was headed by journalist-novelist, and later White House consultant, John Franklin Carter. Among the imaginative projects that emerged from Carter's office was a program for making high-quality still photographs of American life—particularly the less agreeable aspects of rural living "to educate the city dweller to the needs of the rural population."[61]

Motion pictures designed to do the same thing were a natural next step.[62] In 1935, this interest in the educational potential of film brought together RA officials and Pare Lorentz, a film critic, newspaper columnist, and writer who had conceived the idea of a motion picture about the Dust Bowl. Significantly, he proposed to create a documentary of sufficient quality and entertainment value to ensure it a place in commercial movie showings. Although Lorentz had never made a film, he convinced Tugwell of the merits of his project and commenced to make *The Plow That Broke the Plains* (1936) for RA, a project he followed with *The River* (1937), made for RA's successor, the Farm Security Administration. *The Plow*, which had its premier performance in March 1936, provided a historical survey of the settlement of the Great Plains, its overcultivation, and the resultant erosion of its soil. It concluded by depicting the attempts by the RA to meet the human tragedy created by this "unnatural" disaster. Critics lauded the film's moving emotional quality and technical merit, but such praise and the plaudits of Democratic politicians, including the President, did not win Lorentz the Hollywood acceptance he sought. The major studios, which owned the large theater chains and thus dominated commercial film distribution, were reluctant to show the film. The reason is not certain, but a number of explanations suggest themselves. Although the studios were not averse to showing documentary fillers, Lorentz's film was clearly propagandistic in intent and tone. The industry, which was not overly sympathetic to the New Deal, had no incentive to show a pro-New Deal film which, at very least, might oblige them to exhibit something produced for or by the "other side." Moreover, the industry was making its own short subjects and was not interested in helping would-be government competitors. Nevertheless, through considerable efforts and ingenuity, Lorentz and his associates were able to get nationwide bookings in independent theaters, providing the film considerable exposure.

Notwithstanding his success, Lorentz was unhappy with his government film-making experience, characterized as it was by niggardly budgets, red tape, and bureaucratic jealousy.[63] Though he was prepared to quit Washington for Hollywood, Tugwell prevailed upon him to make another film documentary based on an idea Lorentz had suggested. This led to the production of *The River*, which may be the most evocative documentary film ever produced in the United States. *The River* traces the misuse of the Mississippi River basin since the Civil War and the resultant waste of human and natural resources. Like *The Plow*, it concludes with a depiction of the efforts of the federal government to render relief to the victims of the decades of ecological abuse and to attack the underlying causes of this national tragedy. On a more subtle level, *The River* is the story of the evil consequences of unrestrained individualism and ignorance, and a testimonial to the value of government planning and activity. It is, in short, a powerful statement of the reformist outlook of Tugwell and the early New Deal. The film, which was far superior in every respect to *The Plow*, won even more enthusiastic endorsement from the critics and even larger audiences at the independent theaters that showed it. Its popular acclaim may account for Paramount Pictures' agreement to distribute it.

The success of these experiments encouraged Roosevelt to seek to improve the quality and expand the distribution of government films. In 1938, he created the United States Film Service and placed Lorentz in charge. The new agency was to coordinate and supervise the film making of existing agencies and to make its own films as well. It also had the authority to approve the use of government personnel and property used, as they often were, in commercial film productions. This latter might conceivably have been used as leverage to encourage the private studios to cooperate with government in the distribution of its films. Lorentz would embark on a number of other film projects, but none would repeat his earlier successes.

Centralized government film making was a politically risky venture in the best of times—and the late thirties was not a good time for the New Deal. Since 1937 the administration, and particularly its propaganda activities, had been under criticism, and the NEC in which the new Film Service was to be located was scheduled to be dissolved as part of a government reorganization scheme enacted by Congress in 1939.

Richard Dyer MacCann, in his important work on government films, attributes the beginning of the decline of government documentaries to the creation of the U.S. Film Service.[64] A number of circumstances, including the fact that the centralization of the government's film making made this controversial activity particularly obvious, exposed administration film makers to the New Deal's enemies. By the end of June 1940, when Congress cut the funds available to the Film Service and in effect killed the project, administration attention had shifted decisively toward foreign affairs. Within a few months of the demise of the U.S. Film Service, as we will see in the last chapter, new arrangements were concluded by which the government was able to make full use of the facilities of the privately owned motion picture industry.

During the early days of the New Deal, Roosevelt, Early, and the dozens of public relations officers throughout the administration built upon and perfected the techniques their predecessors had begun to develop. Capitalizing on the President's unmatched sense of news and media affairs, and on the fact that the New Deal was itself something of a public attraction, they encouraged the newspapers and radio to carry a constant and voluminous flow of information on the new regime's activities. The effective selling of the New Deal depended on the administration's ability to cultivate whatever interest in serving government needs the various mass media representatives might possess. Where this instinct for cooperation was present and skillfully exploited, as it was in regard to the press (at first), radio, and the newsreels, government propaganda was credible, relatively unassailable, and enjoyed widespread public exposure.[65] Where the basis for cooperation was lacking, as it was in the feature film industry, the full potential of the medium went unrealized. Success in each case depended in part on the administration's efforts and in part on circumstances beyond its control. A favorable combination was by no means assured or easy to maintain, and, as the New Deal and its problems evolved, so too did relations with those who were to carry FDR's messages.

2

Redefining White House–
Press Relations, 1934-1940

The love affair between the President and the press could not have survived at its initial intensity very long, but it need not have degenerated into the often acrimonious squabbling that would characterize their relationship during Roosevelt's second term. The White House had helped establish the conditions for a lasting and mutually agreeable match. But the marriage required enormous patience and self-restraint which neither party, but particularly the President, found easy to exercise. The honeymoon, which lasted longer than most, appears to have survived largely on the willingness of the press to restrain its critical judgement on administration activities. This somewhat unnatural forbearance proceeded from the seriousness of the national crisis in 1933, the sympathy reporters felt for the President, and, most of all, from their satisfaction with the news the White House supplied.

Roosevelt was most attractive to the press when he first entered office—a fresh breeze dispelling the gloomy atmosphere created by Hoover. Reporters initially saw FDR as a sincere, vigorous leader, capable perhaps of solving the problems that had baffled his predecessor. He was a reformer that the somewhat cynical journalist could admire: a practical, good humored, approachable man in touch with reality and with none of the sanctimony they associated with the "do-gooder." For most, this image of the happy warrior would persist, but for many it would dissolve as the challenge of office revealed other facets of this deceptively complex individual. For them, Roosevelt would emerge as a compromiser and a manipulator, as a fallible and sometimes devious politician who, despite his accomplishments, failed to bring about recovery. Adversity and defeat would reveal a man slow to acknowledge mistakes and unable to suffer his critics silently. Reporters' expectations were in many cases excessive, and their disillusionment profound. Having prided themselves on hard-headed realism, they could not forgive themselves for having gone soft on this mere mortal in the White House. As it dawned on them that they had succumbed to sentiment and faith (egregious sins in journalists), they responded with the hyper-skepticism of those determined not to play the fool again.[1]

But if some reporters were disillusioned, many more were also disappointed by the President's failure to live up to his promise of a "new deal" for the press. Most found their dealings with Roosevelt and his press secretary pleasant and productive. They were satisfied with culling stories from handouts and briefings and pleased with the new cordiality extended them. They expected, however, that news from the White House would not only come to them easily, but equitably; that their independence and integrity would be respected; and that the President would not try to manipulate or circumvent them. In short, while willing to serve, reporters were wary of being used.

Many feared that this was happening. Hard times for the New Deal and increasingly stiff political opposition seemed to erode FDR's commitment to the press. Newsmen who initially were uncomfortable with the principle of government-press friendship, seeing the adversary relationship as more natural and healthful, soon found their suspicions justified. Even those who welcomed various White House innovations now saw their manipulative implications and the government's helping hand as stifling. A plentiful supply of just plain information became a smokescreen hiding real news—a way of managing the press and reducing journalists to "intellectual mendicants."[2] As one reporter noted, although routine relations with government were never better, neither in recent times "had the door been shut so tightly against information" other than that officially sanctioned.[3]

Evidence of news management abounded. The control of public access to information, while not always conscious policy, was implicit in the administration's information strategy, which entailed not only the widest distribution of information, but also its selection and even suppression in service to administration public relations goals. Discussions among the President and his lieutenants suggest that while news management may have made them uncomfortable on occasion, they were able to justify it by the higher purposes it served. Administration leaders saw themselves as custodians of a people's government, above partisanship, and with a special moral claim to office. Roosevelt expressed the outlook when he told his colleagues that his "government was being run less for political purposes" and more for the general good than any in some time. "We are thinking about government," he insisted, "and not merely about party." Of course he realized, as he also told them, that his apolitical image promised to "catch more votes" than a partisan political stance.[4] Unfortunately, the cultivation of this image led Roosevelt to employ techniques that tended to stimulate the natural cynicism of the press and erode the too easy faith many reporters had invested in the new regime.

The effort to ensure that only appropriate impressions reached the public took a variety of forms. At its most innocuous it was reflected in the White House policy on photographs of the President. Although Roosevelt did not seem especially sensitive to his incapacity, Stephen Early tried to screen his paralysis from the public. Pictures showing FDR in a wheel chair or leg braces were banned, a policy with which the photographers regularly covering the White House readily cooperated. So effective was the plan that many Americans were not aware of the extent of the President's handicap.[5]

It is easy to sympathize with the White House's desire to hide FDR's condition. At the same time, the policy reflected a larger concern with image making and a willingness to employ censorship at the source to effect its purposes. Seen from this perspective, it was a short step from the relatively harmless ban on photos to the more questionable control of data bearing on the nation's economic health. In October 1933, the President directed that no Cabinet officer or agency head issue any statistical information until it had been cleared by the Executive Council statistician. The order was explicitly aimed at forestalling the publication of data which might be incorrect, inconsistent with other government releases, or, worse still, might undermine confidence in the recovery effort. A related policy, frequently ignored, called upon officials to clear their major political statements with Early.[6]

The issue of statistical candor arose in January 1936 when the Emergency Council prepared a report which showed the farm prices on March 15, 1933, shortly after the New Deal had begun, were in most instances lower than they had been a year earlier under Hoover. The report also revealed that after many months of New Deal effort, manufacturing was 25 percent below the level of 1929. Early, looking over these figures, noted that they tended to undercut the administration position that "things were at their low ebb on March 4, 1933"; that is, on the day Roosevelt took office. He suggested the Council's figures be revised to conform to this position, and reminded the Executive Director that it was his responsibility to make "absolutely certain that no agencies . . . are permitted to say anything at cross purposes with each other."[7]

Although the restriction of information might at first glance appear inconsistent with the informational strategy, there was in fact no conflict. The suppression of information and its profligate effusion were two sides of the same news management coin. Strategy never called for all the truth, just a superabundance of those truths fit to be told, and it sometimes required a fine sense of political realities to render the appropriate judgement. One such case arose in June 1934, when the Director of the Emergency Council, Frank Walker, sought permission to release a breakdown of federal expenditures on drought relief in the various states. Congressmen anxious to prove their worth to their constituents had requested the information and Walker, who had only recently established an Information Service to fill just such requests, felt constrained to provide the data. Roosevelt, however, pointed out that publication of this seemingly positive information might boomerang since the administration was bound to make "a very bad showing in some states and much too good a showing in other states." Thus, while insisting that he was not trying to "hide anything," Roosevelt concluded that responding to the request would require "too many explanations." Apparently, the solution adopted was to release selected figures from the expenditures of various drought fighting agencies but not to issue a state-by-state listing that would lend itself to invidious comparisons.[8]

The restrictive and hence manipulative side of informational propaganda was also apparent in the President's press conferences. These much celebrated affairs were a joy for reporters. Almost everyone who attended was delighted by FDR's wit and intellectual virtuosity. Most left the meetings entertained, uplifted, and usually better informed than when they had arrived. But a few were troubled by the conferences, seeing them as an unequal contest between the poised and confident President and his often uncertain interrogators.

Roosevelt had a better grasp of current affairs than the journalists charged with examining him. News, which at one time had been overwhelmingly political, was now as much as 90 percent economic. Most reporters had neither the academic training, the experience, nor the sustained interest to match the President's understanding.[9] He knew it and so did they, and frequently conferences touching fiscal, monetary, and budgetary subjects resembled nothing so much as an encounter between an overbearing professor and his none-too-bright students. A tentative question posed by one of the reporters would be followed by a well-informed mini-lecture by the President. Follow-up questions, which were in any event discouraged by the number of reporters clamoring to be heard, were rare. However, on occasion a particularly dense or persistent reporter might persevere, thus leaving himself open to a presidential invitation to put on the dunce cap and "stand in the corner." All of this was carried on in good fun, but with a detectable undercurrent of intimidation.[10] Cognizant of their ignorance, in many instances reporters were dependent upon Roosevelt for explanation. Most no doubt appreciated his simple elucidation replete with homey illustrations. Those who accepted the Roosevelt treatment received considerable compensation in the form of the "enlightened" stories they could file and their professional association with the great man. The President's efforts were rewarded in the next edition of the newspapers, where likely as not he would find administration views, often on matters of some controversy, faithfully reproduced.

Like any competent teacher, the President was also adept at directing his "students" along lines of inquiry he wished to pursue while avoiding issues he thought better left unexplored. The parameters were sometimes established by Roosevelt's introductory statement which would usually elicit a series of related questions. The President might also arrange through Early to have a friendly correspondent pose a question concerning some matter FDR wished to examine. On the other hand, where a line of questioning appeared heading astray, Roosevelt might withhold comment, supply a non-responsive riposte, or designate his response as "off the record." This meant that the information imparted was for the reporters' enlightenment only and might not be repeated. Such off-the-record remarks occasionally had the effect of burying unconfirmed reports that reporters had brought to the President for confirmation and elucidation. These and other practices that tended to ensure that the conferences served his purposes led some journalists, including Arthur Krock, David Lawrence, and Dorothy Thompson (three not among FDR's greatest admirers), to call for the abolition of the meetings. But theirs was a minority view for, despite their onesidedness, the conferences were important events which most newspapermen, whatever their misgivings, were loath to forgo.[11]

Although the White House helped shape much of the political news, stories did appear which FDR found hostile or otherwise unacceptable. For all its practical effectiveness, the informational strategy provided little opportunity to see such slanders "nailed," and although Roosevelt claimed the "skin of a rhinocerous in regard to press criticism," he was often angered by and determined to respond to instances of unfair reporting.[12] This reaction, Early warned, was worse than futile. It accomplished little more than to suggest a sensitivity unbecoming a politician or, worse still, a dictatorial intolerance of legitimate criticism.

Although the President had virtually unlimited access to the news media, his opportunities to answer his critics were limited. Conscious of the dignity of the office, concerned with maintaining an image of nonpartisan leadership, and aware that answering his critics would often simply lend importance to them, Roosevelt was obliged to hold his tongue. For the most part he did, although he could not resist arranging on occasion to have prominent individuals send letters arguing his case to the editors of leading newspapers. The ploy suggests his sensitivity to criticism. His insistence that these arrangements be carried out in spite of Early's reluctance indicates the importance he attached to the exercise.[13] On one occasion, Early, directed by FDR to arrange for such a reply, laid the request aside apparently hoping the President would forget it. Roosevelt responded angrily, demanding that Early "get somebody in Washington to send it to the Times [sic]," adding, "I have asked you to do this before and I want it done." The following day it was.[14] More commonly, Roosevelt's rebukes came as impromptu lectures at his bi-weekly press conferences. These remarks would occasionally single out a particular offending journalist or newspaper but often were generalized indictments of journalistic standards. He characteristically employed a patronizing tone reserved for the exceptionally benighted and what he said probably served only to satisfy him, while it irritated his hearers.[15]

Roosevelt took what he considered unfair reporting seriously enough to collect examples and to confront the offenders with the evidence of their misdeeds. Personal pique seems to have been his chief motive, but he also believed that confrontations of this kind might lessen the likelihood of repeated offenses. As he told Early in 1942, corrections of this sort now and then were valuable if for no other reason than that editors "may know they are being watched."[16]

The *New York Times* was a frequent recipient of Roosevelt's lessons in journalistic ethics. His first rebuke to the *Times* went off a year after his election and although he insisted on that occasion that he had a policy of not complaining to publishers, it initiated a series of such missives he dispatched to the *Times* and other papers over the next ten years.[17] Mostly these were the result of impulse, but in at least some cases FDR pursued the practice of preparing his indictment on the basis of evidence of repeated transgressions.

Roosevelt's first serious complaint appears to have arisen during the 1934 congressional election campaign. FDR had anticipated political sniping in this first popular referendum on his program and once the campaign had begun he became convinced that the "interests" had enlisted the support of the press in "a very definite effort . . . to scare the housewife or . . . the head of the family." He singled out a story in the New York *Sun* which included a map of the United States captioned: "Here are the Focal Points of Depression-Bred Ferment Throughout the Nation" and announced in headlines: "Spirit of Unrest Grips the Nation," and "Country Disturbed by Conditions Not Experienced in More Than a Century." From the current perspective these headlines appear unexceptional, and most historians would support these characterizations. With their expectations raised but unfulfilled by New Deal reforms, many Americans were attracted to the banners of "extremist" elements—"thunder on both the Left and the Right," one historian has called it. Nevertheless, and perhaps correctly, Roosevelt put an anti-New Deal construction on the *Sun* story and told his colleagues he had written the paper's publisher charging that such accounts "will do more to breed ferment in our country than have all the depression years put together." It was, he suggested, part of a deliberate effort "to inject fear into the population," and he intended his letter to "lay the foundation so that later on if it is advisable I can say: 'this is nothing new; this goes back to a definite series of small occurrences which might almost be classified by the Attorney General under the term "conspiracy." ' "[18] Convinced that he had identified a conscious effort to undermine the New Deal, FDR had begun to build a case against the *Sun* for which he might eventually call it to account.

Although on many occasions Roosevelt had just cause for complaint, in general his journalistic standards were unrealistic. His expectations

are best illustrated by the "case" he built against that paragon of journalistic virtue, the Associated Press. The wire service wielded enormous
influence. Its stories appeared in more than a thousand newspapers daily
and its professional reputation was equal to that of the *Times*.[19] Roosevelt
was understandably sensitive to AP reporting and did not always like
what he found under its byline. During 1936 his displeasure led him to
collect a series of objectionable pieces to which he appended brief
analyses indicating the source of his unhappiness. These provide valuable insight into Roosevelt's expectations and suggest at least one basis
for a breach between the President and the press. In one article, he
singled out for critical comment an AP reporter's assertion that Democratic Party Chairman James Farley faced a revolt within Democratic
ranks and growing strength among the Republicans. In another, the
assertion that labor leader John L. Lewis stood at "a crossroads in his
political life." In a third, the claim that White House opposition to the
renomination of Senator Guy Gillette in the forthcoming Iowa Democratic primary made the contest a significant "test" of the New Deal
strength in the farm belt.

FDR conceded the truth of the Farley story, but insisted that it was
"not for the AP to say except with straight away facts." He also accepted
the accuracy of the Lewis story, but complained that the idea of a
"political crossroads" might at different times have been used in reference to a wide variety of public figures and was, therefore, little more
than an indirect slap at Lewis. Alluding to New Deal ties with organized
labor, Roosevelt concluded that "although it is hard to pin, the evil
political intent or effect toward the Administration is greater in this case
than in the Farley story." As for AP's account of the Iowa primary,
the President found it "innocent on its face," but arbitrary in that it
selected one event upon which to stake the future of the New Deal. In
each instance the President concluded that "the old AP would never
have done that."[20]

Roosevelt's complaint reflected a simplistic but widely held ideal of
objective reporting that had inspired journalists since the early nineteenth
century and which was in particular vogue at the beginning of the
twentieth. FDR came naturally to this standard for, as he never tired
of telling reporters, he had himself been a journalist (he had edited
Harvard's *Crimson*). From a modern perspective the pursuit of objective
truth was a will-o'-the-wisp which led its followers to lose sight of the
prejudices which shaped their work. The quest for "factuality," often

confused with objectivity, gained a good deal from the widespread use of the pioneering news service, the Associated Press. Since AP subscribers served in a variety of communities and supported a spectrum of editorial positions, the news supplied them, while not value free, had to reflect prevailing political norms and could not be overtly tendentious.

This kind of reporting standard gained from the endorsement of the prestigious *New York Times* and from the professionalization of journalism at the end of the nineteenth century. Thus, Joseph Pulitzer, in establishing a school of journalism at Columbia in 1902, insisted on "special emphasis on accurate and reliable reporting, as the fundamental concern" of the new school. Walter Lippmann, who perhaps should have been skeptical of the idea, was among those voicing approval of the goal of "objectivity" in the training of journalists.

Nevertheless, the ideal was increasingly challenged by intellectuals in Europe and the United States. Propaganda activities during World War I deepened skepticism concerning what one historian would label the "noble dream" of objectivity, and by the 1930s many critics of journalism, reflecting the relativism now dominant in the social sciences, characterized the effort to report events simply as they happened as lending itself to propaganda under the guise of objectivity. The unwanted effects of simple, straightforward reporting were most apparent in instances where journalists merely repeated information supplied them by various informed but interested government sources. Awareness of pitfalls of this kind contributed to the rise in the 1930s of a new critical interpretive journalism boldly espoused by Henry Luce's influential *Time* and widely practiced by political columnists who appeared in great numbers during the decade. Formal professional recognition came as early as 1933 when the American Society of Newspaper Editors urged its members to do more to interpret the news so that the reader would not only know what was happening, but also its background and meaning.[21]

Totally unbiased reporting was beyond the capacity of the nation's newspapers and, in any event, was probably not what Roosevelt wanted. Short of the partisan reporting of his more committed supporters, the best the President could expect was that newspapers would not systematically and blatantly color their accounts against him. In this regard both the AP and the *Times* enjoyed a high reputation, at least in the journalistic community. Although each had drifted from the "strictly news" standard of a generation earlier, both retained a reputation for fairness and reliability. According to a survey of journalists done by Leo Rosten, the major objection to AP writing was its "calculated emasculation of tone" designed to "avoid any semblance of bias." From the perspective of the profession, AP reporting was, if anything, too sterile and dull for contemporary standards. To urge either the news service or the *Times* to move even farther in this direction was tilting at windmills.[22] The President's complaints, valid or not, would not change press performance. But they probably did appear to journalists as self-serving—part of a larger White House effort designed to gain favored rather than fair treatment in the nation's newspapers.

More important than FDR's habit of lecturing on journalistic failings were his violations of the standards Early had adopted for White House press relations. A key element in the new deal they had been promised was the pledge that reporters would have equal access to the news. Early recognized that exclusive interviews and other privileged access to the President undermined press morale and encouraged those not so favored to pursue the kind of investigative or interpretive reporting that was likely to be bad news for the administration. In 1935, he reaffirmed the White House commitment: "Mr. Roosevelt takes the newspapermen as they come. There are no favored groups . . . called into private seances. . . . Equal treatment for all, and respect for the rights of all are rigid policy."[23] That pledge was more an expression of hope than a description of reality and the gap between the two was to grow wider in the months that followed. In the process, a major underpinning of the cooperative relationship Early had developed with the press was destroyed.

Early's equity principle ran afoul of the President's stubborn insistence on obtaining advantages from the press relationship. This the press corps as a whole was not prepared to tolerate. Despite the objections of his press secretary, Roosevelt repeatedly sought to parlay privileged access to his thoughts into favorable treatment in the press. Collaboration with prominent writers was tempting because it offered FDR a way of injecting his own views into apparently independent journalistic accounts, often with his role remaining unknown to the reader. Roosevelt frequently used George Creel and *Collier's* magazine in this way. Creel, a journalist and Democratic politician, had served as the head of the infamous World War I Committee on Public Information—a propaganda and censorship agency that came to bear his name. Now a freelance writer, Creel published a number of articles in the 1930s describing aspects of New Deal plans and policy. Roosevelt provided inspiration, substance, and sometimes whole paragraphs that Creel incorporated verbatim from the President's dictation. John Franklin Carter, who wrote a syndicated column and broadcast political commentary under the pseudonym Jay Franklin, enjoyed a similar arrangement.[24] Such relationships, whatever their value in influencing public attitudes, were evidence to the press at large of FDR's willingness to play favorites.

Nor was the practice confined to these regular sympathetic outlets. Although all journalists railed against the practice of collusion and favoritism, few were likely to pass up the flattering and rewarding opportunities the President could offer. An important instance of press–White House collaboration occurred in 1935 when Roy Howard, head of the Scripps-Howard newspaper chain and the United Press news service, helped FDR attempt to bridge the widening gap between the administration and the business community. Howard supported the President and the New Deal, though his editors were independent and frequently critical of government policies. In early September 1935, the Scripps-Howard publications carried an exchange of letters between the publisher and the President in which Howard wrote of the uneasiness in the business community caused by recent New Deal legislation and FDR responded with the reassuring promise of a "breathing spell" in reform activities. The event drew headlines and praise from editorial writers and businessmen throughout the nation. Presumably both parties to this journalistic coup benefited. The genesis of the exchange was not known at the time, although some journalists suspected that it was not entirely spontaneous. It was, in fact, the product of a closely collaborative effort in which FDR helped write Howard's letter and fixed the timing for the public release of the "correspondence."[25]

Roosevelt made similar use of Arthur Krock, chief of the Washington bureau of the *New York Times* and author of a respected column for that paper. Krock was known professionally for the objectivity of his work and personally for his crusty demeanor. A succession of presidents and politicians found him a sharp and often painful critic. Roosevelt described him in 1940 as someone who "never in his whole life said a really decent thing about any human being without qualifying it by some nasty dig . . . a social parasite . . . a cynic who has never felt warm affection for anybody—man or woman."[26]

Roosevelt developed these feelings early. It was a Krock column in

1934 that produced Roosevelt's first protest to the *Times*. Krock, on learning of the complaint, claimed to be mystified by Roosevelt's apparent animus. A short time later, however, he provided both an explanation and a justification for it in a radio address which roundly denounced the emerging government-press relationship. Krock charged the administration with "more ruthlessness, intelligence, and subtlety in trying to suppress legitimate, unfavorable comment than any other I have known." Understandably, he singled out Roosevelt's practice of complaining to editors and publishers.

Stung by Krock's attack, FDR was nonetheless determined to win him over or at least somehow dilute his venom. Convinced that Krock was susceptible to flattery, he first tendered him an invitation "to run up to Hyde Park." When friendliness failed, he turned to the ruthlessness which Krock had ascribed to him. Turner Catledge, then Krock's assistant in the Washington Bureau, reports that late in 1936 Roosevelt suggested an arrangement whereby he would supply Catledge with special access to White House news if he would use it without Krock's knowledge. Catledge rejected this "bold faced attempt to undercut" his friend and superior. Undaunted, Roosevelt now sought to appeal to Krock's journalistic instincts. In 1937, in the midst of the furor created by his attempt to pack the Court, FDR offered Krock an exclusive interview. The story, which Krock allowed FDR to edit, provided Roosevelt with an influential medium for his views on the Court issue and won for Krock a Pulitzer Prize. It also, as Early feared, brought down upon the White House the wrath of other journalists. As the *Christian Science Monitor* put it, the episode tended to "explode" the White House's much vaunted claim that it "scrupulously avoided playing favorites." Roosevelt apologized to the press, but the damage was done.[27] As for Krock, his hostility toward FDR remained unchanged.

In spite of press discontent, Early's strong opposition, and the President's pledge, the practice continued. In the fall of 1938 conversations with Anne O'Hare McCormick produced two lengthy articles in the *New York Times Magazine* covering Roosevelt's views on domestic and foreign policy.[28] This latest violation of the "no exclusive interviews" rule provoked the *Herald-Tribune*'s correspondent to demand equal treatment. Early forwarded this symbol of the breakdown of White House news policy to the President with the admonition to "read it and weep."[29]

Roosevelt was, however, not inclined to reform. Press criticism merely confirmed his suspicions that the nation's newspapers were in league with his political enemies. The more hostility he encountered, the angrier he became and the more inclined he was to listen to intolerant counsel. Raymond Moley, a onetime close advisor, recalled FDR's "growing petulance about all criticism" during 1935 and his "perverse interest in derogatory stories about himself and his family which some of his close associates carried to him." His morning encounters with the newspapers, Moley reported, would produce angry comments about the consistent unfairness and falsity of newspaper reporting, as well as hostile comments directed at various publishers.[30] Although unfairness was not typical of the press, there was no shortage of items to feed the President's petulance. Roosevelt made little effort to mask his hostility and in August 1935 Roy Howard warned Early that FDR's habit of castigating the entire profession for the sins of a few was bound to alienate even his friends. Early agreed, attributing Roosevelt's attitude to the influence of an "army of advisors" many of whom read only a single opposition newspaper and knew little of the "situation as a whole."[31]

Early had identified an important factor which limited his own influence. Although an "army of advisors" knew less about the workings of the press than Early, they knew a great deal more of its effects. Early, the apolitical friend of the press, rarely experienced the hostility that Roosevelt and his political associates were forced to endure daily. Nor was he as concerned as they with what this criticism was doing to the New Deal and the prospects of reform. To these enterprises, he was an outsider. The anger and frustration experienced by all New Dealers over press misrepresentation provided a sympathetic bond among them that Early could not share. The exchange of anti-press stories among fellow sufferers ensured an emotional climate that smothered the press secretary's appeals to common sense and moderation.

New Dealer Jerome Frank gave expression to the discontent. Frank was one of the bright, young, committed people recruited by the new administration. He soon came to believe, as did the President, that newspaper owners motivated by selfish interests and prejudices were deliberately distorting news of the Roosevelt revolution. This, he argued, deprived the public of the value of a free press and justified government action to ensure the people's enjoyment of their First Amendment right. Frank proposed legislation requiring every newspaper engaged in interstate commerce to print a given quantity of government-supplied news, without charge. He also sought to open up the predominantly conservative press to new liberal competition by attacking the Associated Press practice of permitting its members to deny the news service to newspapers attempting to enter their markets. Since access to the AP wire was highly valued, this veto power in effect enabled members to perpetuate the existing conservative control of American journalism. Frank suggested that this was a species of illegal restraint of trade and that the AP should be required to extend its membership at a reasonable fee to any newspaper requesting it.[32]

Such ideas reflected the impatience within the administration which Roosevelt shared. The issue for them was not simply one of personal pique and political expedience, although these elements certainly played an important role. It was, as Frank suggested, a matter of defining a new concept of the constitutional right to a free press which would serve the public's interest. Although the founding fathers had undertaken to protect the press from Congress and presumably from the federal government, liberals in the 1930s suggested that the right to be informed, along with other traditional rights and values, was now threatened not by government, but by the newspaper owners themselves.

By the end of 1935 the President had decided that there was more to be gained by venting his feelings and acknowledging the enmity between himself and the press than by attempting to mitigate or conceal it. Forcing fairness on the newspapers was impractical, but the issue could be taken to the one tribunal in which Roosevelt was a consistent winner, the court of public opinion. He decided to confront the press directly and openly with his charges, leaving it to the nation's publishers to reform or face repudiation by their readers. In either event the confrontation itself was likely to increase his popularity—no small consideration with a presidential election in the offing. The tactic resembled one he employed about the same time with the business community. Early in the New Deal FDR had hoped to enlist the cooperation of business in his recovery efforts. By 1936, however, it was clear that he had not succeeded. Abandoning fruitless efforts to placate the Right, he attempted instead to take full advantage of the break. This decision was reflected in his 1936 reelection campaign, which he deliberately cast as a contest between the mass of the people, whose rights he championed, and the forces of wealth and privilege represented by his Republican opponent.

Relations with the press took a similar course and for much the same reasons. At first Roosevelt tried to win and keep the support of powerful publishers, but he was soon convinced that the same selfish concerns that motivated obstructionist businessmen dictated the news. Having decided that the newspaper owners were his implacable foes, FDR determined to confront their opposition head on and turn it to his political advantage. The idea seems to have crystallized in the spring of 1936. His thinking at that time is suggested in a conversation recorded by Raymond Moley, who, after leaving government in late 1933, continued to serve the President as occasional advisor and speech writer. During a weekend cruise on the Potomac their discussion turned to the unfairness of the press. Roosevelt declared that the unremitting opposition of the publishers was past the point of hurting him. Indeed, he said, the press had so discredited itself in the public's eyes that he welcomed its hostility much as he did the undisguised hatred of bankers and businessmen.[33]

During the 1936 campaign, Roosevelt told a cheering crowd in Madison Square Garden, New York: "Never before in all of American History" had the forces of "organized money . . . been so united against one candidate as they stand today. They are unanimous in their hate for me and I welcome their hatred." Recognizing and accepting the nation's polarization, FDR decided to court it: "I should like to have it said of my first Administration that in it the forces of selfishness and of lust for power met their match. I should like to have it said of my second Administration that in it these forces met their master."[34] In 1932 the designated enemy had been the "Depression." Now it was the privileged few—including the press moguls—who opposed his efforts at recovery. Roosevelt's overwhelming victory at the polls in November 1936 undoubtedly encouraged him to openly break with the press and to use its opposition to political advantage. The election not only demonstrated his own enormous popularity, it also served as a repudiation of the press which had largely opposed his reelection.

If his victory made the President confident he could take on his press antagonists to his advantage, the political difficulties he suffered after 1936 gave him compelling reason to do so. Soon after his second inauguration, FDR suffered a series of setbacks that indicated the power of a resurgent conservatism in American politics. The first came early in 1937 when FDR asked Congress for legislation aimed at changing the ideological makeup of the Court. The plan, which was poorly presented, met with a storm of protest led by, but not confined to, those elements most hostile to the administration. The reaction eventually produced defeat for the proposal and a severe setback for the President. Among those in the forefront of the opposition were the nation's editorial writers.[35]

The initiative gained by administration critics in the Court fight was sustained in succeeding months by attacks on FDR's proposal for the reorganization of the executive branch.[36] Even before the furor over this had subsided, national concern turned to the economic decline which began in the fall of 1937. The resultant "Roosevelt recession" was severe and the political shock was commensurate with the economic trauma. Roosevelt's critics now had "proof" of their persistent cry that New Deal policies, particularly the growing administration hostility toward business, were retarding economic recovery.

Much of FDR's opposition in Congress came from conservative Democrats, and in mid-1938 the President intervened in several Democratic primary contests, in what was inevitably labeled an attempted party purge. The "purge," FDR's attempt to "pack" the Court, to impose "one-man rule" through executive reorganization, together with the apparent failure of his recovery program, helped shift the political balance to his opponents. The President, now for the first time, was on the defensive.[37]

The conservative attack was as wide ranging as it was often irresponsible, but its major themes were New Deal wastefulness, inefficiency, and its tendency to mimic the totalitarian regimes found elsewhere in the world. Administration news policy, particularly the size of the government public relations apparatus and the volume of information it produced, were offered as further proof of these charges. The campaign to smear the administration by attacking its propaganda apparatus had begun in 1936.[38] In May the anti-administration Philadelphia *Inquirer* reported having received over 2,000 pages (30 pounds) of franked mail from various government agencies in the span of a single month.[39] Exposés of this kind continued during 1937, taking their place alongside the mounting attacks on Court packing and executive reorganization. As critics warmed to their task, they found fuel for their anti-propaganda blasts in a report by the Brookings Institution. The work had been commissioned and released by the Senate Committee to Investigate the Executive Agencies of the Government headed by conservative Democrat Harry Byrd of Virginia. The Committee was at the time also considering the President's plan for executive reorganization. The Brookings study found that in the three months ending September 30,

1936, the government had issued 7 million copies of about 4,800 public releases. It also reported that the Executive employed 146 people full time and 124 more part time to work on publicity in fiscal 1936. Salaries for these publicity officers ran to more than $600,000. These figures actually grossly understated the volume of publicity and its costs. The Works Progress Administration, which did not respond to the Brookings questionnaire and was not represented in its totals, alone spent well over $1 million in a year just for printing.[40] The findings were given widespread coverage in the press in what in some instances was probably part of a concerted campaign led by congressional Republicans.[41] Criticism focused on the expenditure of taxpayers' money to sell them on their own government. But the analogy between New Deal propagandists and the propaganda ministries of the European dictators was, in the context of the times, hard to miss.

The issue of the propriety of government propaganda was a sensitive one first raised when public relations initially found its way into the service of the federal bureaucracy. In 1913 and 1919 Congress forbade the use of federal funds for the payment of "publicity experts," unless it specifically approved, and prohibited executive agencies from issuing any publicity designed to influence the legislature. These laws had been ingeniously avoided over the years, but they did express a congressional intent to strike at any administration information program which became too effective.[42]

Insofar as the President's critics succeeded in curtailing the informational program, they encouraged his growing conflict with the press. If the newspapers, which to Roosevelt's mind were already slanted against him, now objected to publicizing what the administration said and did, it was time to acknowledge openly and make the most of the breach. From mid-1937 there were indications that FDR had decided on this course. Not only did FDR's complaints about reporters' work seem to increase, he now supplemented them with public statements attacking the motives and credibility of the press in general.[43] The once "private" quarrel now took on the aspect of a publicity campaign aimed at discrediting the press. His message seemed to be—recognize newspaper owners as your enemies and do not trust what you read in your papers. In an October 1937 fireside chat Roosevelt suggested that the American people were capable of forming political judgements independent of newspaper direction, noting that "five years of fierce discussion and debate, five years of information through the radio and the moving pictures'' had ''taken the whole nation to school in the nation's business.'' His omission of newspapers in his listing of the media of political education was almost certainly intentional and was, in any event, taken by journalists as a deliberate slap at them.[44]

At a press conference just before Christmas 1937 Roosevelt made his indictment of the press more explicit. Although he had claimed, and would again, that newspapers were losing their influence, he now assigned to ''a large percentage of the press, and a small minority of businessmen'' responsibility for the loss of public confidence which, he said, accounted for the current economic recession. To reporters who asked what these groups had to gain by promoting ''a psychology of fear,'' he answered that ''most of the country was wondering the same thing.''[45]

By the beginning of the new year, FDR's attack on the press was in full swing. In January 1938 he told a Jackson Day audience that the nation's great newspapers historically had been allied with the enemies of liberalism. Linking his own struggles against the privileged few with those of Jefferson and Jackson, Roosevelt noted that in each of these great battles prominent contemporary journals had lined up on the side of the anti-liberal minority. ''Against Jefferson were almost all the newspapers and magazines of the day . . . and we know that the handful of printers and editors who helped Jefferson and his associates were harried and arrested under the sedition law with the full approval of the great papers and magazines of that time.'' These efforts of the privileged ''to curb the essential freedom of the press'' had failed, he said, ''just as any similar effort would fail today.''[46]

Roosevelt enlarged upon these thoughts in the introduction to the 1936 volume of his *Public Papers* which he completed in early 1938 and which also appeared in *Liberty* magazine. FDR not only linked the press to the forces of privilege, but went on to suggest that the alliance forfeited journalism's claim to credibility and public leadership. He welcomed the opposition of ''85 percent'' of the press, he said, since the irresponsible actions of opposition leaders and newspaper owners and editors actually helped him in the 1936 election campaign:

the voting public quickly grasped the situation, resented it, and gave the obvious tactics no further consideration. From the point of view of votes, the New Deal gained. From the point of view of public confidence, the opposition leadership and the majority of the press lost.[47]

Roosevelt's observations were probably intended as much as a lesson to publishers as a description of the developments of 1936, but should the import of his remarks have escaped those to whom they were addressed, FDR soon had a singular opportunity to drive the point home. The occasion was a special news conference the President held for the members of the American Society of Newspaper Editors in April 1938. The editors' questions ranged over a variety of political issues until one prompted the President to tie the success of his tax program to its treatment in the nation's press. This led one member to ask somewhat ingenuously whether Roosevelt thought the American press had treated him unfairly. There followed a lengthy discussion in which the President set forth his views on government-press relations, reviewing themes which had come to characterize his thinking. While refusing to use the word "unfair," he labeled newspaper treatment of various issues "one-sided" and attributed this persistent bias to the orders given to editors by newspaper owners. The effect of this policy, he said, was to make the newspapers "more responsible for inciting of fear in the community than any other factor."

William Allen White, the much respected editor and publisher of the Emporia (Kansas) *Gazette*, attempting perhaps to ease the tension, indicated that Herbert Hoover had complained to him in very much the same terms and that it was the nature of the press and of the presidency, not publishers' prejudice, that had produced the coverage of which FDR complained. Roosevelt would have none of it. Unfair reporting, he suggested, regardless of which president it victimized, was harmful to the country. The press, he said, should cut out "the petty stuff," and get "their shoulders in behind national recovery." He warned the editors that Americans were getting to the point of looking to their newspaper for entertainment rather than enlightenment. They were beginning, he said, to dismiss much of what they read with a doubting: "Oh, that's one of those newspaper stories." Asked how many newspapers he classified as untrustworthy, he again used the figure of "85 percent" but this time sought to exempt much of the rural press by indicating it was 85 percent of the papers subscribing to a major news service. The discussion then turned to other matters, but before the meeting ended Roosevelt returned to the issue. Anxious to impress on his hearers the gravity of the situation, as he saw it, he declared, "I feel very, very strongly about it for the sake of the public and even for the sake of the press; and if, from now on, we can have a presentation from the press on both sides of the news it will be perfectly magnificent."[48] From FDR's perspective, the political function of newspapers in a democracy was the education of the electorate through "balanced" coverage of the government's activities. From the editor's point of view, public enlightenment required independent criticism. The dialogue left the newspapermen convinced that he did not understand their role and that his antagonism toward the press would continue.

At first glance the President's charges against the press appear well founded. A conservative bias was in fact built into the system. Many newspapers were large commercial enterprises and all were dependent in one way or another on the business community for their success. Understandably, most publishers shared the conservative political outlook of business and were disposed, as were other businessmen, to oppose the New Deal. Evidence of this was most apparent during election years when editorial positions were frequently dictated by publisher preference. In 1932, 55 percent of those newspapers with an announced choice supported the reelection of Herbert Hoover. Election-eve support for Roosevelt's opponents would increase in each succeeding election until in 1944 68.5 percent declared for Thomas E. Dewey.[49] In addition, a number of newspapers, including most notably those of the Hearst chain and the Chicago *Tribune*, were unremittingly and virulently hostile to the New Deal and the President.[50] This opposition was reflected not only on the editorial pages, but also in prejudicial headlining and editing of news stories. But consistently irresponsible coverage was exceptional and FDR's indictment of the press seems to have been based on his own self-serving definition of press responsibility.

During the New Deal's first two years most of the nation's editors had given the President the benefit of the doubt. Between October 1933 and August 1934 the administration's Press Intelligence Division, in an effort to keep officials informed of press opinion, surveyed 6,532 editorials. During this period New Deal programs were well underway and their faults well known. Nevertheless, the report found 30.7 percent of press comment favorable, 25.1 percent unfavorable, and the remainder neutral. From the examples of negative opinion cited in the report, it appears that many of the editorials designated "critical" were in fact temperate and responsible. Most of them complained, with some justice, of the confusion generated by shifts in administration policy and of the ineptness of some National Recovery Administration personnel, particularly the intemperate and blundering director, General

Hugh Johnson. On the other hand, the relief program generated little hostile comment and most of that was aimed at local implementation rather than at administration policy. Thus the report concluded that while editorial criticism was increasing:

> the majority continue to express their faith in the President. . . . In other words, newspaper editors seem to have lost faith in his experiments, but to keep faith in him. And what they are beginning to demand more and more is that he keep his word to scrap such emergency measures as have been proven failures and to do it as quickly as possible.[51]

The amount of criticism and the nature of the comments suggests skepticism, impatience, perhaps a regrettable lack of faith, but not widespread, congenital, or irreversible hostility. Moreover, it is worth noting that according to a list that Early prepared late in the summer of 1935, the administration enjoyed the support of almost all of the nation's largest and most prestigious newspapers.[52]

It is true that from 1935 until the administration's preoccupation with foreign policy after 1939 reversed the trend, editorial writers would become increasingly critical. Nevertheless, criticism never reached the dimensions suggested by FDR in his attacks on the press. This conclusion is supported in a recent study by Graham White. White treats the entire twelve years of the Roosevelt administration as a unit and does not delineate the significant differences between the press response to domestic and foreign policies. Nevertheless, the figures he arrives at are a valuable corrective to the President's portrait of press hostility. Examining a sampling of 167 editorials, White concluded that 33 percent were favorable, 36.5 percent unfavorable, and the remainder too general to assign a negative or positive value.[53]

But what of Roosevelt's repeated charge that the news columns were also slanted against him? This allegation was far more serious. Editorials were chiefly significant for their influence on a politically conscious few and their most notable effect seems to have been their infinite capacity to annoy politicians from the President on down. But the faithful reporting of the information provided by the administration was at the heart of the informational strategy. If reporters and editors were in fact distorting what administration spokesmen had to say, they were certainly apt to undermine public confidence in the government and what it was doing. The evidence, however, suggests that there was relatively little anti-administration bias in the reporting of the news. Editors, as mentioned above, were not prone to undue criticism of FDR on the editorial pages. They could hardly have been expected to undercut him with unfair news coverage. This conclusion is borne out by White's findings. Sampling 47 newspaper accounts of several of Roosevelt's speeches, White found 26 to be fair and accurate, 13 seriously biased against him, and the remainder a mix of mild bias one way or the other. Treatment of his press conferences was even less subject to distortion. Of 108 front-page articles covering presidential news conferences, White found only 6 with a serious anti-FDR tone.[54]

Such evidence suggests that in spite of serious faults press coverage by and large served the administration's interests. This conclusion is especially compelling when we consider that much of the political material that appeared in the nation's newspapers was neither byline stories nor editorials, but merely the more or less verbatim reproduction of government handouts. The informational strategy was working, but FDR was too thin skinned to passively accept the criticism that increasingly greeted his faltering domestic program. His attacks on the press, his weakness for playing favorites among its members, and ultimately his attempt to turn the press into a political scapegoat were the result.

Roosevelt's relations with the press approached their nadir just at a time when his concerns were shifting from domestic to foreign affairs. In the fall of 1938 came the Munich crisis. A few months later, having undermined its independence by diplomacy, Hitler seized Czechoslovakia. The Munich agreement and subsequent events discredited the policy of "appeasement" and revealed Hitler's apparently insatiable territorial appetite. In September 1939, Hitler invaded Poland and rather than passively accept further German expansion the British and French declared war. The advent of this second World War forced Americans to reconsider whether the national policy of isolationism that had evolved in the late thirties encompassed an adequate response to the emerging situation. Roosevelt clearly thought not and was now confronted with the task of moving the American people to this realization.

Although personally committed to a positive role for the United States in world affairs, FDR was wary of directly challenging the national predisposition toward non-involvement.[55] Instead he chose to lead by indirection, noting his alarm at the course of events overseas but repeatedly declaring his commitment to peace. Even as he sought modification of the neutrality laws and extension of aid to the Allies, he presented these as measures to keep Hitler's war as far from American shores as possible. Although he could hardly help but recognize that if his actions failed to contain Hitler they would almost assuredly bring war to the United States, he was understandably ill disposed to explore this possibility.

As he cautiously and uncertainly framed a foreign policy, FDR naturally cast a wary eye on the press. Nazi aggression spoke for itself, but some kinds of reporting could undermine its impact on the American people while other "facts" emphasized Hitler's aggressive designs. From his perspective, news reflecting Hitler's aggressiveness and duplicity was educational. News of Germany's peace offers and of the indecision, disunity, and incompetence of its adversaries was isolationist propaganda. The American press, for its part, continued to view events as they bore on foreign policy as they viewed all stories. News was a commodity—gathered and sold. Its "influence" on events was of secondary importance. What mattered was its timeliness, its quantity, and its potential interest. With the New Deal waning, reporters were naturally interested in what the White House could tell them about events abroad, particularly as they affected, or might be affected by, United States policy. FDR, however, was not inclined to candor, partly because his intentions were probably not clear to him and partly for fear of disrupting delicate diplomacy or playing into the hands of his foreign policy critics.

FDR once referred to "government by public opinion" as the "very fabric of democracy."[56] But experience had circumscribed his view of the public's right to information on which to form that opinion. For years he had seen his views, and even the facts he conveyed to the press, distorted or ignored. In many instances he believed this had been done deliberately by editors serving partisan political motives. He had of necessity tolerated this situation, but his annoyance was never well disguised. By 1940, his patience was worn thin and the crisis in world affairs made him less inclined to openness. He had learned, he explained to isolationist Congressman Bruce Barton, that excessive candor provided his enemies with ammunition with which to attack him and undermine the national interest. Rejecting Barton's request for clarification of an important issue, FDR said he found it "hard to explain technical matters to the Congress in view of the distorted values which are promptly given to one phase or the other of a complete picture.'' This disposition to keep his own counsel grew as the opportunity for secrecy expanded and naturally extended to FDR's relations with the press.[57]

The President's distrust of the press, and reporters' heightened interest in administration foreign and military policies, was to lead to a series of sharp encounters. An incident early in 1939 set the tone. In January, an experimental American bombing plane crashed in California. Among the victims was an official of the French Air Ministry. His death revealed for the first time that the President had authorized the sale of some of the nation's most advanced military equipment to a country likely to be involved in another European war. Responding to criticism of the clandestine arrangement, FDR invited members of the Senate Military Affairs Committee to the White House so that he might explain the circumstances surrounding the incident. Although the conference was confidential, some of the conferees leaked its contents to friends in the press. Worst of all, the accounts, which made headlines across the nation, attributed to the President the assertion that ''America's frontier was on the Rhine.''

This remarkable observation naturally evoked considerable comment in the American and foreign press with critics charging that the United States had no clear foreign policy. The President in turn categorically denied making the remark and rejected the imputations of confusion. Asked at a February 3 press conference how such a report could appear, FDR blamed politicians who deliberately misrepresented the truth to newspapermen, and editors who turned rumors into ''facts.'' Roosevelt said that newspapers normally made little distinction between fact and rumor, and this probably accounted for the erroneous press reports. Assertions that the foreign policy of the United States required clarification he labeled a ''deliberate lie'' attributable to political and newspaper ''agitators'' who, ''appealing to the ignorance, the prejudice and the fears of the American people, are acting in an un-American way.''[58]

At the President's next press conference, reporters, seeking to resolve the controversy as to what FDR had in fact said to the Senators, asked him if there was a stenographic record of the meeting. Roosevelt replied that he did not think so. A reporter pressed him to ask his stenographer Henry Kannee, who had been at the meeting and was now present in the conference room, if he had taken notes. Roosevelt jokingly said that Kannee did not know, and reporters laughed. In fact Kannee had taken notes and according to his transcribed record FDR had not used the phrase "frontier on the Rhine." He had, however, indicated that America's "first line of defense" included "the continued independent existence" of the large group of nations threatened by Hitler and Mussolini—preeminently England and France. Roosevelt's refusal, for whatever reason, to reveal the contents of the transcript left reporters free to believe whatever they wished. Upset by the incident, the President sought to protect himself, according to Robert Butow, by installing a taping system which enabled him to secretly record what was said "at sensitive White House meetings."[59]

Other allegedly false press reports fueled the growing conflict. In July 1939, the United Press carried a story reporting disagreement between the President and Secretary of State Cordell Hull concerning modification of the neutrality legislation. Reports of differences between FDR and the Secretary on various aspects of foreign policy were to become increasingly common. They usually originated with interventionist members of the Cabinet, particularly Secretary of the Interior Harold Ickes who blamed Hull for what he thought was the State Department's excessive caution. In this instance, FDR, eager to preserve an image of administration unity, issued a 250-world denial which charged, among other things, that this was only the latest in a series of episodes in which "the United Press had been guilty of a falsification of the actual facts."[60]

The onset of war in Europe in September 1939 intensified both the administration's involvement in foreign affairs and the President's need to keep elements of his activities from the public. In two public statements delivered in early September, Roosevelt affirmed his commitment to press freedoms and insisted that he contemplated no censorship. Nevertheless, he cautioned both the press and the public to check with authoritative government sources before accepting anything they heard or read.[61] Roosevelt's strictures might seem appropriate in view of the international crisis. There were and would continue to be rumors, many of them false, not only of war, but of peace and of the innumerable incidents and personages that ranged between the two. However, defending oneself against rumors presupposed the ability to distinguish them from authentic news. The President recognized this and offered to act as the ultimate source of verification. Although he did not make this entirely clear, FDR apparently hoped that people would suspend judgement on reports until they heard confirmation from him or some other administration spokesman.

The President was advising press and public to credit only the official line; for "authoritative sources" naturally excluded those within government who, while in a position to leak authentic reports, could not claim to speak with authority. In FDR's view, information from such sources was no better than rumor, and he insisted in effect that the public depend completely on those responsible for American policy for their knowledge of that policy. Since such officials were unlikely to comment on matters they found embarrassing to the United States, America's friends, or to the administration, the range of information and critical perspectives available to the public under FDR's prescription would have been severely limited. The government's disposition to secrecy was as strong as the press's penchant for seeking inside information. Both contributed to the ubiquitous news leaks that had become a Washington institution and the source of much of what the President called "rumor" and much of what the press characterized as "news."

FDR's advice was a reiteration of a definition of "freedom of the press" he had originally put forth in the 1930s.[62] In his view, immunity from government control entailed a press obligation to act "responsibly." As Roosevelt indicated at a press conference early in 1940, the American people had a right to expect and newspapers an obligation to supply "honest factual news."[63] Since by the President's standards such news should come from or be confirmed by government, Roosevelt was inviting the press to join government in the service of the public's interest. Should it fail to do so, he seemed to say, it ran the risk of public repudiation and perhaps even the forfeiture of some of its valued independence. Under this formula, the White House would supply all the news fit to print, and the press would print it. No need for journalistic probing or rumor mongering and no call for expressions of doubt.

Most reporters, while happy to accept the government's handouts, were unwilling to accept the administration as the final authority on what constituted legitimate news. Arthur Krock illustrated their objections in an account of his efforts to get at the story of one relatively minor international incident. In October 1939, journalists sought to confirm reports that the Scandinavian governments had requested the United States to intervene with the Soviet Union on behalf of Finland. When Krock and others sought verification at the State Department, they could find no one willing to comment. Inquiring at the White House, they found "Mr. Early as often before" unavailable for comment. Krock pointed to the episode as an example of the "one-sided 'cooperation' over an issue that warranted no secrecy.''[64] The inability of authorities to deal positively with Krock's inquiry may have reflected confusion within the bureaucracy or a desire to prevent the premature disclosure of a sensitive diplomatic move. Whatever the reason, this was only one of a number of incidents indicating the conflict between the President and the press.[65]

In the spring of 1940, FDR sought to intercede with Italy's leader, Benito Mussolini, to ensure continued Italian neutrality. The President attempted to keep this effort secret, but on the first of May the *New York Times* published an account of the American diplomatic efforts.[66] The White House denied the story, and several days later Roosevelt, obviously angered, wrote to publisher Arthur Hays Sulzberger to insist that the press accept secrecy in the national interest. FDR wrote that the *Times* report had not hurt him personally but had hurt "the President of the United States, . . . the policy of our government and the policy of other [the French and the British] governments.'' The *Times*, he said, had unnecessarily "helped the cause of Germany,'' and had it simply "checked with the proper authorities in Washington,'' the incident could have been avoided. Apparently, the President meant that administration officials would have assured the reporter that his account was false.[67]

The White House went even further in its response to an unwanted story in the Chicago *Tribune*. This journal was less the self-described voice of the Middle West than the personal vehicle for the eccentric and vicious sentiments of its owner, Colonel Robert R. McCormick. After a brief period of support for FDR, McCormick had become convinced, as he wrote, that "Mr. Roosevelt is a Communist.''[68] His hatred for the administration thenceforth knew no bounds, and the *Tribune* bore daily witness to McCormick's ire.[69] In mid-June 1940, Walter Trohan, writing in the *Tribune*, alleged that the State Department had learned that France was about to conclude a separate peace with the Axis, leaving Great Britain to fight on alone. Early, who was friendly with Trohan, not only denied the truth of the story but publicly impugned the motives of its author. At his June 13 press conference he accused Trohan of printing a story which the State Department had already told him was false. This led him to wonder, Early said, "whether all news published in the United States is published from a pure American patriotic point of view, or from foreign points of view.'' The day following Early's rebuke, the *Tribune* reaffirmed its story, asserting that its source had also said that it would be vigorously denied. Trohan wrote to Early

to assure him that he was not a member of the German-American Bund
or any other such organization and that he was proud of his Americanism. He also noted that the "White House which was once wont to
label all its critics 'economic royalists' and 'tories' is now rather free
with implications of treason." Four days later the peace negotiations
of which Trohan had written began.[70]

Trohan's report anticipating the event was of no great value to his
readers and made things more difficult for the French and British and
perhaps embarrassing for the United States. From Roosevelt's perspective, the truth of the report did not justify its publication. In this and
similar circumstances it was entirely understandable that the White
House would do what it could to make its views on press responsibilities
understood. Nevertheless, it was unreasonable for FDR to expect that
the majority of the press would share his perspective. If the press was
to be something more than a government mouthpiece, the price was
unwanted, perhaps even unwarranted, publicity.

The President seemed unable to accept this thinking and was repeatedly upset by examples of what he regarded as irresponsible journalism. His problems came most often from syndicated columnists.
These journalists had developed valued sources of information, usually
highly placed government officials, and most, whether friendly to the
President or not, made their living by revealing to their readers what
they learned. The interests of successful columnists and those of the
President were frequently antithetical. Exclusive stories and critical
commentary accounted for much of their popularity and were at the
heart of their craft. Roosevelt, however, thought that the "decent columnist" should refrain from printing any story inimical to the national
interest. His definition tended to be rather broad. Thus, to his way of
thinking the columnists who in one instance reported the first encounter
between an American warship and a German submarine and in another
disclosed the battle raging inside the administration over the creation
of a morale agency, had violated the standards of journalistic decency.
He believed self-censorship was called for even though, as in these
incidents, the reports happened to be true.[71]

Continually looking for ways to make his feelings known, the President, immediately following his reelection in November 1940, ordered
columnist Paul Mallon barred from a regularly scheduled White House
news conference. Historians would find precedent for this action in a

similar ban ordered by Theodore Roosevelt, but the rationale now employed was disturbingly different. No specific offense was cited, as it had been in the earlier episode. Rather, the White House alleged, without example, the "inaccuracy" of Mallon's reporting. On this ground the President could well have banned several others and indeed, according to his personal secretary Marguerite (Missy) Le Hand, he had considered excluding, in addition to Mallon, columnists Ray Tucker, Hugh Johnson, Westbrook Pegler, and Arthur Krock.[72]

Commenting some years later, Roosevelt blamed his troubles with this particular breed of journalist on the fact that with few exceptions "they do not tell the truth or else do it in such a way as to hurt their neighbor." This, he said, combined with the fact that "there are always people in private life who believe anything they read," made political columns particularly destructive.[73] Actually, however, it was not the truthfulness of columnists that annoyed Roosevelt, but the thrust of particular exposés. He enjoyed close relations with some members of the fraternity, and his favorite, Walter Winchell, was known neither for his veracity nor his sensitivity. Indeed, Winchell's gossipy column and weekly radio broadcasts were notable for nothing so much as their sensationalism and character assassination. But he was slavishly devoted to the President and unswervingly promoted interventionism. His wisdom in these matters seemed to have overcome Roosevelt's concern for objectivity and journalistic ethics, and Winchell enjoyed an intimacy and ease of access to the President commanded by few others.[74]

Mallon's banishment was short lived, and the President did not act on his wish to exclude others. His actions were in a sense restrained. He was unhappy with the newspaper treatment of his foreign policy, yet he avoided action that could lead to a complete rupture. Nevertheless, the Mallon affair appeared to some reporters to be part of an emerging White House policy of holding the press at arms length.[75]

Although the President was not happy with the state of White House-press relations, his concern was no doubt eased by the fact, which he suspected, that newspapers had passed the peak of their political influence. Roosevelt had warned journalists repeatedly since 1937 that their irresponsible ways were destroying their credibility. Whatever truth there may have been to this analysis, two other developments in the late 1930s, over which newspapers had no control, almost certainly did undermine their political importance. The first of these, the development of radio as an important source of news and information, will be examined in chapter 5. More speculative but also worth exploring is the development of scientific opinion polling, to which we now turn.

A major factor accounting for the traditional power of the press was its role in assessing political performance. Until the 1940s, Roosevelt, like most politicians, looked to the editorial and opinion pages of the major daily newspapers for a continuous evaluation of government. Ego certainly played a large role. More importantly, he knew that with mass opinion an unknown quantity, the reputation and prestige of the administration rested largely with the judgements of the nation's leading newspapers. Political leadership depends in large part on an image of success. Insofar as bureaucrats, congressmen, and business and labor leaders believed that Roosevelt was fully in command and likely to succeed, they were apt to cooperate. Doubts encouraged defections and opposition.[76] Such attitudes could not always be based on personal observation, and it was tempting to rely on political pundits. Inevitably, FDR's allies and adversaries, as well as fence straddlers, derived their impressions of how well the President was doing from what they read in the editorial and opinion columns of their newspapers.

To the extent that this was true, Roosevelt's political standing rested on the sympathies of a handful of journalists. This situation he found intolerable, particularly in view of the fact that press criticism was usually at odds with the public's assessment of his performance—so far as he could tell. This conclusion, based on his public contacts, was borne out by election results. Unfortunately, the opportunities for such popular endorsements were widely spaced, and in the time between the elections assessments of presidential performance continued to rest largely on newspaper comment. What FDR needed was a continuous, credible reflection of his popular support.

The obvious way to determine what people thought between elections was to ask them, and politicians and journalists in pursuit of an elusive "public opinion" had for some time employed "straw votes." These were not necessarily, as the name implies, minor or informal undertakings. In some cases considerable effort went into ensuring accurate results. Such was the case with the polls conducted for Roosevelt during his governorship and before the 1932, 1934, and 1936 national elections. The motive of the pollsters in these instances was to use voter preferences to determine campaign strategy. Unfortunately, the pollsters could not ask everyone, and their samplings, while extensive, were not scientifically selected. Results, according to party chieftain James Farley, ranged from exceedingly accurate to dismally misleading. The predictions of the 1936 vote based on straw vote polling fell into the latter category.[77]

The election was to prove fatal to the most widely known straw vote, the one conducted by the *Literary Digest*. In an effort to increase subscriptions the journal had for some time been compiling lists of names drawn from telephone directories and automobile registration records. To these people the *Digest* had periodically sent questionnaires on political issues along with subscription forms. The device worked well—subscriptions increased and the poll results, which the magazine printed, had become widely accepted and a popular magazine feature. In 1936, however, the class bias inherent in *Digest* sources together with the fact that the election more clearly divided the electorate along income lines than any other in the past, produced a forecast grossly at odds with election returns. Ironically, the device once successful in building the magazine's fortunes now contributed to its demise, taking down with it the pretensions of all straw polling.[78]

The same election that did in the straw vote, however, witnessed the emergence of scientific polls which would not only take their place, but would quickly end the newspaper's role as principal arbiter of political success.[79] The principles upon which scientific polling was based had been known for some time and psychologists had made considerable use of opinion sampling in attitudinal studies. In the 1920s, commercial advertisers began looking to polling to test consumer response to products, advertising themes, and techniques. In 1935, three organizations which were to perfect the application of these methods to political issues were formed. The agencies of George Gallup, Elmo Roper, and Archibald Crossley promoted their services by conducting polls on public issues which they sold to newspapers and journals. These interesting forays into the public mind were intended to familiarize potential commercial customers with the pollsters and their products. Since credibility was an important element of a poll's saleability, considerable thought and effort were put into refining the technique.

The creation of *Public Opinion Quarterly* in 1937 testified to a growing academic interest in developing reliable means to divine popular preferences. The issue of bias-free methodology preoccupied the growing body of experts and the results were encouraging. Although the people in the samples now appear to have been wealthier and better educated than the populace in general, they closely approximated the voting portion of the citizenry and the polls recorded impressively accurate predictions in both the 1936 and 1940 elections; in each instance missing the popular vote by less than 3 percent.[80]

Election predictions attracted the most attention and provided the best demonstration of the accuracy of scientific polling, but the pollsters did not confine themselves to predicting political contests. They also sampled opinion on a variety of contemporary issues ranging from how well the President was doing his job to the preferred form of welfare for the unemployed. The scope of polling and its apparent accuracy piqued the interest of both public and politicians. In FDR's case, the interest was encouraged by pollsters who deliberately sought to make the President aware of their product, often supplying the White House with pre-publication releases. Beginning in the 1940 election campaign and increasingly thereafter, Roosevelt received large numbers of poll results. Some, as suggested, came from the polling organizations. Others were supplied by political associates usually intent on encouraging the President to follow a given course of action.[81]

The most important source of polls reaching the White House was social psychologist Hadley Cantril, who in 1940 had created the Office of Public Opinion Research. Cantril was a liberal, loyal to FDR, and concerned with making polls serve the President. He designed his polls for maximum political utility and conducted many of his surveys at the White House's suggestion. Employing a special technique, he was able to produce fairly accurate preliminary findings more rapidly than other polling agencies. He often submitted these results in a format designed to help FDR take them in at a glance. Issues of continuing interest were the subject of repeated polls and provided the data for trend charts which Cantril personally kept current at the White House.[82]

More importantly, such polls were now a regular feature appearing in various forms in journals, notably Roper's polls in *Fortune*, and in newspapers. Henceforth, every politician, from FDR on down, could know the public's judgement on every issue almost as soon as it arose. The effect on the President's prestige and power is not certain. It is clear, however, that Roosevelt and other politicians were no longer obliged to rely on newspapers to assess their success or prospects. As the political community came to look to the polls for guidance on the President's performance, the influence newspapers once enjoyed, especially at the White House, very likely diminished.[83] Now the press was seen by the President less as a judge and more as only a medium. And even in this role, it no longer exercised the near monopoly it once had.

3

Confronting the Challenge of Isolationism

In the months following the outbreak of war in Europe, President Franklin D. Roosevelt faced a pair of closely related problems upon whose solution the fate of the nation might well rest. How might America's great strength most effectively secure Hitler's defeat? How could the American people be made to support the action the President decided to take? Roosevelt had long been convinced that Hitler was a moral abomination and Germany a menace to civilized values and to American security. At first he hoped that France and Britain, with U.S. moral and diplomatic support, could bring the Third Reich to heel. But by the summer of 1940 it was clear that this was beyond their capacity and that if Hitler was to be stopped, the United States would have to take a direct hand. Timely intervention on even a limited scale might mean the difference between a relatively short, bloodless victory and a drawn out bloodletting of uncertain outcome.

The key to determining whether America's defensive frontier would be along the Rhine, the English Channel, or somewhere in the Western Hemisphere did not lie with strategic planning or military preparedness alone. Indeed, public opinion might well prove decisive. The American people shared the President's revulsion against Hitler and were conscious of the aggressive and threatening nature of the Nazi regime. They were, however, neither inclined to contemplate the long-range implications of these circumstances nor to precipitate conflict so long as there was any hope of avoiding it. The experience of World War I had contributed to public hostility and organized resistance toward involvement in another conflict. Most Americans in the late 1930s believed that war was a costly and fruitless undertaking that the United States could avoid by minding its own business. In these circumstances the events of 1939–1941, although they convinced many of the need for limited U.S. involvement, were not sufficient to unite the nation in support of immediate military intervention. In time perhaps they would. But it was time that Hitler's adversaries, current and potential, did not have.

The nature of the Nazi regime, the power of German arms, and the evidence of Hitler's apparently unlimited ambition went a long way toward undermining isolationism, but the "facts" never argued clearly for armed American involvement. Until Germany declared war on the United States it was possible to argue, as isolationists did, that Hitler either did not wish, or was at least unable, to attack the United States or the Western Hemisphere successfully: an impression that the Fuehrer himself sought to encourage. This problem was intensified by the fact that the administration's immediate programs were in a sense the enemy of its long-range goals. Rhetoric in favor of re-armament and aid to Britain was inevitably couched in terms which suggested that these were a substitute for the much feared American expeditionary force. In fact, however, such an expeditionary force might some day be required and the President was confronted with the job of encouraging partial involvement in the war without limiting his freedom to pursue more aggressive policies should the situation call for them.

Achieving this goal was made difficult, at least at first, by the fact that the informational strategy which the administration had used to good effect during the New Deal years was, in the circumstances of early 1940, of greatly diminished utility. White House–press tensions were a factor, but more important was the fact that the administration was less able than earlier to exploit the propaganda value normally attached to government affairs. Informational propaganda presupposed purposeful activity. However, industrial and military mobilization were slow to get under way and plagued by serious problems, while policy in regard to the deployment of U.S. forces was confused and uncertain. This gave the administration little to advertise, and for a time during 1940 FDR groped for a propaganda policy that would effectively serve the nation's needs.

His efforts produced first a campaign of public speeches in which he and a corps of interventionist spokesmen sought mainly to discredit the isolationist opposition. This enterprise enlisted the support of and was eventually largely supplanted by independent interventionist organizations which operated with encouragement and direction from the White House. The growing crisis created by Hitler's successes, however, led many interventionists to demand a more active White House propaganda program and in the fall of 1940 the President began considering creation of an official morale building agency. The Office of Civilian Defense emerged in May 1941.

Isolationism was at the heart of the administration's problems. Its adherents were indistinguishable from other Americans except in their attitudes toward U.S. foreign policy.[1] Its leaders were a widely disparate group which included progressives like Montana Democrat Burton K. Wheeler and right-wing Republican Senator Robert Taft; Sears Roebuck Chairman Robert Wood, and Socialist Party leader Norman Thomas; intellectuals like University of Chicago President Robert Hutchins, and technologues like Charles Lindbergh. Such people, though recognizing that their advocacy benefited Germany, were not necessarily pro-German, unconcerned with the fate of democratic nations or institutions, or even particularly anglophobic. Admirers of Hitler were clearly outside the mainstream of isolationism, and most isolationists, as they tirelessly repeated, preferred an Allied to an Axis victory. They differed from their interventionist adversaries chiefly in their willingness to accept British defeat if attempts to avoid it seemed likely to lead to American military involvement. They believed the risk in lives, wealth, and basic American freedom was too great, especially since it was unnecessary. By the spring of 1941 most approved of material assistance to Britain as long as it did not vitiate American preparedness, but their fundamental faith rested in America's inherent strength and defensibility. These, they argued, provided the nation with a luxury unique among world powers. The United States alone could avoid war through its own actions without giving up anything except the impulse to meddle in other people's affairs. Unlike the interventionists, they saw neither moral default nor national peril in a neutrality that left a substantial portion of the western world under Nazi control. Having judged war to be the worst possible consequence of national policy, they were calloused to circumstances that others took as incitement to involvement.

Understandably, Roosevelt did not view the isolationists with the detachment of a recent scholar. He believed the worst of them and derived both emotional satisfaction and political value from this conviction. Although he believed that only a few of his critics were consciously collaborating with Berlin, he thought that some were so preoccupied with their own narrow interests that they had willfully blinded themselves to those of the nation. Others he saw as pure of heart but hopelessly naive. From his perspective, the distinctions were of little consequence since the effects were all the same.

In the months of debate finally resolved by the attack on Pearl Harbor, Roosevelt's rhetoric reflected these convictions. Of course, he argued on a number of fronts: defending aid to Britain as prudent and commonsensical, likening Lend Lease to providing a hose to a neighbor whose house was on fire, and dramatizing the Nazi peril by characterizing the U-boats as "rattlesnakes" of the Atlantic. But throughout, insofar as he directly met the challenge of isolationism, he sought mainly to impugn the motives and destroy the credibility of its proponents. It was a tactic reminiscent of the one he had employed against the enemies of the New Deal a few years earlier.

Not long after the commencement of hostilities in Europe, Roosevelt, referring to the coming debate over American foreign policy, predicted "a dirty fight."[2] This characterization was a reality almost before the echoes of the opening salvoes in Poland had died away. The initial skirmish came in regard to the administration's attempt to modify the neutrality laws to permit the sale of munitions to the Allies. Revision was jeopardized by a deluge of messages urging Congress to resist the proposed change. The White House responded by labeling this apparent expression of public sentiment a product of Nazi intrigue. In September, Stephen Early told reporters that the government had intercepted cabled instructions from Berlin to "its friends in the United States" directing organized opposition to revision, suggesting that the letters and telegrams received on Capitol Hill were the result. At the same time, although he had indicated publicly that the White House did not intend to play a role in the public discussion of the embargo issue, he joined Assistant Secretary of State Adolf Berle in arranging to have the German cable story "leaked" to Walter Winchell and others.[3] Thus from the very outset, the administration, while pretending to stand above debate, sought to impress upon the public the un-American character of its opponents.

This technique is also apparent in Roosevelt's January 1940 State of the Union address. After touching on a number of problems facing the nation, the President spoke of the need for national unity. Roosevelt warned Americans to be alert to the "apologists for foreign aggressors," whom he described further as "those selfish and partisan groups at home who wrap themselves in a false mantle of Americanism to promote their own economic, financial, or political advantage." Borrowing a phrase from the isolationist lexicon, the President charged these sinister forces with "trying European tricks upon us."[4] FDR's idea that the isolationist-interventionist struggle was merely a continuation of the ideological struggle of the New Deal era was not convincing. Indeed, as Berle noted with some misgivings, interventionist supporters included "the Morgans, the Harvard New Englanders," and others of that ilk, who had "really influenced our entry into war in 1917."[5] Nevertheless, Roosevelt would never abandon the idea growing out of his earlier experience that opposition to his policies was rooted in class interests and partisan politics.

Events in Europe soon provided Roosevelt with a more compelling explanation for isolationism. In the spring and summer of 1940, Hitler amassed a series of surprisingly sudden victories beginning in Norway and ending with the collapse of France in June. Germany's head start in the arms race and its superior leadership and tactics were given some credit for this shocking turn of events. Those who had witnessed or had been victimized by the blitzkrieg provided another rationale—internal subversion, a phenomenon dating to antiquity but recently named the "fifth column." Although the term originated in the Spanish Civil War, it seemed particularly applicable to the German aggression. Nazism was an ideology which found sympathizers throughout the western world. It appealed especially to German nationals living outside the fatherland. Inevitably, these elements were blamed for the disintegration of resistance in the face of the Nazi attack. Such speculation drew credibility from largely fictional journalistic accounts, of which Leland Stowe's stories on the Norwegian debacle were prototypical. Based on rumor and speculation generated by civilians and soldiers fleeing the Nazis, such stories assumed tidal wave proportions at the time of the fall of France.[6]

Americans were intrigued by the idea that nations, including presumably the United States, could be delivered to Hitler by a handful of his agents and their sympathizers. Government officials, who on this issue knew little more than what they read in the newspapers, shared popular thinking. Stories emanating from the war zone suggested that the German march of conquest had not begun with Nazi troops crossing frontiers; this was merely the second stage in a process initiated earlier with subversion and propaganda. It seemed that America, with its own dissidents and alien populations, might conceivably already be at war without realizing it.

Although there was little substance to the idea of an American fifth column, the concept was plausible, had captured the public's imagination, and FDR found it useful. It served to bolster the President's appeal for faith in his leadership and unquestioning loyalty to his policies. America was threatened, Roosevelt's argument ran, and those who continued to express doubts on this score were part of the problem. They were encouraging Americans to run the risk taken (and lost) by the complacent French during the "phoney war" that preceded their humiliating defeat. The isolationists were not only wrong, they were contributing mightily to the apathy and disunity jeopardizing national survival. Thus, while his opponents sought to focus public discourse on the plausibility of the foreign threat, the President attacked the very concept of foreign policy debate. His thinking is reflected in a May 16 address to Congress. In asking for additional appropriations for defense, Roosevelt justified the request in part by reference to the unprecedented Nazi capacity to reach out and engulf the United States. The new techniques that made this possible, he said, included not only long-range aircraft, but "the treacherous use of the 'fifth column,' " which had made older concepts of defense and security dangerously outmoded.[7] Those who rejected this view were, as FDR soon after described Charles A. Lindbergh, "Nazis" or, at best, their dupes.[8]

In a fireside chat at the end of May, Roosevelt again spoke of the unprecedented threat confronting the nation, emphasizing that American security rested ultimately not on technology but on domestic unity. The menace to the United States, he said, was "not a matter of military weapons alone," it included "new methods of attack," including the "fifth column that betrays a nation unprepared for treachery." Roosevelt made it clear that he spoke not only of "spies, saboteurs, and traitors," with whom he promised to deal vigorously, but of all those agents of discord who were creating a situation wherein "sound national policies come to be viewed with a new and unreasoning skepticism." He charged that his critics had "deliberately and consciously closed their eyes" to the realities of international affairs "because they were determined to be opposed to their government, its foreign policy and every other policy, to be partisan, and to believe that anything that the government did was wholly wrong." The result, he warned, was that "men can lose confidence in each other . . . and in the efficacy of their own united action. Faith and courage can yield to doubt and fear. The unity of the State can be so sapped that its strength is destroyed.'' This process, he said, was currently at work in America to ''divide and weaken us in the face of danger as other nations have been weakened before.''[9]

By the spring of 1941, circumstances were propitious for the effective use of informational propaganda, and this gradually supplanted the earlier negative campaign led by the President. The educational effort, loosely orchestrated by the White House, was carried out by public relations officers of both the new and the long-established defense agencies. Almost all of the propaganda they produced was of the kind that had earlier promoted the New Deal—it did not advocate policy, it merely provided (or withheld) information in ways calculated to build support for the administration. Without dwelling on the possibility of U.S. military involvement, it helped to undermine isolationism by building confidence in the administration's ability to deal with the Axis threat.

True, policy remained uncertain, but there were by now a great many things to which the administration might point with pride. Men and women were going to work in defense plants, reporting for duty in military training camps, buying defense bonds, and cooperating with government programs for the conservation of strategic goods. Activities in the great arsenal of democracy supplied a great deal of non-controversial copy, and the public relations officers for the various defense agencies, many of them recently recruited from the older peacetime departments, now went to work publicizing the great national defense story. Although their efforts would not gain the notoriety of the Creel Committee, they were, in the judgment of one expert, ''probably only slightly less effective'' than CPI in carrying the government's message to the people.[10]

The greatest single source of information on the defense effort was the Division of Information (DoI) of the Office of Emergency Management (OEM). DoI maintained a central press room from which the Washington press corps could obtain news releases, pictures, charts, and other data originating in the sixteen mobilization agencies affiliated with OEM. Its staff was efficient and productive—turning out between ten and twenty stories a day, almost all of which were carried by the press associations. In one month in 1941, it supplied reporters with 190 press releases. DoI also produced the full range of products common to the propagandist's craft, including a slick weekly magazine, called

Defense, designed to provide state and local officials with "all (and I mean ALL) the news fit to print about defense."[11]

DoI propaganda was complemented by the work of Lowell Mellett's Office of Government Reports. OGR was the successor to the National Emergency Council, which had coordinated New Deal propaganda at the state level. Among Mellett's functions, like that of the old NEC, was to see to it that local communities were kept informed of administration programs. In this case, the message was almost entirely related to defense preparedness. Mellett had arranged with the National Editorial Association, a news service which catered to small daily, weekly, and semi-weekly newspapers, to distribute to its own subscribers a brief weekly summary of information bearing on national defense. He also provided a daily digest of defense information to a select but considerable list of newspapers and other institutions, public officials, and "persons having a need to be kept informed."[12]

Every agency whose activities touched on defense contributed to the effort led by DoI and OGR. Employing methods proven effective since the outset of the New Deal, these public information offices secured data from the organizations they served, put these dry facts into more or less palatable form, and supplied them to the national wire services and large metropolitan dailies. The written word was supplemented in many instances by agency-produced posters, short films, and radio programs. The Treasury Department, for example, as part of its efforts to sell defense bonds, provided newspaper copy and other publicity releases urging sales and indicating how great the public response had been thus far. The Post Office contributed a series of three defense stamps (about 20 million were issued beginning October 1, 1940) celebrating the contributions of "industry and agriculture" (1 cent), the "Army and Navy" (2 cents), and "security, education, conservation, and health" (3 cents). And so it went in agency after agency.[13]

One educational project worthy of special attention was that carried out by the Army in the nation's defense plants. Soon after his appointment in the summer of 1940, Secretary of War Stimson placed the Army's Bureau of Public Relations under his direct supervision and encouraged it to increase its public educational functions.[14] In June 1941 the Office of Production Management (OPM) reported to Army officials that worker complacency was impeding military production.[15] Edward F. McGrady, a special labor consultant to the Secretary of War, wrote to Under Secretary Robert Patterson warning of the need for immediate action. Pointing to strikes in 25 munitions plants, McGrady charged that "labor morale was dangerously low [and] likely to become worse." At the root of the problem, the former union leader declared, was the fact that no sustained effort had been made to show labor its stake and role in the defense program with the result that labor relations were proceeding on a "strike-as-usual basis."[16]

In early September the War Department, in cooperation with the labor division of OPM, undertook to remedy the situation. Although a number of traditional devices were employed, its effort rested mainly on personal contact. Morale specialists and military officers began visiting defense plants ostensibly to conduct inspection tours but actually to impress upon the workers the urgency and significance of their work. Typically, the groups included Air Corps cadets, an officer from the War Department's Bureau of Public Relations, and a labor representative of OPM. They spent about two hours in each plant while members of the party spoke informally to individual employees as they went about "inspecting" their work. A short speech on the dangers facing the nation and the workers' contribution to national security was sometimes followed by festivities which included flags, pennants, band music, and singing in which workers participated. According to a confidential report, workers exhibited considerable pride in the Army's interest in their work and were especially pleased to learn of their contributions to the defense program. One union leader reported that the program made it easier to keep the men working when grievances arose.[17]

The activities of the government's publicists and morale builders were extensive and pervasive. Their educational effect, however, was of a special limited kind—one little different from that achieved by the colorful posters and advertisements that adorned factory walls and the pages of the nation's magazines. They suggested purposeful activity involving the whole population and effectively mobilizing the massive military strength of the nation, but provided little instruction, save in the most general sense, in the priorities, purposes, and progress of that endeavor.

This was partly attributable to the constraints imposed by national security considerations. In late May 1941, Grenville Clark, an active and influential spokesman for interventionism, wrote Assistant Secretary of War John J. McCloy, the War Department's expert on morale, urging a comprehensive statement on the progress of rearmament. Clark and other interventionists argued that the government must rebut the isolationist contention that the nation was militarily unprepared to risk confrontation with the Axis and reassure the public that the nation had the capacity to assist Great Britain immediately, without sacrificing American security. The Army, however, was concerned that publication of facts and figures on war production would aid the nation's potential enemies. A compromise solution was reached. Instead of baring its statistical soul, the Army sought to convince newspapermen that all was well by providing them with impressive tours of America's munitions plants to give them a "look behind the scenes of defense."[18]

But it was more than a desire to keep valuable intelligence from the enemy that shaped the defense information strategy. A unified, meaningful account required a single rationale for the release of information, and this did not exist. Defense officials did not agree on essential themes of the "defense story," including the proper pace of mobilization (whether to emphasize how much had been accomplished or how much had yet to be done), priorities in weapons procurement, and the like. This issue might have been resolved by presidential dictation and possibly, as was suggested, by the appointment of an "information czar."[19] Roosevelt was determined, however, to harness everyone—the "all outers" and the "business-as-usualists"—to the war chariot and would not provide the government's information policy with a consistent theme. Defense public relations personnel were left to tell "all the facts," producing information that was often redundant and, worse, inconsistent.[20] The result was that Americans found themselves with more information but less real knowledge on mobilization than on any issue in their history. Certainly most citizens, even the more concerned and erudite among them, could divine little from the deluge of vagrant information on steel tonnage, airplane engine production and the like. There was, nevertheless, a message in this madness. The information blizzard, blinding in its particulars, left the clear impression of successful activity. As in New Deal days, defense propaganda produced a sense that the nation (including the individual citizen) was involved in an enormous endeavor, not entirely comprehensible, perhaps even a little muddled, but, like the social experiments of the 1930s, a great enterprise.

As extensive as the government's propaganda effort was, it was not an adequate response to the isolationist challenge. The facts and figures released by defense agenices were limited by uncertainty and a necessarily non-controversial approach. The speeches of the President and his associates suffered the stigma of special pleading. Polls indicated that more Americans would vote for war than thought the United States should enter the war. This curious anomaly was interpreted by one analyst to mean "that people were more willing to go to war if they felt they could personally play some part in making the decision.[21] That is, while Americans were willing to accept the logical necessity of conflict, they were unwilling to be drawn into it by their governmental leaders. In these circumstances, the effectiveness of official spokesmen was limited. The White House made every effort to recruit people who were not connected in the public's mind with the administration, but after a time, as Early told the President, the task had become a considerable burden.[22]

These deficiencies in government propaganda were in part offset by the appearance of a number of unofficial interventionist organizations which from the winter of 1940–1941 on were to originate much of the administration's side of the great debate. These groups, with White House help, were adept at arranging public appearances for a wide variety of celebrities, many of them non-political, who spoke in favor of interventionism without committing the President to any policy line. The organizations were also able to expand on the government's informational program with a grassroots publicity campaign rather more pointedly directed at intervention.

The privately organized interventionist movement began with the formation of the Committee to Defend Democracy by Aiding the Allies. By the summer of 1940 this group, now commonly called the "White Committee" after its chairman, journalist William Allen White, had 300 local chapters, each involved in organizing meetings, arranging letter-writing campaigns aimed at Congress, and planting material in local papers. All of these activities were designed to place Great Britain in a favorable light, document the Nazi threat, and urge the American interest in the outcome of the European struggle. National headquarters pursued the same objectives on a larger scale. During the campaign for Lend Lease, for example, the Committee distributed a sixteen-page pamphlet delineating the ease with which Germany might invade the Western Hemisphere and a short movie, *It Could Happen Here*, on the vulnerability of the United States to Nazi attack.[23]

The efforts of the White Committee helped to secure adoption of the initial administration measures designed to aid Great Britain. But following passage of Lend Lease, Roosevelt proposed no new foreign policy initiatives and the Committee drifted. FDR's policy, particularly on the salient issue of naval policy, was known only to him, and the absence of leadership stymied his supporters. Like the administration, White's group seemed to tread water waiting for something to happen.

In the meantime, White himself had incurred the wrath of the more militant members of his Committee by announcing that he saw aid to Britain as an alternative rather than a prelude to American involvement, and he was forced out of the organization.[24] The vanguard of the anti-isolationist effort had by now passed to another organization—one favoring immediate American armed intervention. This was the Fight for Freedom (first known as the Century Group), which evolved from meetings in the summer of 1940 among interventionist writers, newspapermen, and clergymen. These "warhawks," as they have recently been dubbed, pledged to seek an immediate American declaration of war against Germany. The chief obstacle to the realization of this goal, they believed, was unenlightened public opinion—a condition they set out to correct.[25]

Taking advantage of extensive contacts among leading journalists, the warhawks concentrated at first on placing interventionist-slanted material in the nation's newspapers, and stories, editorials, cartoons, and features inspired by the organization but not attributed to it appeared widely. Distribution techniques soon extended to include the extensive use of radio and public meetings. By mid-1941 Americans could hear warhawk spokesmen two or three times weekly over nationwide broadcasts. In addition, Fight for Freedom sponsored local radio programs, public meetings, petition drives, and street corner rallies, all echoing the national propaganda themes.[26] Typically, Fight for Freedom spokesmen dealt with the British war effort, the efficacy of the underground resistance movement in Europe, and the fallacies of isolationism.

The warhawks also provided sustained and systematic attacks on the isolationists and their principal organization, the America First Committee. Complementing a similar effort directed from the White House, Fight for Freedom sought to unearth evidence which might be used to discredit the isolationists and their cause,[27] or, in any event, to "pin upon each of the major isolationist figures the image of a Nazi, a Fascist sympathizer, or a dupe of the Axis."[28]

Their effort was assisted by British intelligence, which was working assiduously to move Americans to accept increased United States involvement in the war. Led by William Stephenson ("Intrepid"), the unit stationed in New York used a number of what might be called "dirty tricks" which would eventually prove somewhat embarrassing to the administration. In September 1941, Berle reported that British intelligence appeared to be trying to create as many "incidents" as possible in order to inflame American public opinion and urged the President to permit him to take steps to rein in the rampaging British operation.[29]

A more elevated approach to the problem of persistent isolationist sentiment was taken by the Council for Democracy. This organization was founded in the summer of 1940 by publisher Henry Luce, editor Freda Kirchwey (*The Nation*), journalist-author John Gunther, playwright Robert Sherwood, and radio commentator Raymond Gram Swing. This illustrious group blamed the persistence of isolationism on widespread ignorance of democratic values and sought the remedy in a greater public appreciation of the American system and the danger to it posed by the Nazi-Fascist ideology.

Luce provided seed money and the services of Time-Life Vice President C. D. Jackson. The Council, in its own name and in collaboration with organizations like the Association of Business and Professional Women's Clubs, the National Association of Manufacturers, the United States Chamber of Commerce, and the National Education Association, organized rallies, forums, and conventions.[30] Its messages were heard over radio, read in newspaper and magazine articles and advertisements, and seen in a variety of other media from films to lapel buttons. Their tone was preeminently positive. The Council, rejecting hate propaganda, chose to emphasize the meaning and value of democracy, to encourage national unity, faith in the American system, and confidence in the nation's institutions and leaders.[31]

Although the work of these unofficial propagandists was not directly tied to the administration and did not commit the President to any particular policy line, cooperation with the White House was close and continuous. William Allen White described his affair with the President as a "morganatic relationship" in which he took for granted Roosevelt's "private support," always conferred with him on the Committee's program, and "never did anything the President didn't ask for."[32]

The leaders of the other interventionist/morale organizations also enjoyed close ties to the White House. Fight for Freedom executives were in touch with various members of the President's staff "at least once or twice a day," keeping the White House informed of their plans and undertaking government propaganda assignments on request.[33] The assistance the propagandists sought was extensive and varied. The Council for Democracy, for example, felt free to seek FDR's help in obtaining financial support from a philanthropic foundation. More commonly, the Council sought and received advice on its propaganda campaigns and the good offices of Roosevelt's staff in arranging for government officials and other prominent individuals to speak at Council functions.[34]

Similar services were provided Fight for Freedom. In mid-June 1941, for example, sometime presidential speech writer Robert Sherwood, who was associated at one time or another with all three of the interventionist groups, wired Early asking for a "star" to appear at the Fight for Freedom's scheduled "negro mass meeting in Harlem." The press secretary offered Oklahoma Senator Josh Lee, whom Early described as "an excellent speaker and 'all-out.' "[35] The warhawks also sought White House aid in securing the endorsement of labor leader Daniel Tobin. Early approached Tobin at FDR's request but found the Teamster executive unwilling to jeopardize his standing with his rank-and-file members of German or Italian origin by accepting outright membership in the interventionist organization. He did agree, however, to let the Committee use his name from time to time.[36]

White House assistance to the private propagandists, while significant, never encompassed the explicit policy guidance which anxious interventionists wanted. In January 1941, James Warburg, a critic of FDR's domestic policies and more recently a prominent warhawk, sent Early a copy of a speech he intended to broadcast in support of pending Lend Lease legislation. He asked Early if the line he was to take suited administration needs and also sought clarification of FDR's position on convoying. The same sort of inquiry came from Charles Poletti, Lieutenant Governor of New York, an interventionist and an important figure in Democratic politics, who wrote to presidential assistant Harry Hopkins expressing his confusion as to what he should or should not be saying in regard to the current crisis. "I have made some speeches in favor of convoys," Poletti reported, "but I understand that the President believes that the more effective course is to have patrols. Is it the plan of the administration that we should stop demanding convoys? If it is let us know." The answer received by Poletti, if any, is unknown. Early did, however, write to Warburg telling him that it was impossible to do more than "advise our friends to keep up the good work they are doing."[37]

Similar requests brought essentially the same response. In early April,

William L. White, a member of the more aggressive policy committee which had taken over direction of the Committee to Defend Democracy from White's father, wrote to Mellett announcing the Committee's intention to initiate a bolder propaganda policy. "Instead of tagging along behind the President and endorsing him," he said, the Committee intended to "get out ahead and do some sod-busting and stump-grubbing to make his task easier." But, according to White, one of the obstacles his colleagues confronted was not knowing just what problems the administration anticipated and what policies it contemplated. Occasionally, they found themselves stymied by their ignorance, at a loss to know whether they should be "plugging for convoys or Singapore or more grease for the Greeks." White asked Mellett if he or some other official might provide the Committee with guidance. Mellett, while inviting White to talk with him, insisted that he could not supply what the Committee wanted.[38] As Mellett recognized, White's inquiries posed the same sorts of questions that, as we shall see, FDR repeatedly turned aside at his press conferences. For reasons sufficient to him but beyond the understanding of many of his supporters, Roosevelt would not answer them. Apart from its other effects, his refusal helped to keep alive the differences among the interventionists and undermined their collective effort.[39]

Roosevelt was concerned both by what he felt was the need to make the interventionist propaganda effort more effective and by the uneasiness among some of his most active supporters.[40] In July 1941, he urged members of his Cabinet to redouble their efforts in the war against the administration's critics, but, realistically, his subordinates could not accomplish what the master undertook with reluctance and little success.[41] In August, Secretary of the Navy Frank Knox, responding to FDR's plea, asked his assistant, Adlai Stevenson, to work out a plan for improved government liaison with the interventionist leaders.[42] Stevenson, working with John H. McCloy of the War Department, examined the issue and recommended creation of a committee comprising equal numbers of officials representing government and the private groups. Significantly, this was to concern itself chiefly with scheduling star performers and not with the critical issue of what they should say. Stevenson, reflecting the administration's refusal to delineate its foreign policy, suggested the broadest possible guidelines. Propaganda, he said, should aim at developing increased public confidence in the nation's leaders—not at greater public understanding of foreign policy. In order "to get the maximum of local support throughout the country," Stevenson wrote, "it would be best to emphasize the slogan 'Support the President in the emergency' and avoid controversy about individual measures, declaration of war, etc." Thus, any improvement in propaganda would be in its form not in its substance. In the absence of a national policy which might instruct interventionist rhetoric, government morale makers were merely to turn up its volume.[43]

Although administration spokesmen would have to live with this prescription, they were not altogether happy with it. Attacking the isolationists was not enough. Indeed, by the summer of 1941 the administration tactic of linking its adversaries to the Nazis was producing an adverse reaction in the generally supportive press.[44] Generalized talk of saving democracy was no more promising. While inspiring to some, it inevitably left interventionist leaders, and presumably others, wanting answers to specific questions. How did the President propose to ensure the delivery of goods to England? What was he prepared to do should the current policy of aid short of war fail to secure Hitler's defeat? What circumstances might ultimately require a declaration of war? If war came, would increased aid involve sending American ground troops to fight in Europe? How much more effective interventionist speakers might be if they were able to shape their remarks to anticipate coming events and policy initiatives. If nothing else, such guidance would enable them to avoid embarrassing either themselves or the President. But those who turned to the White House for answers looked in vain.

Roosevelt's stance reflected the fact that on some issues he could not honestly predict what he would do, as he had not settled on a course of action. On all issues, settled or not, he believed more was to be lost than gained through candor. Statements of policy and intent gave his opponents text for niggling criticism and pretext for divisive debate. The President believed that isolationism was a species of defeatism, a counsel of despair, a reactionary holdover of a bygone historical era. It could best be destroyed not with rational argumentation but by raising public morale. What Americans needed was not increased understanding, but greater national pride, self-confidence, determination, and faith in government. When he thought of public enlightenment he thought of old-fashioned "patriotic" speeches designed more to inspire than to instruct. As in 1933, he wanted Americans to rid themselves of doubts and fears and rally to the support of their leaders. Isolationism, like the conservative economic policies of his Republican predecessors, had been tested and proved wanting. The nation, in the midst of crisis created by the outmoded ideology, could ill afford the luxury of debating its wisdom. Propaganda which dwelt upon policy simply distracted most of its listeners from this fundamental fact.

Nevertheless, attitudes toward the defense effort continued to betray troubling signs of weakness. Strikes in defense industries, the strong resistance of draftees to an extension of their service, and the disappointing response to a government appeal for voluntary fuel conservation were all seen by worried interventionists as evidence of "complacency."[45] Most disturbing of all was the persistent outspoken opposition of the isolationists. Although their credibility, even their loyalty, was constantly impugned and their rhetoric all but buried by the avalanche of pro-administration propaganda, they continued to be heard and, more disconcerting, listened to. Their allusions to American mistakes in World War I, the selfish goals of perfidious Albion, the futility of resisting Hitler's military might in Europe, and other such messages drew large and receptive audiences. FDR had probably concluded that the only certain immediate solution to public apathy and isolationism was increased military involvement, particularly the limited engagement of American ground troops. This alone seemed certain to generate the enthusiastic support the administration sought. With this in mind, Roosevelt examined a number of schemes for the overseas deployment of American troops, but events intervened and no suitable opportunity materialized until the Japanese attack solved the problem. In the meantime, while the President groped for a policy and a program of action he was vulnerable to demands that he supplant, or at least bolster, current public relations activities with a more direct approach.[46]

In need of a device that would galvanize the public and satisfy his supporters' demands for effective leadership, FDR encouraged discussion of a national morale (or propaganda) agency with wide-ranging powers to combat isolationism. At the very least, such an organization would quiet his interventionist critics and free him of the burden of personally leading the attack on his opponents. His attempts to realize this concept, however, quickly ran into problems growing out of sharp differences within the administration as to the proper approach to the morale problem.

Much of the debate revolved around interpretations of the American experience with propaganda in the first World War. Long before the United States had joined that conflict, the American people had been subjected to intensive propaganda, much of it from abroad, particularly from Great Britain. Once the United States had become a belligerent, the burden of telling Americans what to think passed to the government. During the years 1917–1918 George Creel's Committee on Public Information (CPI) worked to heighten and sustain enthusiasm for the war effort and support for America's wartime leadership. The propaganda worked so well that it aroused intense public criticism of its anti-democratic implications and the false perceptions and hysteria it had produced. Resentments were kept alive in the thirties by anti-war literature which left Americans feeling ill used by propagandists, foreign and domestic.[47] Reinforcing this negative reaction was news from Germany suggesting that enthrallment with Hitler and Nazism was in large part the work of Dr. Goebbels' Ministry of Propaganda.

Some Americans were offended by efforts to manipulate opinion. Others saw propaganda as a means to make the democratic state more effective. Indeed, many of those professing the strongest loyalty to liberal values and aspirations, most notably the progressives of the Theodore Roosevelt–Woodrow Wilson era, rejected the sovereignty of mass opinion. Walter Lippmann, among others, had argued that the public, acting out of ignorance, indifference, or under the influence of powerful factions, might ignore or even be led to oppose its own interests. In these circumstances, many progressives, including FDR, felt a responsibility to actively combat popular delusions and to shape public attitudes to an enlightened vision of the national good. The Creel Committee itself had been largely made up of progressives who sought to use it to promote democratic ideals and social reform.[48]

Those who subscribed to this practical idealism, while not necessarily endorsing the propaganda effort of the World War, recognized in it a model for the efficient molding of popular attitudes. After all, propaganda was widely credited with helping take the nation into war and with inducing militancy in a people thousands of miles removed from the conflict. More recently, commercial advertising served as a constant reminder of the susceptibility of the mass mind to purposeful manipulation. The implications for government were made clear in 1927 by Harold Lasswell's very influential study of *Propaganda Techniques in the World War*, in which he asserted that "There is no question but that government management of opinions is an unescapable [sic] corollary of large scale modern war." In this and other works Lasswell urged a scientific approach to thought modification.[49]

Interest in propaganda techniques and analysis increased dramatically in the United States following the outbreak of war in 1939. Most of it focused on how Americans might defend themselves against the various totalitarian "isms." But there was also considerable concern for developing stronger attachment to American values as a protection against these ideologies. Thus, while those worried by the growing threat of totalitarianism warned the public against the wiles of alien demagoguery, they found it appropriate to consider how propaganda might be used to promote American democracy.[50] Some hoped for the revival of some sort of Creel Committee. In 1939, two social scientists published a sympathetic account of the CPI in which they described the organization as "a social innovation brilliantly conceived and in many ways brilliantly executed." War, they argued, required the full participation of all citizens and the state could either generate it through propaganda or secure it through coercive power.[51] Propaganda was an alternative to coercion—a benign tool for freedom's defense—and Creel's Committee provided a positive model for organizing the effort.

While social scientists and others discussed the potential of organized propaganda, the need for some morale effort was driven home to the President by the flood of offers the White House received following the fall of France from Americans anxious about the fate of the nation and seeking some way of participating in its defense. White House advisors recognized both the potential value of this human resource and the danger of enthusiasm turning to frustration and disaffection should it fail to find appropriate outlets. A number of suggestions reached the President and from them grew the idea of a national agency which would capitalize on the voluntarist spirit and provide a center for national morale building.[52] Archibald MacLeish, the distinguished poet and Librarian of Congress, urged appointment of what he called a "coordinator of civilian volunteer activities for defense." MacLeish, who also served as one of FDR's speech writers, was passionately committed to a more active American role in the destruction of Nazism. Though he professed a strong faith in the inherent wisdom of the American people, he believed that the public needed guidance, and he was anxious to avoid the repetition of hysteria, vigilantism, and violations of civil liberties of World War I. A federal coordinator, he suggested, could apprise communities of the kinds of voluntary activities genuinely needed, head off excesses, and "produce a calmer and more united front" among the concerned elements in the population.

Similar proposals were being considered by the White House.[53] Indeed, on the day that MacLeish wrote, the President had asked Adolf Berle to explore ways of channeling this "huge volume of volunteer national defenders" into useful defense activities. Berle recommended that groups like the American Legion be encouraged to undertake the "Americanization of aliens" and "combatting foreign propaganda." He urged that these and other volunteer activities be coordinated and supervised by state-wide committees appointed by the Governors and overseen by a three-man federal board.[54] Work among the unconverted was, after all, the greatest service the volunteers could provide.

A number of proposals aimed in one way or another at creating what Stephen Early called "a far-flung Americanism education program" were considered by the White House in the summer of 1940. Their common concern was that Americans, partly because of their diverse ethnic origins, lacked the inherent unity of spirit and purpose required in the current crisis. Their common conviction was that the remedy lay in proper indoctrination in democratic ideals and aims.[55] Roosevelt believed that both this propaganda objective and the task of supervising existing voluntary activities might be undertaken by a single federal morale agency, and he explored the idea with Louis Brownlow, the public administration expert whom FDR had earlier consulted on his plans for executive reorganization. Their discussion produced the outlines of a federal morale-building scheme.[56]

The Brownlow plan sought first to increase the public's reliance upon, and faith in, government-supplied information. To do this, it proposed consolidating existing government information services and speeding up release of data on the defense effort. In addition, the blessing of voluntarism was to be exploited by a new federal agency which would encourage and coordinate the activities of the volunteer patriotic organizations. Brownlow also envisioned the systematic collection and analysis of information on the nature and source of anti-administration propaganda. This intelligence was to be used by the new morale agency to create an effective counter-isolationist campaign. Thus, the President's current haphazard approach was to take on a more thorough and systematic aspect.[57]

Following the November elections, Roosevelt asked Secretary of War Stimson, Secretary of the Navy Knox, Secretary of Labor Francis Perkins, Selective Service Director Clarence Dykstra, and Interior Secretary Harold Ickes to consider the Brownlow proposal. Their objective: to plan an agency which could conduct a "constructive campaign for loyalty . . . as a defense against subversion and Fifth Column activities." Ickes served as Chairman.[58] Expert opinion was provided by Assistant to the Secretary of War John J. McCloy who sat in for Stimson at the morale conferences. McCloy had recently come to Washington at Stimson's request to advise the War Department on counter-intelligence. Experiences with German subversive activities (he had been involved in the investigation of the notorious World War Black Tom sabotage case) inclined McCloy to see similar forces currently at work. He told the group that the United States was being outdone, perhaps undone, by Nazi propagandists who, with characteristic efficiency, were busily supporting various peace and isolationist groups in the United States. He urged the importance of counter-propaganda and suggested that German propaganda techniques should provide inspiration and perhaps a model for the American effort in this field.[59].

Actually, McCloy's remarks were somewhat off the mark. The Nazis employed relatively little propaganda in the United States for both they and America's anti-war elements realized that any hint of foreign, particularly Nazi, involvement assured a hostile reception.[60] Nevertheless, McCloy's admiration for what he took to be the very model of a modern propaganda system was generally shared by the Ickes Committee, which recommended a centralized propaganda agency commanding considerable authority. "Adequate defense against subversive propaganda," the Committee reported, required creation of an agency which could cooperate with existing intelligence and investigative offices to "analyze and combat propaganda, . . . fortify the national morale, . . . create a positive defense for democracy, . . . [and] acquaint the people of this country with the nature and sources of the present threat to their liberties."[61]

The Committee's recommendation reflected a consensus that the problem of morale originated principally in the subversive rhetoric of the isolationist elements. Ickes and his colleagues agreed that American attitudes were sound—that Nazism had made few converts in the United States and was not likely to make many more. They were concerned, however, as was Roosevelt, that the public might be misled by the defeatist utterances of a handful, and in answering and discrediting this minority both he and now the Committee found the key to domestic unity.[62] This approach, which was essentially a more systematic extension of the current anti-isolationist campaign, would also keep the focus of the national debate off administration policy and on the evils of isolationism.

Ickes submitted this report to the President in November. Inasmuch as it paralleled Roosevelt's thinking and followed closely the recommendations supplied by Brownlow, Ickes probably looked for speedy approval. Instead, he had no response from FDR for the next several weeks. When he did hear again of the President's thinking on morale, he was shocked, although he should not have been surprised, to learn that Roosevelt's attention had wandered far from the thrust of the Committee's proposal. The President was in essential agreement with Ickes and the Committee, but he was too eclectic and too preoccupied with other issues to keep his thoughts focused on a single solution. Whatever its merits, his "flexibility" exasperated the officials involved and set them to fighting among themselves.

Ickes' first indication that the issue of morale had not been settled came when he learned that Roosevelt was entertaining Florence Kerr's proposal for a "great volunteer organization with a challenging program of action to do all that needs to be done for home defense." Kerr, a long-time friend of Harry Hopkins and his deputy in the Works Progress Administration, believed that national unity rested in part on national well-being, and the Home Defense Commission which she proposed would include the promotion of voluntary social services work. The agency would thus provide federal encouragement to the settlement house reform principle popular in the progressive era. The scheme was still-born, a victim of the opposition (real or anticipated) of officials who feared it would overlap or compete with existing programs.[63]

No sooner had the Kerr plan been laid to rest than Roosevelt turned to the idea of utilizing the more traditional propaganda solution represented by the activities of the Committee on Public Information. At a luncheon meeting with Ickes in early February, the President suggested bringing George Creel into government to do the job he had done during the first World War. Ickes was shaken by this suggestion, noting that the administration could ill afford to remind the public of their earlier propaganda experiences. But Roosevelt countered by defending Creel, noting that the jingoistic techniques that had made him infamous might now be in order—the nation, he said, "could stand a little flag wrapping."[64]

Ickes' thoughts by now were fixed upon what he fancied was a more sophisticated, more systematic way of dealing with public attitudes.

Strongly influenced by the prospects of applying social scientific techniques to the molding of opinion, he was impressed by the work of the Committee for National Morale. This private organization, affiliated with the interventionist Council for Democracy, had been formed in July 1940 on the premise that psychologists, sociologists, political scientists, and other experts on public opinion could diagnose and remedy morale problems. The committee brought together about 100 specialists, including Gordon Allport, Ruth Benedict, Hadley Cantril, Leonard Doob, Erik Erikson, Erich Fromm, Geoffrey Gorer, George Gallup, and Margaret Mead, who proceeded to collect data, formulate basic principles, and publish their findings on morale and propaganda.

Their thinking, reflected in a report the Committee supplied to Ickes in January 1941, emphasized the complex and technical nature of the morale problem. Inadequate public support for national policy was not simply a function of ignorance, inadequate patriotism, or other superficial deficiencies. Poor morale reflected underlying tensions within society, including the generation gap, familial conflict, and the inherent struggle between workers and managers. Diagnosing and dealing with such socially pathogenic conditions required continuous research as well as immediate action, undertaken by "highly qualified specialists in close touch with reality."[65] In short, propaganda could not be left to speech makers, journalists, ideologues, politicians, or the others associated with the craft in the past. It must be entrusted to practical experts who understood how to motivate and manipulate the public. These social scientists thought of themselves as custodians of an arcane craft, possessed of an intellectual resource similar to that offered by the physical scientists currently being recruited by government to improve the nation's weaponry. The national crisis, particularly as reflected in inadequate morale, seemed to offer an opportunity for them to prove it. Roosevelt, having publicly acknowledged the new and important role of psychological warfare, apparently agreed that the social scientists had a contribution to make and he provided the Committee with $5,000 in unvouchered White House funds with which to compile a complete roster of experts.[66]

Ickes intended to make use of this intellectual resource if and when the President approved the morale agency. However, the fate of the scheme was still very much in doubt in the spring of 1941.[67] Serious objections had been raised by officials whose cooperation was essential to the plan's success. Much of the information upon which the morale experts would base their analysis was to be provided by the Justice Department. But Attorney General Robert Jackson told the Ickes Committee that he was reluctant to have his agency participate. He pointed out that quite apart from the violence done to democratic principle by surveillance and investigation of political dissidents, the project was bound to subject the administration and the department to serious public criticism.[68] Later, when Ickes consulted Solicitor General Francis Biddle, he encountered much the same response. Most of the work proposed for the new super morale agency, Biddle said, was currently being carried out by a number of private and governmental organizations. This he thought was appropriate. However, uniting investigation and propaganda in one centralized government authority would tend to intimidate government critics. "The most serious propaganda in America today," he wrote, did not originate in Germany, but was "the vigorously expressed opposition in and out of Congress of the isolationist groups." A morale service "on the scale and within the scope suggested," Biddle said, "would tend to smother and suppress this opposition [and] I am not prepared to advocate such a course."[69]

Although these objections threatened to rob the proposed agency of much of its isolationist-fighting capacity, Ickes was undeterred. Anticipating perhaps that White House support would produce the intelligence capacity he needed or that the social scientists would devise some alternative, the Secretary continued to press for his scheme. He had not, however, reckoned on the opposition of Lowell Mellett who, in challenging the basic premise of the super morale agency, was to pose the most serious obstacle to its realization. Since early in 1940, as head of the Office of Government Reports and Administrative Assistant to the President, Mellett had been charged by Roosevelt with overseeing administration public relations. In this capacity, he had been quietly and efficiently ensuring that the administration's messages were carried voluntarily in every medium from radio to wall posters. At the same time, he encouraged and cooperated with the propaganda efforts of several private morale and interventionist groups that had been formed in the summer of 1940. While these activities had not as yet produced a dramatic conversion of public attitude, he was confident that his subtle but pervasive propaganda campaign, employing the informational approach espoused by the administration since 1933, made the Ickes plan unnecessary.

Mellett had not made these views known at the inception of the morale agency planning, probably hoping that it would fade away without his intercession. But in February, Ickes, hoping to enlist his support, sent him a report by the Committee for National Morale outlining the philosophy and methodology of the proposed morale agency, and Mellett had also met with the Committee's Chairman, the internationally known, politically active, Harvard-based expert on Persian art, Arthur Upham Pope.[70] Mellett had come away from these encounters convinced that the morale scheme would not work. Ickes' social scientists impressed Mellett as idealistic amateurs. This conviction was strengthened by a report from a member of the Committee which declared that in spite of its prestigious membership its work was in fact being done by second- or third-rate individuals. The informant characterized Pope as sincere but naive, consumed by a passion to do something but unable to distinguish between a good scheme and a bad one. Most meetings, he said, resembled faculty club bull sessions: the results so chaotic and simplistic that their implementation could only undermine national morale.[71]

Mellett objected to more than the alleged silly incompetence of the experts. The chief problem with a government morale agency, he believed, was the difficulty it would encounter in having its messages accepted. He pointed out that the German methods so admired by the morale planners were totally inappropriate to the United States. Americans, he said, unlike Germans, had not been conditioned by two centuries of obedience to authority, nor would American propagandists enjoy the virtually uncontested access to the public mind that totalitarianism assured to Nazi propaganda. Such obvious oversights, Mellett suggested, revealed a fundamental ignorance of the ways American opinion might, and might not, be influenced. In Mellett's view the existing media, particularly the press, played the key role in determining the scope and character of government propaganda. But Ickes proposed to either bypass or, worse still, coerce the press. In a post-war interview he recalled that one of the experts associated with the Ickes scheme had told him he intended to eliminate morale-weakening newspaper items, like photographs of the tearful departures of draftees, by having local morale officers remind editors of their duty to suppress such material. Mellett disdainfully noted that the man admitted he had never seen a newspaper office and did not know any editors. The least bit of journalistic experience, the former newspaperman observed, would have made the "expert" realize that any official who came to an editor with any such suggestion would be "thrown out on his ear—and rightly so."[72]

Mellett offered another even more compelling reason why nothing beyond the rather diffuse educational campaign already under way could be undertaken. There could be no national propaganda policy, he told the President, "until there is an accepted national policy." Direct, centrally controlled propaganda for intervention presupposed a national consensus that transcended agreement on the need for defense. Until the nation clearly manifested its acceptance of interventionist policy, the administration would remain merely a faction in a continuing national debate. The strength of the opposition, particularly in Congress, indicated to Mellett that the requisite consensus did not exist. In these circumstances, he argued, the proposed propaganda effort would be construed as a misuse of government power, resented by Congress and the public and likely to divide the country further. The palliative that "morale building" would supply for interventionist anxieties, he concluded, was not worth the serious adverse consequences it was likely to entail.[73]

Ickes, having learned of Mellett's hostility, characterized him as a "dull-witted and pusillanimous man" with neither imagination nor "spark."[74] But, in fact, Ickes had met his match. Mellett was close to FDR and his arguments were persuasive. Confronted with his opposition, FDR compromised, hoping somehow to satisfy Ickes without offending the logic propounded by his media advisor. He was aware of—Mellett would not let him forget—the extensive propaganda efforts that Mellett was currently orchestrating on behalf of the administration's foreign and defense policies. Nevertheless, Roosevelt was under great pressure from his supporters to "do something" about faltering American morale and was aware of political problems he courted should he fail to satisfy Ickes and others that he was doing everything possible. Moreover, although he had concluded that he must limit his own speech making, he was convinced that the new morale agency might carry out a campaign of public addresses to good effect.

He therefore approved Ickes' plan—in principle—but put off its implementation. Ickes, at first delighted at his success, soon had reason for despair. FDR insisted on consultations among the interested parties (including some, like Mellett, who opposed the whole project) and conducted what turned out to be a protracted search for "the right man" to direct the new agency. What emerged was a pale reflection of the scheme originally proposed, directed by an individual with none of the social scientific expertise advocated by the Secretary and his advisors on the National Morale Committee.

In late March 1941, the President asked William C. Bullitt, recently Ambassador to France, Director of the Budget Harold Smith, and Presidential Assistant Wayne Coy to draw up an executive order creating an Office of Home Defense. The draft they submitted in early April, while incorporating some of the elements of the Ickes scheme, did not include its more controversial aspects. There would be no intelligence gathering or analyzing and no elaborate opinion-manipulating function. What was left was an agency to be called the Office of Civilian Defense (OCD) which would undertake the protection of the civilian population in the event of air raid or other defense-related emergency. The OCD was to oversee the execution of these plans by existing state and local defense agencies and encourage citizen participation in the defense program. The agency, as its name suggested, was to concern itself principally with organizing the citizenry for home defense. Its authors hoped that this would have a positive effect on morale as well. Participation was expected to heighten the public's awareness and sense of involvement. The patriotism of those who volunteered would be reinforced, directed, and restrained, while even those not directly involved would find inspiration in the quasi-military, emergency character of civilian defense.[75]

But if "propaganda of the deed" was to be OCD's main contribution to American morale, the President insisted that it not be its only one. Fond recollections of the inspiring oratory of the World War led him to seek a director with a "big name" able to "attract public attention as a good ballyhoo artist and speechmaker."[76]

Whoever Roosevelt chose would take on a task enshrouded in confusion. Largely as a result of FDR's unwillingness to reconcile conflicting advice and personal impulses, the character of the new agency remained unsettled even after the President had approved the order establishing it. Continuing discussions indicated that those concerned were not certain how much a defense agency and how much a morale agency OCD was intended to be. Apparently, the decision would rest with the first Director.[77]

On May 20 the President finally signed the executive order establishing the Office of Civilian Defense and named Fiorello LaGuardia as its Director. The appointment was a defeat for Ickes and the propaganda philosophy he represented. The dynamic New York Mayor was a colorful figure, an accomplished orator, and a committed interventionist, but his selection suggested that the agency would not have a full-time Director nor one dedicated to a systematic approach to propaganda. Moreover, while the Mayor could make a good speech, he was no expert on public opinion and was obviously far more interested in civil defense—preparing the cities against air attack—than in morale.[78]

Misgivings about LaGuardia's appointment were soon confirmed when it became apparent that he was neglecting his morale function in favor of his defense responsibilities.[79] Pressure for reform produced a reorganization of the young agency designed to restore its propaganda function. In July, LaGuardia established a Bureau of Facts and Figures within the OCD. The bureau was to "keep a check on every meeting held in the United States on foreign policy" and to supply information concerning the isolationist opposition to a "speakers bureau" which would arrange for timely responses. The Bureau of Facts and Figures was also to monitor and correct media coverage of the defense effort. These activities were rather feeble approximations of the intelligence functions originally proposed for the morale agency.

By now, however, the morale enthusiasts doubted that any project under LaGuardia's direction would adequately address the problem, and their continued dissatisfaction led the President to take the propaganda function away from the OCD and vest it in a new independent office directly responsible to him. In late October, FDR created the Office of Facts and Figures (OFF) and appointed Archibald MacLeish as its Director.[80] Although still a far cry from the elaborate propaganda agency envisioned by FDR a year earlier, at least the new agency had in MacLeish an individual who appreciated the important role social scientific techniques might play in educating the public. Some months before taking office, MacLeish had asked Harold Lasswell what needed to be done to create an effective morale-building program. The renowned propaganda expert stressed the need for a centralized agency which could pinpoint propaganda needs, analyze "unfriendly propaganda," and test the efficacy of government appeals.[81] The agency established by MacLeish reflected Lasswell's advice. Its major function was to be the analysis of public attitudes and the appropriateness of government propaganda.[82] Education would be left, for the most part, to existing administration publicists who would simply rely on MacLeish's office for direction, advice, and occasionally for information. OFF would also generate a limited amount of propaganda on national themes which transcended the interests of any single agency propaganda office. These activities were an extension of the informational propaganda approach which Mellett had espoused and which the administration had long been practicing.

The Office of Facts and Figures was destined to a short, impotent existence. With little to do beyond monitoring public opinion, OFF became a superfluous and unwanted rival to those who thought that they had the educational effort well in hand. In June 1942, the agency was absorbed by the Office of War Information in a reorganization of the entire propaganda apparatus.

In a discussion of OCD written some years ago, I saw the fate of the agency as evidence of FDR's "indecisive and inept handling of the morale problem."[83] Having now examined the episode in a broader context, it is clear that the history of the project, and particularly its fate, is better viewed as a reflection of FDR's understanding that by the spring of 1941 the proposed elaborate morale-building service was a potentially troublesome duplication of existing propaganda efforts. As Mellett reminded the President, the current informational propaganda centering on, but going well beyond, the defense mobilization program promised everything the morale agency did, except satisfaction to the militant interventionists. From a variety of sources inside government and out, effectively utilizing, as we will see in the next chapters, all the existing communications media, the administration and its inter-ventionist allies were able to envelop the American people in a torrent of facts, arguments, and symbols undermining isolationism. By the time OCD had become a reality, it had also become redundant.[84]

4

The Uneasy Alliance: FDR, the Press, and Foreign Affairs, 1939–1941

Although the supporters of administration policy would continue to lament the persistence of isolationism, by the summer of 1941 it was clear that FDR and his interventionist allies were winning the propaganda war. True, there was no mass conversion to intervention by which to measure victory. But judged by their success in shaping the images upon which popular judgements rested, the interventionists' triumph was certain.

From the outset, FDR's publicists had proceeded on the assumption that the truth of the government's cause did not ensure its public acceptance, and that, while they could not concoct a convincing story out of nothing, neither did the facts speak for themselves. The practical key to selling the President and his policies, they concluded, was their ability to gain for their version of events full, and preferably uncontradicted, access to the mass media. In the months preceding American involvement in the war, the administration succeeded in this as never before.

The reasons for this success vary from medium to medium. Certainly a common factor was their willingness to carry information about the defense preparedness effort as a public service. In this very important aspect of its propaganda effort, the administration's responsibility was chiefly to provide copy and to encourage media representatives to meet their voluntarily assumed obligation fully. But the more profound issue confronting all those party to the great foreign policy debate was what contribution beyond this the media would make.

Radio broadcasters and movie makers would, as the next chapters explain, far exceed administration expectations. The majority of newspapers, on the other hand, as we will presently see, would never quite fulfill FDR's long-standing quest for an objective vehicle of government views.

I

From the outset of the war in Europe, the President and the press informally exchanged ideas on the responsibility of each in keeping the nation informed on foreign and defense matters. It was apparent that their ideas were far apart. Roosevelt insisted that the European conflict created a national emergency which required circumspection in the government's release of information and restraint in newspaper reporting. Reporters, noting the absence of fighting following the conquest of Poland and not at all certain that a "real" war would ensue, saw in the diplomatic maneuvering of the winter of 1939–1940 not the national emergency invoked by the President, but a kind of international charade, and his demands for an end to journalism-as-usual struck them as unreasonable. In the months to come, press attitudes changed as journalists came to share FDR's view of the nation's peril. But it was a change initiated independently of the White House by individual publishers and editors in response to events as they perceived them. As a result, press cooperation was always on the press's terms, and ultimately Roosevelt would find the press, for all its good will, an uncertain ally in the propaganda war.

The improvement in White House–press relations came as a direct response to German military success. In early May 1940, following swift victories in Denmark and Norway, German forces rolled over the Low Countries and skirted the Maginot Line. In late June, the French laid down their arms. Only Great Britain now stood between Hitler and total victory. For American journalists, as for many others, the war in Europe had suddenly become very real. Prospects of a protracted stalemate and negotiated settlement evaporated. German power had given newspapermen a new perspective on events. What many had seen as perhaps the last act of a European melodrama now appeared to be only the first act of what might prove to be a world tragedy. For most, mere observer status no longer seemed appropriate for either the United States or for American journalism.

The effect was soon apparent. Publishers who a short time before had been cool toward the President and his policies now put aside past differences as they sought ways to cooperate. Beginning in the late spring of 1940 a number of offers reached the White House. One was from Harry Chandler, the owner of the Los Angeles *Times*. Chandler thought that Roosevelt's New Deal resembled "the antics of a Mad Hatter," but he was anxious to support the President in meeting the Axis threat.[1] In May 1940, he wrote a friend in the administration suggesting a press campaign to enliven public interest in the European crisis and the need for national preparedness. Chandler's proposal of a meeting between newspaper and government representatives to work out a cooperative effort found its way to the White House. Roosevelt was interested, but his advisors were reticent. As Early wrote to Chandler, "if the government made the first move, it would be certainly construed in some quarters as the opening wedge to censorship and other forms of control of the press."[2] Chandler would be left to promote preparedness and interventionism on his own, as best he could.

Some offers of help also came from those intent on capitalizing on the current crisis. Thus, for example, the North American Newspaper Alliance offered the White House syndication of a "semi-official" column which would speak for the administration on preparedness-related themes[3] and Crowell-Collier publications expressed a willingness to distribute a "controlled publication, adroitly conceived" and designed to act as the administration's mouthpiece on national defense issues. The last offer was predicated, according to Lowell Mellett, on the conclusion of "certain special arrangements" advantageous to the company. Mellett, like Early, was wary of such special arrangements, conscious of the antagonisms they might generate among other journalists. Confident that the White House now had the ability to get its public releases published almost without limit and without tying itself to any such deals, Mellett turned down both offers.[4]

The press's desire to awaken the public to the nation's peril was immediately apparent to the President in the stream of newspaper clippings and press reports that came to him from a variety of sources in the summer of 1940. Chief among these were the editorial opinion surveys done by the Office of Government Reports (OGR). This service, which had begun earlier in the National Emergency Council, was under the supervision of Miss Katherine Blackburn, known affectionately around the White House as "K. C." They were based on conscientiously conducted surveys of a large number of newspapers from around the country. Blackburn had no interest in skewing the results, and her work reflects cautious assessment of "positive" and "negative" opinion which did not force ambivalent or neutral expressions into one category or the other. While her techniques may not have met today's sampling standards, there is no reason to doubt the general accuracy of her findings.

Stephen Early was alerted to the change in press attitudes in early July when the heretofore vehemently anti-administration Philadelphia *Inquirer* ran a two-column, front page editorial entitled "America Must Help the Allies to Beat Hitler." Sensing a trend in this dramatic pronouncement, Early ordered a survey of press attitudes to determine the extent to which the press was rallying behind the administration cause. The results were most gratifying. The Office of Government Reports (OGR) sampled editorial opinion in April, May, and the first week in June. The results showed that although sentiment against armed intervention remained high, a "steadily mounting number of papers" was endorsing "immediate and unstinted aid to the allies." The OGR survey showed that at the end of the first week in June, 83 newspapers supported such aid, while 49 remained "isolationist." The report predicted that while the isolationist group would remain firm, numbers of hitherto uncommitted newspapers would join the "aid to the Allies" camp.[5]

From this point forward, the press in general would set aside earlier hostility and increasingly urge the rapid mobilization of American military might and the extension of all possible assistance to Great Britain short of war. The odyssey of Eugene Meyer and his Washington *Post* illustrates this process. Meyer, a successful investment banker, purchased the moribund *Post* in 1933. A fiscal and monetary conservative, he was opposed to what he regarded as Roosevelt's reckless economic experimentation and annoyed by the President's penchant for blaming the business community for the nation's ills. In 1936, along with most other papers, the *Post* supported (without outright endorsement) the candidacy of Roosevelt's Republican challenger, Alfred Landon. However, following Hitler's humiliation of the Allies at the Munich Conference in the fall of 1938, the *Post* ran a series of articles in support of American military preparedness, and, in early April 1939, a *Post* editorial on the European crisis won praise from FDR who included it in the record of his press conference.

Meyer's major step toward interventionism came, as it did for so many of his colleagues, in response to events in the summer of 1940. In mid-July, Felix Morley, editor of the *Post*, ran an editorial in which he argued that the Monroe Doctrine, which administration spokesmen sometimes invoked to justify U.S. policy, not only declared the Western Hemisphere off limits to foreign intervention but also pledged the United States not to interfere in European or Asian affairs. For Morley, American military strength provided security. But Meyer had by now concluded that preparedness alone was not enough and he found Morley's non-interventionism unacceptable. In August, he was fired and henceforth front-page editorials urged readers to think in terms of what the *Post* argued was inevitable American military involvement in the European war. "We are in a state of war," the paper stridently declared, "whether we call it war or defense or what-have-you . . . the only alternative open to us is surrender or resistance." Meyer, of course, did not accept New Dealism and refused to support Roosevelt's bid for a third term. But when it came to foreign policy, the President could count on the *Post*.[6]

For about a year following the French debacle, the tide of emotionalism in the American press rose, reaching a peak in May 1941 when 73 percent of a sampling of newspapers could be described as "thundering against defeatists," urging that the gravity of the situation demanded decisive action to save Britain, "and otherwise espousing the interventionist cause."[7] The migration of attitudes included, to some degree, almost all journalists. One government-sponsored analysis noted that "today's isolationist follows the precepts of yesterday's interventionist. He favors ineffectual intervention." Even the consistently and bitterly hostile Chicago *Tribune*, though it had opposed Lend Lease, came to support the delivery of war material by American ships to Iceland. At the same time, those who had all along supported aid to Britain now insisted on convoying and did not shrink from support of overt naval warfare.[8]

In July 1941, Congress considered a controversial administration measure extending the service of military inductees beyond the one-year term stipulated in draft legislation adopted the previous fall. The one-vote margin by which extension passed the House in August has frequently been cited as an indication of isolationist power. Yet the same yardstick (support for the draft) revealed how far the movement toward preparedness among the nation's editorial writers had gone. During the week ending July 24, a survey of 157 newspapers found that of 223 editorials on the draft law, 152 (68 percent) categorically approved, while only 34 (15 percent) opposed it. The remainder offered some sort of qualified opinion. A week later, as debate on the issue reached a peak, editorial comment more than doubled and approval of extension rose to 84 percent.[9]

By the fall of 1941, the eve of full-scale American involvement, the press appeared to be taking its lead from the White House. In mid-November, government analysts reported that the dominant mood was that "the foreign policy issue is now settled," and that, apart from a small minority, the nation's newspapers could be "counted upon to support any positive measure taken by the President within the broad framework of established and accepted policy." Whether this included a declaration of war against Germany is not clear, but it seems likely that a majority were even prepared to embrace this ultimate step.[10] It is important to note, however, that support seemed to be tied to administration initiatives and action. To the extent that this was in fact the case, the press remained restive where it detected inaction, indecisiveness, or indirection in the President's leadership.

In some instances, cooperation went even further than editorial support and included what appeared in news columns. At the end of May 1940, for example, Barry Bingham of the highly regarded Louisville *Courier-Journal* told White House advisor Lowell Mellett that he was trying to stop the press practice of likening the emergency measures taken by France and Britain to those of the dictatorships. Bingham said that he had written about a dozen of his publisher friends warning them that comparison tended to mislead the American people by lumping the Allied and Nazi causes.[11]

More significant were two incidents involving the *New York Times* which exemplified a willingness to redefine the proper relationship between press and government. In mid-December 1940, several administration officials met with Arthur Sulzberger at a Washington hotel to set the publisher straight on the "role and responsibility of the press in general and the *Times* in particular. In a rather heated discussion, Sulzberger responded to attacks on the newspaper's handling of various issues by claiming what amounted to a constitutional obligation to critical independence. Several months later, however, Sulzberger's views of how the press might best serve democracy seemed to have changed. Like a great many others, Sulzberger naturally preferred to stand with the nation's leader in a time of crisis on issues laden with patriotic import. The December 1940 rebuke, friendly chats at the White House and Hyde Park since then, and, most importantly, the increasing gravity of the international situation apparently had their effect. In September, at one of their meetings, Sulzberger told Roosevelt of his paper's investigation of the military training camps springing up across the nation. The story, he said, documented shocking conditions at the facilities and low morale among the recruits, but, in deference to the national interest, the *Times* did not intend to publish the account.[12] The newspaper no doubt continued to see itself as the guardian of the public interest. This role now seemed, however, to require more than simple adherence to the traditional "objectivity," independence, and concern for "all the news fit to print."[13]

II

Neither the *New York Times* nor the vast majority of other papers, however, had become mere tools of administration propagandists. Unlike the other media where uniform cooperation with White House propaganda needs was the rule, journalists had no taste for self-discipline. Each publisher and editor, and to an extent the newspapermen they employed, continued to exercise wide latitude in presenting the news. A handful of isolationist papers remained adamantly opposed to administration policy and continued to condemn the government as the occasion arose. Even those disposed to cooperate could not always be counted on. Thus, in November 1941, not long after Sulzberger withheld the account of military camp conditions, the *Times* angered White House officials with a story providing figures on United States tank production.[14] Releases of this sort, as well as critical commentary directed at the pace of industrial mobilization or alleged indecisiveness in White House leadership, reflected insensitivity to administration problems or excessive interventionist zeal. In either case, with no systematic means of controlling or even advising the press, the administration found itself repeatedly embarrassed and its propaganda goals undercut. As Roosevelt bitterly complained to Helen Reid, publisher of the staunchly interventionist New York *Herald Tribune*, "the factual reports" issued by the government were irresponsibly challenged in the press, and "when we venture an opinion, we are frequently criticized and charged with spreading war hysteria." Stephen Early thought that much of this was attributable to those who were trying to "make trouble for the government . . . to confuse, mystify, and inject poison into the defense setup."[15] Such motives, though they no doubt existed, were the exception, but, whatever their cause, coverage of this sort posed a considerable problem for the President.

From mid-1940 on FDR sought ways to make the pro-administration sympathies of the press more clearly and consistently reflected in what appeared and, particularly, in what did not appear in the nation's newspapers. During the New Deal, Roosevelt used information to encourage journalists to depend on the government's perspective of events. Having seized the initiative in dealing with the economic crisis, he was able to stimulate confidence and hope by instructing the press on his relentless struggle on the public's behalf. Press officers for various defense agencies continued to operate on this principle, but the technique posed difficulties for the President in dealing with the White House press corps on issues of foreign and military policy. His foreign policy options limited by distance, military weakness, and isolationist sentiment, FDR was in many instances no more than an anxious observer of foreign events. Often he had relatively little to tell. Information on foreign and military policy was always sensitive, often uncertain, and usually confidential. In these circumstances, the President's press conferences, which had once served the New Deal and continued to serve defense preparedness, had become a burden in regard to other war-related issues. Reporters had many questions but, for much of what they wanted to know, the President had few answers. What little he felt able to say had to be carefully presented so that a press and a nation anxious to divine portents from the most minor events or the slightest nuance of speech would not make more than he intended of the information he supplied.[16]

Faced with the problem of controlling press curiosity and reporters' penchant for misinterpreting or "overinterpreting" his remarks, FDR looked for ways to manage the release of news on foreign and military policy more effectively. At first he appears to have entertained the idea of using an authoritative spokesman who might be able either to put off or to satisfy press inquiries without committing him or endangering his prestige.[17] In June 1940, Roosevelt took the issue to Louis Brownlow, the public administration expert whom FDR had consulted on plans for a national morale agency. Roosevelt told Brownlow that he was concerned by the persistent misinterpretation of his press conference remarks on foreign policy and asked the former journalist to devise a system that would shield him from potentially embarrassing questions. After discussions with several government officials, Brownlow endorsed

Stephen Early's idea that the President appoint a spokesman to whom he might refer questions demanding particularly careful handling. The person chosen, Early said, would have to be someone of extraordinarily high reputation, particularly among journalists; someone, he suggested, like Republican senior statesman Henry L. Stimson. An internationalist with a reputation for integrity and good press relations, Stimson had once served as Secretary of War and more recently as Herbert Hoover's Secretary of State.[18]

Such a plan required press cooperation and, although Roosevelt liked the idea, he insisted that it have the prior public endorsement of newspaper owners. Brownlow moved to satisfy this requirement by meeting with Eugene Meyer, Helen Reid, and Henry R. Luce of Time-Life. All had in varying degrees been hostile to the New Deal, but all were now strongly committed to intervention. Their reaction to the White House approach was sympathetic but cautious. They accepted in principle the appointment of a "statesman type" like Stimson, or a "super journalist type" such as William Allen White, to serve as an intermediary between Roosevelt and the press. But they insisted on further discussions with FDR himself, and perhaps with others, before they would ratify any plan. Roosevelt, however, wanted the initiative to appear to come from representatives of the medium, and he refused to be personally drawn into discussions before he had a firm commitment to the scheme. The publishers, unwilling perhaps to speak for the entire press, and possibly suspicious of the President's motives, refused to proceed on that basis and at this point the discussions ended.[19] The episode suggests the persisting dilemma confronting the President and the press. Both recognized the urgent need to shape an interventionist consensus and the value of White House–press cooperation toward that end. But suspicion and independence, rooted at least in part in early frictions, undermined the tendency toward unity created by the national crisis.

Nevertheless, the incident was not without result for, although no spokesman was officially appointed, the man mentioned most prominently for the job did join the Cabinet. Within a week of Brownlow's discussions with the publishers, Roosevelt offered Stimson the post of Secretary of War. On June 20, 1940, FDR announced that both Stimson and another Republican, Chicago publisher Frank Knox, had agreed to serve; Stimson at the War Department and Knox as the Secretary of the Navy. Whatever other reasons Roosevelt may have had for the appointments, he probably also anticipated that the two men would lend bi-partisan credibility to the government's discussion of its policies and tend to make news management more palatable.

FDR's failure to secure press approval of a special White House spokesman left to Press Secretary Stephen Early the task of speaking unofficially for the President. It was apparent, however, that he lacked the understanding or the tact necessary to convey the subtleties of the administration's none-too-certain foreign policy. His efforts to interpret the President to the press in one instance created an international incident. At a press conference on July 6 he told reporters that the United States "thinks there should be an application of the Monroe Doctrine in Europe and Asia." The Chinese government, interpreting the widely published remarks as an endorsement of a Japanese sphere of influence, protested this apparent change in U.S. policy. Secretary of State Cordell Hull, who had only the day before specifically denied any similarity between the Asian and Latin American situations, rushed to the White House to secure a repudiation of Early's remarks. The Press Secretary attempted, without success, to clarify administration policy on the issue, and newspapers now turned to criticizing FDR for this evidence of offhandedness in his public discussion of serious foreign policy issues.[20] Thus ended the President's attempts to hide behind a "spokesman" on foreign policy issues.

Alerted to the President's interest in ducking the foreign policy issue, the press inevitably suspected that he intended to turn to some system of censorship to curb "irresponsible" disclosures. Such fears were elaborated on by Walter Davenport, who charged in a February 1941 article in *Collier's* that the administration was actively considering the creation of an office of censorship and named Lowell Mellett as the man most likely to head the agency.[21] The designation of Mellett was not surprising. In recent months he had come to assume an important, if somewhat enigmatic, position in the circle of presidential aides and advisors. His background and current duties made him seem a likely choice for a government censor, but speculation to this effect also fed upon doubts concerning his commitment to press independence. Unlike Early, he had failed to establish a friendly relationship with the White House press corps, which tended to describe him as scholarly, bland, and aloof. Moreover, unlike the apolitical Early, Mellett was seen as an ideologue—he had been a crusading liberal editor, had lost his job because of his political convictions, and was now a staunch New Dealer. Such a man, journalists probably assumed, was likely to subordinate the rights of the press to the needs of the man and the cause he served. These factors, together with the fact that Mellett's rise coincided with the precipitous decline in White House–press relations, encouraged the press to identify him with the anticipated advent of censorship.[22]

Press suspicions appeared repeatedly during 1940 and early 1941 and drew repeated affirmations of respect for the freedom of the press from the White House.[23] The concern was understandable but unfounded. What FDR wanted was not government censorship, but press self-restraint. His attitude was reflected in his response to an episode that occurred during consideration of the Lend Lease legislation in early 1941. In the course of hearings on the measure, Chief of Staff General George C. Marshall appeared before a Senate Committee in a closed-door session. The next day, much to the chagrin of administration officials, some of the details of Marshall's secret testimony appeared in print. This event occurred within a few weeks of the Davenport article on alleged administration censorship plans and at a time when the controversy over press freedom was at a peak. In these circumstances, the President, at a conference with reporters the day following the exposé of Marshall's testimony, raised the issue of press rights and duties.

Obviously wishing to avoid charges that he was trying to coerce or intimidate the press, Roosevelt insisted he was simply exploring the issue. He noted that primary responsibility for the confidentiality of official secrets rested with government and said he understood the desire of reporters to file stories based upon leaks. However, he questioned the ethics, morality, and patriotism of newspaper and news service editors and owners who authorized the publication of such material. Reporters challenged the President. Without insisting on a right to publish military secrets, some suggested that not all revelations of information regarding military affairs jeopardized the national security and argued that greater administration candor might lessen the danger of the publication of material genuinely harmful to the national interest. More fundamentally, correspondents asked the President just what *did* constitute a "national defense secret?" The following exchange ensued:

PRESIDENT: . . . it is things that have been kept secret on the advice . . . of the Army and Navy.

REPORTER: . . . if we take the attitude that any testimony . . . given on the Hill in executive session remains secret, isn't the final test what the government wants to give out and what it doesn't want to give out?

PRESIDENT: No, only if the government didn't give out or held secret things
that there was no reason for holding secret.

REPORTER: Then what *is* the test?

PRESIDENT: The test is what the Commander in Chief of the Army and Navy
thinks . . . would be harmful to the defense of this country to give out.

Following this unsatisfactory colloquy reporters turned to the issue
of what was to be done. Roosevelt refused to endorse the need for
censorship, saying that he had only raised the issue in hopes that public
discussion would lead to a solution which did not employ government-
imposed controls.[24]

In fact, FDR had long since considered, and rejected, censorship. In
early April 1940, before the onset of the Nazi blitzkrieg in the West,
an interdepartmental committee concerned with internal security had
discussed the creation of a censorship mechanism for possible future
use.[25] Shortly thereafter, the Army-Navy Joint Board approved a plan
drafted before the war which would have authorized the complete censorship of publications, radio broadcasts, motion pictures, and all communications leaving the United States. The scheme also outlined a
comprehensive war propaganda apparatus. On June 10, the Joint Board
submitted this ''Basic Plan for Public Relations Administration'' to the
President together with a request for an initial appropriation of $50
million. What happened next is unclear. Years later, Lowell Mellett
recalled that FDR had been horrified by the thought that the plan might
become known to his critics. Convinced that the idea was politically
naive and potentially ruinous, he gave it to Stephen Early with instructions to bury it. On February 1, 1941, having failed to receive any
response to its plan, the Joint Board resubmitted it. Three weeks later
(shortly before the appearance of the Davenport article), Roosevelt
finally replied. Denying he had ever seen the original proposal, he
sharply rejected what he called the whole ''wild'' idea. ''Obviously,''
he wrote, ''the Joint Board knows nothing about what the American
public let alone the American press would say to a thing like this.''[26]

Nevertheless, secrecy in some instances was justified. The President
and others charged with the conduct of foreign and military policy
assumed an obligation to keep the confidences of other nations and the
confidentiality of American military plans and preparations. Unwanted
exposure could embarrass friendly nations and work to the advantage
of America's potential enemies. However, there was no infallible way

of distinguishing between matters vital to the national security and those secrets that merely served the administration's interests. Critics were ill disposed to leave this judgement solely to government officials, particularly when the nation was not at war.[27]

Roosevelt, realizing that censorship was politically impossible, sought to accomplish his purposes through a system of voluntary press restraint coupled with a government policy of withholding sensitive information at the source. Under this program, described to the press by government public relations officers in mid-March 1941, primary responsibility for the secrecy of troop and ship movements, delicate negotiations, and other military and diplomatic affairs was to rest with the officials directly involved. They were to apply a system of security classification, which the military had devised in 1940, by which sensitive material was classified as either "secret," "confidential," or "restricted." These categories denoted the sensitivity of the information and suggested the care to be exercised in its handling. None of the classified information was to be released to the press. This system was supplemented with repeated appeals to the media to refrain from publishing classified material that came into its hands in spite of government precautions.[28]

Mellett, for one, was optimistic, believing that voluntary self-censorship would accompany the growth of press support for the administration's foreign policies. At the height of the censorship controversy early in March, he reported to the President that with the exception of a few "naturally bad elements," the press was "seeking ways of getting gracefully into line." The momentum in this direction was such, he believed, that the majority of the nation's newspapers would soon be willing to impose "some restraints of their own on the bad elements." Mellett went on to observe that the administration had gained more by encouraging the trend toward self-discipline and restraint than it would have from censorship or other government interference in the dissemination of news.[29]

His report proved too sanguine. Although newspapers were increasingly supportive, collectively they made little effort to ensure an end to "irresponsible" journalism. Mellett would eventually lament that neither the American Society of Newspaper Editors nor the American Newspaper Publishers Association seemed to command the unity or courage to effect the self-discipline for which he had hoped.[30] The result was that the system worked imperfectly. Information potentially detrimental to American security continued to appear in American newspapers, and "leaks" remained a problem in spite of sporadic attempts to eliminate them at the source.[31] The failure was attributable at least in part to the almost unassailable motives of the culprits. In almost every instance, leaks were supplied by high-ranking officials acting out of conviction that their actions served the national interest. The exposure of the guilty in such instances ran the risk of revealing fundamental differences within the administration and of giving further publicity both to the unauthorized information and to the cause its release was intended to serve.

The dilemma is illustrated by the case of the greatest leak of all—the pre–Pearl Harbor publication of the "Victory Program" outlining American strategic intentions in the event of involvement in the war. Details from one of the most sensitive documents generated by the government to date appeared on December 5 in the Chicago *Tribune*. At Roosevelt's direction, the FBI sought the source of the leak, but an intensive investigation ended prematurely without action against those responsible. Evidence suggests that the FBI traced the disclosure to the office of the Army Air Corps Chief of Staff, General Henry H. (Hap) Arnold. Apparently, Air Corps officers, unhappy with the role and supplies allotted their service in the Victory Program, had sought to correct the situation through public exposure. Pursuing this matter further would have done the war effort no good, and the administration quietly let the matter drop.[32]

The system of classifying and withholding information and relying on press patriotism worked imperfectly at best for material which might legitimately be characterized as "security sensitive." However, it did not even address the core of Roosevelt's problems with the press—the unacceptable representation of government policies and activities. Instances of this kind sometimes originated with a reporter's misinterpretation of the President's press conference remarks or with an editor's failure to provide them with an administration slant in publication. Moreover, even those journalists who wished to conform to FDR's standards of responsible journalism could not always be sure their reports would prove acceptable. Unless they were willing to submit their copy to the White House for clearance before publication (which they were not), the misunderstandings of which Roosevelt complained were bound to recur.[33] Minimizing the problem required the skillful handling of the major source of newspaper commentary on national affairs, FDR's twice-weekly meetings with the press, and it was upon this that the President's success in managing the news would ultimately rest.

Unable to effect a workable scheme for avoiding unwanted press coverage, Roosevelt sought to minimize the opportunities for reporters to misconstrue his remarks. Although the surest way of achieving this was to cut down on, or eliminate, his meetings with the press, Roosevelt rejected this expedient. By 1940, the twice-weekly conferences had become something of a ritual, and even occasional cancellations provoked critical commentary. Rather than risk a serious confrontation by unilaterally altering the press conference formula, he chose instead to strip them of much of their news value on critical issues of diplomatic and military affairs.

Meetings during 1940 and 1941 remained much as they had been earlier—numerous, well attended, and lively. Reporters continued to appear, drawn perhaps by the prospect of some great revelation or at least by the sure knowledge that everything the President said, or refrained from saying, could somehow be construed as "news." When occasions arose for the President to promote his programs, he could still be counted on for some headline-making comment and he remained forthcoming on the trivial matters that always made up a significant portion of news conference banter. However, on substantive issues relating to the U.S. response to the wars in Europe and Asia, Roosevelt generally refused to make any but the most general comments. At one time the source of "inside" information and incisive commentary, the conferences had conveyed a sense of FDR's appreciation of the value of the press relationship. Now they were enlightening on nothing so much as his fear of candor and his negative attitude toward the press. This is not to say that the President abandoned his role as leader of national opinion; only that he no longer employed the Washington press corps as often or as well as he once had.

Negative aspects of the conferences, always present, now came increasingly to the fore. Conferences frequently began with Roosevelt announcing that there was nothing of significance to report. When issues arose that he did not wish pursued, he would turn them aside with a "no news in that." Sometimes his remarks were more pointed and occasionally intimidating. In the past he had attributed unwelcome inquiries to "orders" from hostile publishers and editors; now he tended to blame them on the ignorance or unprofessionalism of the working press. The difference was significant. Once excused for their stubbornness or obtuseness, reporters now were likely to encounter some personal rebuke apt to discourage lines of inquiry that might antagonize the chief executive. It is impossible to say how many of the more timid succumbed, but surely FDR's attitude did not encourage free inquiry. In any event, even those who screwed up the courage to tackle Roosevelt on touchy issues were unlikely to elicit an informative response.

The vast majority of subjects raised by reporters at their twice-weekly meetings with the President dealt with the world situation and America's response. They included requests for comment on diplomatic negotiations, aid to Great Britain, and developments in the undeclared war with Germany. All were matters of critical importance to the American people; all were repeatedly broached by reporters. Often, the President was ready with an informative response. But where he suspected a critical reaction or further probing into areas he wished left unexplored, he ducked. Many inquiries called for speculation and prediction which the President steadfastly refused to supply, labeling them "iffy questions" requiring unwarranted "crystal-ball gazing." In many instances, such responses were justified. But often FDR would evade issues—on the nature of a diplomatic appointment or mission, for example—with no more apparent justification than his desire to avoid public discussion. Whatever the rationale in each instance, the total effect was to keep Americans in the dark concerning the course of administration policy.[34]

Roosevelt's refusal to analyze events deprived the press and the public of an important aspect of the news. While reporters often used him as a convenient source of information, the chief value of the press conferences lay in the opportunities they provided to probe the President's thinking on the nature and direction of national policy. Roosevelt's views were precisely what reporters and readers most wanted. But such remarks were most readily misinterpreted, and, for this reason, the President was determined to avoid them. He made exceptions, of course, when these served propaganda purposes. Thus, for example, when public doubts were expressed concerning the dedication of the Soviet Union to freedom of religion, Roosevelt, seeking to smooth the way for the extension of American aid to the Russians, arranged for a planted question on the subject and responded with a full discussion of the issue.[35] Discourses of this kind did occur, but the initiative usually came from FDR and they were far outweighed by the number of subjects on which the President insisted that the "facts speak for themselves."

FDR's response to questions bearing on the possible modification of the neutrality laws reflects his determination not to say anything that might be used against him. In early February 1940, the President was asked if he still believed, as he had stated at the outset of the war, that the United States could stay out. Roosevelt passed up this opportunity to discuss American policy and its prospects by curtly declaring that his earlier "statement still holds until there is another one." Asked more specifically about the operation of the Neutrality Act, he commented, "off the record," that the law was a technical matter that had best be discussed with officials at the State Department.[36]

In early September 1940, the President announced the exchange of American destroyers for British bases, an action he likened in importance to the Louisiana Purchase. On this momentous occasion, however, his announcement to the press went little beyond the message he was to submit to the Congress. In refusing to answer one question, he declared that a reply would involve "all kinds of things that nobody here would understand, so that I won't mention them. It is a fait accompli; it is done this way." A further inquiry he dismissed as an "if" question, to which he would not reply.[37]

Early in 1941, Congress and the nation began debate on Lend Lease, a major step toward armed involvement in the war. The President, however, sought to contribute as little as possible to press discussion of the measure. Asked at the beginning of February what he would do first under the proposed legislation should it pass, the President answered: "Go out in the middle of Pennsylvania Avenue, and stand on my head."[38] His response drew a laugh, but remarks like this led Secretary of War Stimson to "gently warn" FDR against the frivolous tone he was imparting to his press conferences. The nation needed leadership, the elder statesman suggested, not clever evasions.[39] On an earlier occasion, he had told Roosevelt bluntly that "the only person that the American people took their information on foreign affairs from was the President of the United States," adding that unless he got into action "pretty soon," the isolationists ("people who have no morals on international affairs") would prevent any effective American response to the international crisis.[40]

Lend Lease became law in March, ensuring that American assistance to Britain would not be limited by British ability to pay. But German U-boat successes soon made it apparent that the principle of all-out aid short of war would not save Britain unless measures were taken to ensure delivery of the goods. This raised the issue of what responsibility the United States would assume for the safety of Atlantic shipping lanes. During the congressional debate on Lend Lease, opponents had argued that passage would inevitably lead to demands for the protection of supply ships. Asked to comment, Roosevelt replied, off the record, that he had not given the matter any thought! He had not considered it, he said, because "when a nation convoys ships . . . through a hostile zone . . . there is apt to be some shooting . . . and shooting comes awfully close to war, doesn't it.''[41]

But in the spring of 1941, the issue could not be avoided and both sides to the foreign policy controversy watched intently to see what the President would do. Interventionists, concentrating on the need to ensure British survival regardless of the risk, demanded naval convoys. Isolationists, determined to keep America out of the war, saw adoption of the measure as a major step toward a dreaded second American Expeditionary Force. Roosevelt refused to contribute to the controversy by revealing the nature of United States naval policy or commenting on its values and attendant risks. His leadership of public opinion was limited to revealing and embellishing upon various naval incidents in hopes no doubt that these ''facts'' would forcefully argue the need for greater American involvement.

As it stood, American naval policy, although provocative, was restrained. From the fall of 1939, Roosevelt sought to keep German ships from operating freely on what he called ''the American side of the Atlantic.'' To this end, he employed patrols by American warships and planes under orders to broadcast the sighting of any submarine or suspect surface ship in uncoded radio signals. The object was to bring such sightings to the attention of British naval units which might then take appropriate action.[42] The advantage of this method of quasi-warfare was that it preserved the fiction of non-belligerency; its fault, that it proved insufficient to neutralize the Axis submarine forces.

By the spring of 1941, Navy authorities felt obliged to take steps to increase the effectiveness of patrols lest the U-boat succeed in closing the sea lanes. On a single night in early April, a German wolf pack sank 10 of 22 ships in a British convoy, and United States Chief of Naval Operations Admiral Harold R. Stark noted that the situation in the Atlantic was ''obviously critical'' and ''hopeless, except as we take strong measures to save it.'' On April 9, the United States established a protectorate over Greenland; on the 18th, the Chief of the U.S. Atlantic

Fleet extended naval patrols eastward from North America to 26 degrees longitude, covering an area which included all of Greenland and the Azores and overlapping the zone in which Germany had declared all foreign shipping fair game.[43]

On April 15, reporters, taking note of current concerns, asked somewhat obliquely if the President believed there was "increasing demand toward the use of American naval power." Roosevelt first said he could not comment, but, warming to a subject to which he was obviously keenly attuned, noted that there had been "more nonsense written, more printer's ink spoiled, more oratory orated over the subject by people who don't know a 'hill of beans' about it than any other subject in modern times." He cautioned reporters against speculation on the protection of shipping, implying that the subject was beyond their competence. He also dismissed the suggestion that he would seek the arming of American merchant ships.[44]

The issue of what the President would do to turn around the obviously deteriorating situation in the Atlantic continued to interest the press. In late April a Washington correspondent asked the President if matters had yet gotten to the point "where it looks as though convoys would have to be seriously considered?" Roosevelt replied with a snappish, "I never lived at Delphi," suggesting that he could not tell what the future held in this regard. Actually, the Delphic oracle to which the President alluded was noted for obscure and ambiguous answers, and in this sense Roosevelt might indeed have qualified, metaphorically, for residence. He also labeled as "too glittering" a question as to whether any steps had been taken to ensure deliveries to England and refused, even at this late date, to describe American naval activity as aimed at complementing British efforts to protect the transatlantic traffic. Instead, he repeatedly insisted that the Navy was merely engaged in the protection of the American Hemisphere, conceding, however, that such protection might be carried out anywhere on the seven seas.[45] Roosevelt sought to deny what was very much a fact: that the issue of war or peace for America rested largely in his hands.

In the midst of this sparring over the meaning and implications of U.S. naval policy, John O'Donnell, writing in the anti-administration Washington *Times-Herald*, charged that the administration had adopted a policy of escorting the merchant ships of foreign belligerents from American ports to a point in the Atlantic where they were picked up by British warships. In an accompanying statement, publisher Eleanor

"Cissy" Patterson declared that the important issue was not the name applied to policy, but simply whether the nation was courting war by placing its warships between the munitions-laden British cargo vessels and the German submarines determined to send them down.[46] It was important for the public to have an answer to this question, but the President was, as he had said on an earlier occasion, convinced that such explanations merely lent themselves to efforts by "a certain element of the press" to "pervert" his remarks, "attack" his position, and "confuse the public mind."[47]

Roosevelt directed Early to tell the press that the O'Donnell accusation was a "deliberate lie." At the same time he did not accept Patterson's challenge to go beyond semantics and clarify American naval policy. Instead, he told reporters that there was "just exactly as much difference" between patrolling (what he said the Navy was doing) and convoying (what the administration critics charged) as there was between a horse and a cow. The comparison, while colorful, failed to address the risks and efficacy of each course. Nevertheless, reporters who accepted the distinction and asked whether the administration had "any idea of escorting convoys" did elicit from the President a categorical "no," to which he added with what may have been a touch of bitterness, "I am afraid [that] will be awfully bad news to some of you."[48]

Three weeks later, with discussion of the convoy issue apparently ruled out, reporters turned to the operation of the administration's patrol system. "How successful do you consider it?" one intrepid reporter asked. Roosevelt refused to comment on this "perfectly silly question." The President, somewhat apologetically now, noted that the situation was too "terribly serious" for comments such as he was being asked to make: "I can't create hypothetical news for all of you good people. You have got to go on facts as they happen. No human being can . . . guess what is going to happen tomorrow."[49]

Criticism of Roosevelt's refusal to clarify publicly administration foreign policy rose, and it did not come from hostile sources alone. In early May, according to a government survey, a significant number of newspapers that supported intervention were openly critical of FDR's failure to lead public opinion. Editorial writers, finding widespread public "apathy, confusion, and timidity," blamed it on Roosevelt, who, they charged, apparently lacked confidence in the people's capacity to understand and respond sensibly to a realistic picture of what had to be done to prevent a Hitler victory. They also resented "the President's 'jocose' or 'evasive' responses to press conference queries'' on foreign policy. As to the substance of that policy, the report noted, newspapers generally approved of patrols but expressed no great faith in their ability to reverse the tide of the war in the Atlantic. Convoying had come to be regarded as the answer, and the government analysis concluded that until the nature of the battle of the Atlantic ''and the elements of naval strategy involved are explained to the public, this view of convoys as the unique solution seems likely to persist.''[50]

During May, as British ships continued to go down with frightening frequency, pressure for a change or at least an adequate explanation of American naval policy increased. Action seemed imminent and many anticipated a dramatically significant announcement from a presidential address scheduled for mid-May. The Chicago *Tribune* predicted a declaration of war, an action interventionists would have welcomed but were too realistic to expect. Yet they hoped for something that would ignite a largely apathetic American people. As Ickes told the President: ''I know we cannot cold bloodedly go to war with Germany, but isn't there something that we could do to clarify the issue, such as declaring a general emergency.''[51] At the same time isolationist leaders urged Roosevelt to use the speech to renew earlier assurances that he would take no step likely to involve the country in war.[52]

Roosevelt delivered the anxiously awaited address before the Governing Board of the Pan American Union on May 27. Those who looked to it for a new departure or a detailed analysis of American policy were disappointed. It was more of a rallying cry; a call for unity and determination that emphasized the Axis threat to the Western Hemisphere, the impossibility of doing business with Hitler, and the consequences for the United States of a Nazi victory. The President reviewed what he had done, including a brief outline of the system of naval patrols, and asserted that he and his military advisors would devise and implement whatever other methods seemed appropriate to ensure the ''freedom of the seas.''

The President did not directly address the issues raised by his critics, apparently not wishing to fuel the debate on the efficacy and direction of American policy. The time for questioning and contention was long past: ''Your government has the right to expect of all citizens that they take part in the common work of our common defense—take loyal part from this moment forward.''[53] What he expected was public confidence in his leadership, not nitpicking analysis.[54] This may account for his decision to minimize press coverage and its attendant commentary. While the radio networks and newsreel companies were invited to broadcast and film the address, only under pressure did he agree to admit one reporter from each of the three press associations, later joined by a correspondent from the *New York Times*. Moreover, Early refused to outline the content of the speech in advance and delayed distribution of a prepared text making it difficult for many papers to meet publication deadlines. Such arrangements seemed designed to discourage editorializing.[55]

After the event, the White House was also reluctant to elaborate on what FDR had said. On the morning after the address, reporters confronted Early with the vagueness of the President's remarks, particularly as they related to naval policy. Rather than attempt to clarify Roosevelt's words, Early referred reporters to a special presidential news conference to be held that afternoon.[56] But those who went looking for answers found few. FDR remained evasive, and at least one friendly observer thought that his refusal to elucidate the issues he had raised in the speech had offset its morale-building benefits.[57] Thus, asked if he saw "any further need of extending the patrol" in the Atlantic, FDR said that was "like asking where Destroyer 446 is at the present time . . . in other words, that is . . . purely a military and naval matter." Roosevelt's use of national security to justify his silence prompted one reporter to ask whether the press might assume that all "the steps you may take from now on of a naval and military character are secret?" Roosevelt denied this but noted that "there were some things that obviously I am not going to tell you about, and you will get accustomed to not asking them after a while." Although FDR was probably speaking in earnest, his remarks evoked laughter from at least some of those gathered.[58] The press, though by and large skeptical, was not embittered by FDR's efforts to manage the news.

In July, the President authorized actions, hinted at in his May 27 speech, that increased the likelihood of conflict with Germany. Early in the month he announced that American marines had replaced the British force occupying Iceland, and that the Navy had been ordered to take all steps necessary to protect communications between the United States and this new American outpost. Although Roosevelt did not elaborate, in mid-July, the Navy began providing armed escorts for all friendly ships moving to or from Iceland. This in effect meant convoying ships, many of them bound for Great Britain, well into the German blockade zone. Naval encounters were almost certain to follow.[59]

The President was not unmindful of this consequence, and while it is too much to say that he took the action in hopes of provoking incidents, he was quick to exploit the "educational" value of those that did occur. The most important encounter from this perspective was one involving the U.S.S. *Greer*. In early September, while on its way to Iceland, the destroyer was notified by a British patrol plane of the nearby presence of a German submarine. *Greer* proceeded to track the U-boat while awaiting the arrival of British craft. After four hours, during which time a British bomber directed to the scene by the *Greer* attacked the U-boat, the German commander, unaware of the nationality of his persistent harrier, turned on the American ship and attacked. The *Greer* replied with depth bombs. Neither thrust found the mark, and the encounter ended inconclusively.[60]

On September 4, the Navy announced the attack. The following day the President began his press conference with an account of the affair, which sought to picture the American ship as the innocent victim of a deliberate German attack. The fact that no damage had been done, he said, was not important; the United States intended to seek out and "eliminate" the attacker. A week later, FDR discussed the meaning of the event in a fireside chat to the nation. The encounter, he said, was part of a calculated Nazi plan "to abolish the freedom of the seas, and to acquire absolute control and domination of these seas for themselves." The next step, he said, was clear—"domination of the United States—domination of the Western Hemisphere by force of arms." The President insisted that the *Greer* had a right to be where it was, that it had been fired upon first, and had responded in self-defense. In the future, American ships would defend themselves by shooting on sight: "When you see a rattlesnake poised to strike, you do not wait until he has struck before you crush him." The time for "active defense," the President concluded, "was now."[61]

Roosevelt on this occasion followed the practice of insisting that his remarks to the public be allowed to stand on their own. He discouraged speculation on their meaning, and refused both before and after the address to answer reporters' inquiries. The speech would be in plain English, Early told reporters on the eve of the address, and would require no translation. Nevertheless, on the day after FDR spoke, several reporters questioned the press secretary about the precise meaning of some of the things Roosevelt had said. Somewhat uncomfortable, Early refused to interpret his chief's remarks: "Frankly, I am not going to answer any questions. You may ask the questions but I am not in position to answer any of them. It was designed that way; that's the design of living for the day."[62] The President apparently believed that the effect he sought from his speech was best achieved through the words Americans heard over their radio and that any additional comment would undermine the mood he had attempted to create.

But questions on the *Greer* episode would not go away, and the President's refusal to discuss the issue did not prevent isolationists in Congress from probing further. In late September, the Chief of Naval Operations admitted to the Senate Naval Affairs Committee that the *Greer* had been fired upon only after it had pursued and broadcast the position of the German submarine. Isolationist elements in the press exploited the revelation, producing embarrassment and anger at the White House.[63]

The President believed that the character of the events engulfing the United States made the details of each incident in the Atlantic war insignificant. What mattered was that the United States was in a shooting war with Germany, and the grave danger to American security this represented overshadowed other issues. FDR had occasion to drive this point home three days after the *Greer* announcement when he disclosed that another ship, the S.S. *Pink Star*, carrying what he called "general cargo" and bound for Iceland in a Canadian-escorted convoy, had been attacked and sunk by a submarine. Roosevelt urged reporters (and inferentially the public as well) to focus on the larger issues involved in this and other encounters and not to be distracted by what he considered petty details. The principal facts, according to the President, were that "a certain group of people is trying to dominate the whole world, and we are trying to defend the Americas against that attempted domination." Roosevelt went on to say that he did not think that there was

much argument that is justified—with honesty—in trying to obscure the main objectives, by talking about whether the ship was in convoy, or was not; whether the ship was armed or not, whether the ship was carrying the Panama flag or the United States flag. They are just "red herrings." Thank you. That's all for today.

Although the President attempted to break off discussion at that point, reporters did elicit his acknowledgment that the administration was considering a change in the Neutrality Act that would permit the arming of American merchant ships.

The importance attached to the various facts that made up these incidents depended a great deal on perspective. The President in an effort to dramatize the importance of the loss of the *Pink Star* described its cargo in considerable detail: enough concentrated orange juice "to supply the vitamin C requirements of 91,000 individuals for 12 days," etc.[64] Isolationists probably found it more important that the ship carried munitions, that it was armed, and that it was headed ultimately for England.[65] For them, these circumstances helped explain the encounter. For the President and his supporters, they were merely distracting minutia. Both sides saw the war at sea as evidence of a design for involving the United States. They differed chiefly on the author of that design. In establishing whether it was Hitler or Roosevelt, the selection of facts for scrutiny was essential.

The fact that the press was overwhelmingly sympathetic to administration goals suggests that Roosevelt's reluctance to discuss certain events was not motivated mainly by a desire to hide embarrassing facts. Rather, it reflected his concern that basically sympathetic journalists, in reporting events, would miss their central meaning because of a preoccupation with controversial detail. The press was behind him, and he knew it. But reporters, in spite of themselves, were still capable of doing great harm, and his news management was directed toward minimizing this potential.

The President conducted his press conferences with extraordinary skill. The mark of his success was how little he managed to say without antagonizing reporters. He was apparently convinced that the conversion of public opinion on foreign policy was being effected without the need for authoritative explanation from him. In this circumstance, he found it expedient to avoid delineating his policies or justifying his actions (even when these were clear) for fear of generating unnecessary controversy and criticism. True, the press conferences were largely uninformative, but FDR was not concerned. He saw his encounters with the press as part of a total administration effort to shape and lead public opinion. Conferences served mainly to satisfy the press without endangering the vague consensus on foreign affairs being shaped through other means. From this perspective, the conferences served best by saying least.

Nowhere was this approach to information more in evidence than in the President's failure to keep the public fully informed of events in the Far East. Problems between the United States and Japan were long-standing and would have disastrous consequences. Yet the same considerations that led FDR to avoid discussions of the Atlantic war led him to tell the American people little of the deterioration of relations with Tokyo.

Although their remote origins date back further, America's problems with the Japanese may be traced most immediately to Japan's quest for mastery of Asia. The United States resisted, first employing diplomatic means and then, in 1940, invoking economic sanctions as well. The two governments continued to discuss the issues alienating them, but the Japanese, firmly committed to creating what they called the "Greater East Asia Co-prosperity Sphere," refused to surrender their hard-won gains or their ambitions for more. The administration declined to accept Japanese imperialism, and the result was a steady worsening of relations leading ultimately to war.[66]

Roosevelt took far eastern developments seriously but saw them as distinctly subordinate to the course of events in Europe. Involved in raising American consciousness of the Nazi threat and the need for greater involvement in Europe, he saw no reason to call attention to the conflict in Asia or to American policy in the region. Roosevelt was aware that the public mood was volatile and aggressive with regard to the Japanese, and it is quite possible that he wished to avoid provoking militant opinion which would in turn push him toward actions he considered premature. In October 1940, Roosevelt learned that the chief of a Japanese press association had suggested that as part of a scheme to diminish tensions in the Far East, the U.S. should demilitarize its Pacific possessions, including the base at Pearl Harbor. The President took the remark to be provocative and expressed concern that something of this kind "might stir up bad feeling in this country," noting that the country was "ready to pull the trigger if the Japs do anything." "Public opinion," he said, "won't stand for any nonsense . . . from the Japs."[67]

During 1940–1941 FDR spoke out publicly only once concerning far eastern affairs and then only briefly.[68] Nor did he raise the problems with the press, a policy abetted by reporters who showed little interest in pursuing the issue. Generally, the press found more drama in the

Nazi blitzkrieg, the air war over Britain, and the battle of the Atlantic than in the protracted war in Asia or the fruitless diplomatic maneuvering it spawned. Moreover, Asian affairs generated less domestic debate and therefore had less news value than the great isolationist-interventionist struggle over policy in Europe.[69] Routine comment came from the State Department, but as long as the press was content to let the issue lie, the White House was not disposed to bring it up.[70]

FDR volunteered nothing and easily shook off the few queries that did arise.[71] Thus, for example, on the day after Mussolini joined Hitler in sealing the fate of France, Roosevelt was asked to comment on "various editorial suggestions" that "in view of the troubled state of the world generally," the administration might explore the possibility of modifying its policies in the Pacific, particularly in regard to trade relations with Tokyo. Roosevelt's only comment was the "off the record" observation that "there isn't any editorial writer in the country who knows one-third as much about it as the State Department and I do."[72]

The most dramatic demonstration of the apparent unity of the totalitarian aggressors was the Tripartite Pact concluded in late September 1940. By it, Japan, Italy, and Germany agreed that if any one of them were attacked, the others would assist the victim. The pact was aimed at deterring American intervention in the European conflict and at clearing the way for Japanese southward expansion. The alliance was viewed in the United States as evidence of a world-wide conspiracy directed from Berlin but operating out of Rome and Tokyo as well. According to one scholar, it "contributed more than anything else to the deterioration of Japanese-American relations."[73] The pact was the subject of considerable public discussion which tended to grossly exaggerate its significance, particularly for the United States. But immediately following its signing, when the issue was raised by the press, the President had nothing to say.[74]

In late July 1941, the strain in U.S.-Japanese relations increased perceptibly. On the 24th, France capitulated to Tokyo's demands for the right to occupy bases in southern Indochina (the Japanese had already occupied the north). The action significantly extended Japanese penetration into Southeast Asia and threatened British possessions and American interests in an area rich in strategic resources. The same day, Roosevelt, apparently moved by this event, broke his public silence on Japanese-American relations in informal remarks to a group of civilian defense volunteers. In a brief statement, which was not broadcast, the President ascribed his caution in dealing with Japan to his desire to avoid provoking additional aggression. This statement suggested that FDR was describing past policy and some journalists concluded that the administration had now embarked on a new, more belligerent course in its relations with Japan. Such speculation produced a firm denial from the President at his next press conference. However, when asked to interpret recent Japanese-American relations and their implications for American security, the President steadfastly refused to be drawn out.[75]

On July 26, Roosevelt froze Japanese assets in the United States, making possible the termination of trade. At a press conference three days later, he was asked to "discuss export control in relation to the Far East," to which he replied, "I don't think there is any news on it." Later at that same conference, asked for comment on Japanese expansion into French Indochina, he demurred saying that this was still "a very current matter" about which "we had better not say anything."[76]

Attempts to ease increasing tensions through diplomacy continued over the next several months. The President, however, refused to comment on the discussions, except to deny (with questionable accuracy) that Japanese demands on China were the chief obstacle to a settlement.[77] At the beginning of November, the President, anticipating further Japanese aggression in Southeast Asia, probably in the direction of British possessions, asked the members of his Cabinet what sort of public response they thought he could expect should he use naval forces to oppose the Japanese advance. Specifically, he wanted to know if such a commitment of U.S. forces required some prior "incident." The Cabinet was unanimous in declaring that the country would be behind the President should he decide to act and that no incident was required. The members did suggest that some sort of preparation was called for, perhaps public statements by the State Department and the White House followed by a radio address by the President indicating the stalemate in negotiations with Japan and the gravity of the crisis confronting the nation. Characteristically, however, even at this late date Roosevelt was reluctant to involve himself in any such educational effort, preferring to have the members of the Cabinet "leak" the seriousness of the situation to the press.[78] Here the matter rested, apparently awaiting more certain signs of the imminent Japanese aggression. In the meantime, negotiations continued as Roosevelt sought to put off the confrontation for as long as possible. These efforts came to an end on November 26 when Secretary of State Hull in effect rejected what was to be the final Japanese proposal. Two days later, with all hope of negotiated settlement gone, Roosevelt broke his silence and provided the press with the kind of discussion that had been absent from his press conferences in the past. Even now he insisted that his long statement be treated as "off the record," suggesting that reporters attribute his remarks to the "best information obtainable in Washington."[79]

The President believed that providing the American people with information on current events was the best way to encourage support for the course he would take. But he was never certain, as David Reynolds has recently suggested, whether and to what extent the United States would become involved in the war.[80] The press demanded specifics, but FDR realized that presidential policy statements would limit his flexibility while providing his critics with focus for their inevitable attacks. Roosevelt was clearly concerned about generating public support but would not undertake to do so by jeopardizing his ability to lead. Press releases, public speeches, statements and acts by unofficial supporters, leaks to the press, and the propaganda implicit in publicizing and promoting the defense mobilization suited his need. Meetings with the press, on the other hand, because they conceded to reporters the initiative in questioning the President, challenged his ability to manage the discussion of public affairs. Unable to find an acceptable substitute for what had become a Washington institution, FDR supplemented the devices he had always used to control the conferences with appeals to patriotism and to a new standard of journalistic ethics. Occasionally, the confrontations his tactics provoked were embarrassing, if not for the President then at least for some of his anxious interventionist supporters who insisted on more statesmanlike leadership from the chief executive. But Roosevelt and his media advisors were more acutely sensitive than Stimson, Ickes, and others to the limitations of the "bully pulpit." They were also aware that the administration was being served by a vast educational effort more immune from criticism and more likely to reach the mass of the American people than explications aimed primarily at satisfying inquisitive journalists.

5

Radio, 1940–1941: Emergence of the Perfect Informational Medium

FDR's relations with the press reached their lowest point just as the international crisis and growing debate over United States foreign policy made administration access to the public critically important. What Roosevelt had wanted from the press was a neutral medium that would give the American people the "facts" unadulterated by offsetting unofficial reports and editorializing. Although the nation's leading newspapers, as we have seen, seemed for a time willing to go some way toward meeting these expectations, Roosevelt was never happy with overall press performance. Journalism's failure was, however, more than compensated for by radio, which would carry the White House foreign policy and defense messages dependably and without the doubt-raising news commentary that had apparently become an inescapable aspect of the print medium.

In part, this happy relationship grew out of the patriotic and interventionist sentiments of broadcast executives pleased to serve the administration's educational needs. But radio's cooperation was also offered against a political background that made such cooperation sound business policy. How much each element contributed to determining radio's course is impossible to say, but it seems certain that the industry's vulnerability to hostile government action—a vulnerability that reached its peak in the years before American involvement in the war—contributed to its desire to demonstrate its public spiritedness and responsibility.

The broadcasting industry had grown to maturity in the early 1930s with an abiding fear of federal encroachment. During the New Deal years, as we have seen in chapter 1, the broadcasters, led by network representatives, had sought to ensure themselves against possible hostile government action by proving the medium's value to the administration. The resultant friendly cooperation, evidenced by industry word and deed, was made particularly impressive to the President by its sharp contrast with the partisan irresponsibility he daily identified in the nation's newspapers. By the end of his second term, FDR was acutely conscious of radio as an alternative to an increasingly hostile press. For their part, the broadcasters may well have credited their unscathed transit through eight politically tumultuous years to the cooperative relationship they had painstakingly cultivated with the White House.

While satisfying the President's demand for an "objective"—that is, uncritical—vehicle for administration views was no guarantee of continued immunity from hostile government action, it did offer the best hope, and the industry, under network leadership, clung tightly to the formula. With this in mind, the broadcasters took on and overcame the challenge to this posture posed by the advent of the radio news commentator. Late in the decade, the industry discovered that broadcast news was a popular and saleable commodity. The networks were eager to exploit this type of programming but soon found that radio commentators could prove as obnoxious to the administration as their newspaper counterparts. They were thus confronted with the need to balance commercial gain, often tied to the controversy inherent in news commentary, against the potential political losses this might incur. Their solution was self-censorship.[1]

Their first victim was General Hugh Johnson. Formerly head of Roosevelt's National Recovery Administration, Johnson had turned to journalism and against the direction taken by the New Deal. He now employed his wit and ability to turn a phrase to criticize the administration both in a syndicated newspaper column and on a regular radio series airing over NBC. In October 1937, Johnson responded intemperately to a fireside chat in which Roosevelt discussed his forthcoming legislative program. The network's Vice-President, Frank Russell, immediately called the White House to apologize for the incident and to announce that Johnson was to be taken off the air. Russell promised that in the future NBC would refuse time to sponsors who intended to use it for controversial discussions. Early, although no doubt pleased, was apparently embarrassed by this acknowledgement of White House–network cooperation and told Russell that the administration had no interest in and would take no cognizance of the action. Nevertheless, NBC replaced Johnson with "Jay Franklin" (John Franklin Carter), a one-time administration public relations officer and a New Deal partisan with close White House ties.[2]

Not long after, the problem of critical news commentary arose again, with the same result. This episode involved Boake Carter, by far the most popular political commentator of the late 1930s and, after Johnson, the only one consistently critical of the administration. Carter had long been a troubling presence on radio, and, as early as the fall of 1934, FCC Chairman Pettey had informed White House officials that he had information which might somehow be used to silence him.[3] The President, however, preferred to try first to win him over to the administration's cause. In 1936, Carter did endorse Roosevelt's reelection, but the following year he vigorously castigated Roosevelt's plan to "pack" the Supreme Court, as well as his response to the Japanese sinking of the United States gunboat *Panay*. At the end of the year, government investigators began probing Carter's background in hopes of turning up material that would justify the deportation of the "unfair and pestiferous" English-born journalist.[4]

According to one scholar who has examined his broadcasts, Carter had become so irrationally critical by 1938 that CBS or his sponsors would have liked to have restrained him long before they finally did. However, Carter was heard at prime time on 85 stations, five days a week, and until the Munich crisis suddenly stimulated public interest in radio news in the fall of 1938, he was the only newscaster commanding a significant audience.[5] Nevertheless, ultimately not even his popularity could save him.

Marjorie Merriweather Post Davies was a contributor to Democratic causes and the wife of the recently appointed Ambassador to the Soviet Union, Joseph Davies. Moreover, she was heir to the Post cereal fortune, and as a former director had considerable influence with General Foods, which sponsored Carter's broadcasts. In late November 1937, Marvin McIntyre asked Early if he could "do anything with Marjorie about Boake Carter's new connection with General Foods." In January 1938, at Mrs. Davies' suggestion, the company's advertising agency concluded an arrangement with Carter regulating the content of his broadcasts. According to this agreement, which Joseph Davies subsequently sent to the White House, Carter agreed that in commenting on government policy he would be "constructive," and would deliver his remarks with "suitable restraint of language . . . without invective, or criticism of the motives, . . . character, . . . and moral attributes of personalities."[6]

Over the next few months Carter toned down his commentary—his audience ratings dropped, and in June General Foods declined to renew his contract.[7] Carter's voice could still be heard, but only on a few stations and at mostly unpopular times. Like Johnson, he continued to write a newspaper column critical of the administration. It served chiefly as a reminder to the White House and to everyone concerned of the stark contrast between newspaper and broadcast journalism. The most obvious result of the episode was that as events overseas came to dominate the news, radio was without a major spokesman in opposition to the nation's emerging foreign policy.[8]

Although the Johnson and Carter episodes were resolved to the satisfaction of both the President and the network executives, both remained acutely aware of the problems that such controversies might cause in the future. The interests of both continued to lie in seeing to it that radio's political content did not stray far from administration orthodoxy. The President would, of course, encourage this objectivity, but under the existing "understanding" it was ultimately the industry's responsibility to ensure it. The large networks responded by pushing for industry-wide self-regulation designed in large measure to guarantee controversy-free (safe) radio programming.

Elements within the industry had long looked to self-regulation as an alternative to government control, but the broadcasters were badly divided among themselves and agreement on this, as on many issues, had proven impossible. In 1923, the industry had been driven by the threat of government restrictions and by the demands of the powerful American Society of Composers, Authors, and Publishers (ASCAP) to form the National Association of Broadcasters (NAB). Divisions within the industry, however, were reflected in bitter bickering at the NAB meetings, and the organization was largely ineffective.

Following the enactment of the Radio Act in 1927, pressure for self-regulation increased and was finally given expression in a code of ethics adopted by the NAB in 1929. Although the code was vague and weak, many independent owners still found it too restrictive and successfully resisted efforts aimed at its strengthening. By the late 1930s, however, a variety of problems besetting the industry tipped the balance in favor of those who supported a stronger unified direction.[9]

The threat came chiefly from Congress, which was expressing a keen interest in the monopolistic aspect of network broadcasting. In part this interest reflected a current revival of anti-trust sentiment in general,[10] but at least some of it may be traceable to New Deal enemies who, conscious of the closeness of the network-administration relationship, saw the investigation of industry and FCC affairs as a way to settle political scores.[11] In any event, during 1937, four congressional resolutions were introduced calling for investigations of monopoly in broadcasting and possible collusion between the industry and the FCC.[12]

From this point forward, the industry would find itself under attack from both Congress and the FCC and, as *Variety* would later comment, radio executives came to be gripped by a "paralyzing fear of extinction at the caprice of a few men in Washington."[13]

When the NAB met in Chicago in June 1937, the spectre of outside interference led the broadcasters to close ranks and finally agree on the need for an industry "czar" to replace the unpaid President who currently served the Association. The czar idea had already proven successful in professional baseball and the motion picture industry. Following scandals and public criticism each had appointed leaders (Judge Kenesaw Mountain Landis for baseball and Will Hays for the movies) in whom they vested extraordinary power to regulate and discipline their respective industries. It was assumed, correctly, that rigid self-controls would restore public faith and eliminate pressure for government interference.

Following the NAB convention, a search committee took up the task of finding the appropriate man to lead radio. Early and McIntyre were among those suggested for the position and, as the search proceeded, industry leaders kept the President fully informed of their efforts. FDR's endorsement would have made the NAB's task easier, and enhanced the organization's political prestige and strength. But, while encouraging the industry's move toward unity, FDR refused to pick its next leader, and when the NAB met again in February 1938 this issue was still unresolved.[14] Now, however, labor problems and public criticism of offensive radio material made some immediate action necessary. Particularly worrisome was the reaction to the generally violent tone of children's programming and an allegedly sacrilegious skit in which actress Mae West appeared in a parody of the story of Adam and Eve. Under pressure to act, the NAB appointed Mark Ethridge, a distinguished journalist, a Democrat, and the owner of a Louisville, Kentucky, radio station, as interim president. In July, it finally appointed

Neville Miller, the former Democratic mayor of Louisville, as its first full-time, paid president.[15] Miller promptly formed a committee to draft a new code of self-regulation.

The industry's belated efforts to improve its image and performance were not enough to alleviate the threat of government encroachment. In November 1938, the FCC, responding to political pressure, created a three-member committee to investigate allegations of monopoly in broadcasting and to recommend appropriate new regulations. The inquiry, which was public, was slow in getting under way and slow to resolution. Hearings concluded in May 1939, but the Commission, obviously not eager to incur the wrath of either Congress or the industry, would not act on its findings for another two years.[16] Meanwhile, proceeding on another front, at the end of February 1939 the FCC announced fourteen types of offensive programs which might lead to punitive action against offending broadcasters. These included the broadcast of defamatory statements, failure to allow equal time for all sides to discuss controversial issues, programs offensive on religious or racial grounds, and programs in which the broadcasters took sides on political, religious, or racial matters.[17] Beset by fears of further interference, the broadcasters again looked to the White House for signs of approval and cooperation. In early March, Ethridge wrote Early that the industry believed its long-range interests coincided with those of the President and that if he and Miller could meet with Roosevelt, Ethridge was certain a mutually beneficial arrangement could be worked out. The President refused to involve himself directly in the industry's woes.[18]

The President's strategy in dealing with radio and its problems was to express sympathy and understanding to all concerned but to stand aloof. The political risks of deeper involvement were too great; the potential benefits were negligible. Should the White House attempt to protect the broadcasters, it would simply lend credence to current charges of political interference in Commission affairs. On the other hand, the President was in no position to join the critics of the FCC or of the networks. His "neutrality" probably encouraged all parties to the controversy, particularly the corporate executives, to believe that ultimately he would do what he could to help them.

This was the theme of Stephen Early's address to the broadcasters' convention which convened in Atlantic City in July 1939. His speech, drafted by Harry Butcher and Paul Porter, CBS's Washington counsel, declared that radio had nothing to fear from government if it continued to fulfill its obligation to serve the public interest. Early noted that the broadcasters' "best insurance . . . is consistently to render the very best public service you can." "Each broadcaster," he said, "knows whether his station is doing the right kind of job and, for my part, I would be willing to leave to a jury of broadcasters any specific instance involving the right of a station to have its license renewed." So long as programs were "interesting, informative and clean—in brief so long as radio serves democracy," Early concluded, "it will remain free."[19]

The broadcasters responded by adopting new "standards of practice." The code covered children's programs, committed the industry (weakly) to improving its educational service, limited the length of commercials, clarified the meaning of "good taste" as it applied to advertising copy, and banned attacks on racial or religious groups. Two sections dealt with political broadcasting and were of special interest to the White House. One, on "controversial public issues," called upon networks and stations to provide time for the balanced presentation of public issues of a controversial nature. Time for the discussion of political issues was not to be sold except during election campaigns. A second section decreed that news programming "shall not be editorial." This was explained to mean that news would not be selected for the purpose of contributing to either side of any controversy nor was it to reflect the opinions of the station or network or any of the people involved in the creation of the program. Broadcasters might analyze and elucidate the news "so long as such analysis and elucidation are free of bias."[20] These two sections provided broadcasters with a rationale for dealing with Father Charles Coughlin, as well as with the potential problems raised by the growing popularity of the radio news commentator.

Some members of the NAB objected to the new restrictions. But the industry as a whole, under network leadership, in adopting these restraints demonstrated its willingness not only to modify its more objectionable practices, but also to censor itself in ways which made it the "objective" medium of information that the administration wanted. Although its problems were not over, radio had established a firm position from which to battle its detractors.

In the fall of 1939, while the industry awaited the outcome of a number of proposed or pending government actions directed at its economic arrangements, it suddenly confronted another problem. The Communications Act of 1934 gave the President the authority to control

broadcasting in the event of a national emergency, and, five days following the German invasion of Poland, Roosevelt announced the existence of what he called a "limited national emergency."[21] The industry
sought reassurances from the White House, and although these were
forthcoming, they were accompanied by statements that left little doubt
that the administration's commitment to radio's independence was con-
ditional. Thus, in September 1939, a few days after the war began, the
President's Press Secretary, responding to a question regarding the possible imposition of radio censorship, said that he was certain that "for
the present" the President wanted no such action. He reminded reporters, however, that the Communications Act did give the chief executive censorship and other control authority, and that the administration
had undertaken contingency planning should such controls prove necessary. Early's closing comments were even less comforting. Radio
broadcasting was a new and relatively unknown medium, he said. Its
behavior in the current crisis was unpredictable, and government would
have to assess its performance before deciding upon policy. Comparing
the industry to a child, Early said that if in time radio proved to be
"well-mannered, it would be left to move along on its own." On the
other hand, should it prove "to be a bad child, there would, I think,
be a disposition to . . . correct it and make it behave itself."[22]

On the day following Early's remarks, the industry indicated that it
understood the warning and accepted the responsibility. Following a
conference on the broadcast of war news, an industry spokesman declared that no censorship of radio would be required in as much as any
problems between government and the industry could be resolved by
the broadcasters "through self-discipline and common sense." The
Press Secretary, in turn, expressed satisfaction with the industry's attitude, noting that he was especially gratified that radio's pledge of self-
regulation had come voluntarily and had "not even been prompted by
government suggestion."[23]

The industry soon took a major step toward redeeming its commitment
to responsible broadcasting. In October 1939, the NAB's Code Compliance Committee issued a statement defining broadcasters' obligations
under the Code of Conduct adopted the previous July. Henceforth,
member broadcasters would not sell time for the discussion of controversial subjects. Instead, to ensure the public's right to know, stations
would provide their facilities equitably and without charge to conflicting
sides of any issue of legitimate public concern. The principal object of

the Code was Father Charles Coughlin. By citing its ban on self-sponsorship of controversial views, broadcasters could more comfortably rid themselves of a long-standing nuisance while demonstrating the industry's oft-expressed commitment to neutral programming.[24]

The President had reason to be pleased by radio's total commitment to public interest broadcasting. Whatever else this meant, it indicated that the industry would not only censor material the administration might find obnoxious, but would continue to air programming (some of it originating with government) that presented the White House version of national affairs. The great value of this cooperation was made clear by opinion polls showing the public's great faith in broadcast news. Indeed, by mid-1941 more Americans relied upon radio for their understanding of current affairs than upon any other medium.[25]

In the weeks following the outbreak of war in 1939, the White House made it clear that it intended to make increased use of this powerful force. In a press conference a few days after the German attack, Early told reporters that radio newsmen would enjoy equal access to war and other news emanating from government.[26] Given the total dominance of news gathering hitherto enjoyed by newspaper reporters, the announcement was an indication of the importance FDR attached to radio broadcasting. This was also evident in FDR's introduction to a series of transcribed broadcasts describing administration operations. On this occasion, Roosevelt declared that limitations of time and space made it impossible for newspapers to carry all the information about government the public needed to know. This, he said, made it essential for the administration to turn to radio to make up the deficiency. In taking to the air waves, Roosevelt said, government would be able "to correct the kind of misinformation that is sometimes given currency for one reason or another." Some communities, he said, were unhappily dependent on a single source of printed news, and in such cases only radio could "overtake loudly proclaimed untruths or greatly exaggerated half-truths."[27]

Broadcasters had always responded generously to hints from eager administration propagandists and during 1940–1941 the industry's difficulties with government and the sympathy many broadcasters had for administration policy objectives reinforced this disposition. None of the skepticism that afflicted newspapers would be apparent in their performance. The broadcasters were uninhibited by any tradition of independent political advocacy or of diligent news-gathering and thus there was, in short, nothing in the White House–radio relationship of the kind that had undermined the President's rapport with the press.

While the basis of a mutually satisfactory arrangement was present, an open alliance was not possible. Responsibility for oversight of the industry was shared between the administration and Congress, and, though the White House exercised the preponderance of influence, some care had to be exercised by FDR and the broadcasters to avoid antagonizing those in Congress who were hostile to accretions of presidential power. Among those was Senator Burton K. Wheeler, whose isolationism made him suspicious of FDR's internationalist-interventionist proclivities and whose position on the Senate Committee on Interstate Commerce put him in a position to make trouble for both the broadcasters and the FCC should industry-administration cooperation too blatantly serve an activist foreign policy. In these circumstances, maximizing the propaganda potential of the medium without bringing harm to the industry or the administration was to test the political skills of both parties in the months to come.[28]

The formula devised by network executives was somewhat analogous to FDR's policy in regard to the European war. Radio's leaders would assist in the struggle against isolationism but under a cover of officially declared neutrality. It was an effective scheme that was well suited to political realities. Congress and most Americans accepted the need for defense and aid to Great Britain. Information on these efforts presumptively served the public interest and was not readily recognizable for the effective interventionist propaganda it was. Radio could, without serious objection, inform Americans of the efficacy of the defense effort and urge their participation in it. Whatever their format or overt purpose, the cumulative effect of such messages was to increase public awareness of the national crisis and build faith in the nation's ability to deal with it. These were the foundations upon which interventionism was based.

The broadcasters' claim to objectivity was based on their policy of airing a balance of interventionist and isolationist speakers. Public speeches were the most obvious manifestation of the "great debate" on radio, and it was on these speeches that the defenders of radio policy and skeptics alike focused their attention. In this one prominent aspect of broadcasting, in fact, the industry's claim was unassailable.

In the late summer of 1941, FCC Chairman Fly, responding to a request by isolationist Senator Charles Tobey (Republican, New Hampshire), a member of the Senate Committee on Interstate Commerce, surveyed the nation's radio stations to determine the coverage afforded speeches addressing the "role of this country with respect to the war abroad." The results showed that during the first five months of 1941 about 950 statements identified as dealing with foreign policy were broadcast; about two-thirds of them originating with local stations. For the most part these had been supplied by national organizations in the form of electrical transcriptions. Of this total, approximately 40 percent were pro-interventionist; an equal percentage, pro-isolationist; and the remainder of no discernible bias. The Mutual Broadcasting System presented the most evenly balanced fare, while CBS slightly favored the interventionists and NBC the isolationists.[29]

The objective stance substantiated by these figures masked a reality of radio bias. Speeches clearly recommending a given foreign policy made up only a very small portion of network radio programming related to defense and foreign policy. Between January and June 1941, the major networks produced an average of only 1.1 discussions of foreign policy per day.[30] This "debate" was dwarfed by the vast quantities of public service and other programming which tended to support the administration's position. An officer of the National Council for the Prevention of War illustrated the non-interventionist's problem when he complained that an anti-war address he had recently heard had been followed immediately by an emotional half-hour dramatization of the capture of German spies who had been doing their dirty work in an American Army camp. "Just the kind of thing to increase the tempo of war hysteria" he observed with some justification, and certainly the kind of programming likely to offset the words of even the most gifted spokesman for isolationism.[31]

The real problem confronting the isolationists, as this plaintive protest suggests, was not broadcast speeches, which were in any event of limited propaganda effectiveness, but the mass of other programming dealing with the United States response to the world crisis. Broadcasts of this kind were numerous, often entertaining, and usually not identifiable as propaganda.

The selling of defense lent itself to network broadcasting. Unlike industrial recovery, agricultural reform, and the like, interest was not limited to certain regions, occupations, or classes. Military mobilization naturally commanded the near universal appeal of patriotism, something to which a New Deal program like NRA could only aspire. Moreover, subjects relating to war were easily adapted for popular dramatization.

Indeed, many of the programs promoting the defense effort were merely variations on stock entertainment themes and enjoyed commercial sponsorship. A brief description of some of the defense-related broadcasts suggests the variety and ingenuity of radio's contribution.[32] During the first seven months of 1941, NBC broadcast nationally 627 programs which the company classified as defense related. Most were prepared in cooperation with either the Executive Office of the President (Lowell Mellett) or with private patriotic and civic organizations. Many originated with NBC itself. In addition to these national broadcasts, NBC's affiliates also produced larger quantities of such material designed for local consumption. For example, its two stations in New York City produced 60 programs and over 1,000 spot announcements, the latter mostly dealing with recruitment for the military, solicitations for the purchase of defense bonds, and contributions to the Red Cross. Similar productions came of course from the other networks and their affiliates and from independent stations around the nation.

The nature of the national campaign on NBC is suggested by the company's description of its regularly scheduled weekly network programming dealing with "civilian defense and morale" and other "general defense" matters. "America Looks Abroad," produced in cooperation with the Foreign Policy Association, provided discussions of international affairs, while "I'm an American" introduced listeners to distinguished naturalized citizens who discussed the meaning of American democracy, presumably for the edification of the foreign born. The National Association of Manufacturers supplied glimpses of the contributions of industry to the nation's defense, each week taking the listener on an imaginary tour of various munitions plants. The Council for Democracy produced a series called "Speaking of Liberty," which NBC described as discussions by the "nation's topflight authors and journalists" of the "problems facing America's democracy." A Council official suggested the purpose of the series when he confided to Lowell Mellett that while this program was not quite "warmongering," it "went beyond anything on radio to date."[33]

Promotion of administration policy just short of open advocacy was not confined to the public service or informational format. Thus, for example, "From Oxford Pacifism to Fighter Pilot" recounted the "blazing spectacular story of one of Britain's gallant air fighters, from pacifist beginnings to a fiery plunge from the skies." This "true story of the actual exploits of one of the RAF's unnamed heroes," which provided the basis for a motion picture as well, suggested the conversion interventionists wished the American people to emulate. Somewhat more down to earth was a serialized romance dealing with the trials and tribulations of Steve Mason, a former automobile mechanic caught in the military draft.

Regular radio series with origins pre-dating the current crisis also contributed to keeping the public's mind on defense. Programs of this type, ranging from the "University of Chicago Round Table" to "Pin Money Party," merely substituted defense-related topics, questions, or settings for the civilian ones to which listeners had become accustomed. Occasionally, script writers with interventionist convictions succeeded in injecting propaganda into even the unlikeliest radio productions. The writers of the popular "Fibber McGee and Molly" comedy series informed Stephen Early that, although network policy forbade it, they had managed to include educational material in the discussions among McGee, Molly, and their friends.[34] Obviously, programming of this kind was not simply providing information; it was, to use the radio parlance, "plugging" a cause. Nor was it merely propaganda masquerading as entertainment. Rather, it was a happy marriage of the two and no more effective medium for the interventionist message was possible. As a result, no one listening to radio in 1940 and 1941 could fail to understand that the nation was embarked on a great and critically important endeavor involving the participation of millions of their fellow Americans. So far as the radio presented these activities, the effort was well in hand, productive, and destined to produce an enormous arsenal with which the forces of democracy could defeat any foe. Almost all of this programming could be and was described as educational—promoting public understanding of the non-controversial aspects of American policy. But much of it can also be fairly described as propaganda—promoting public support for a policy (deeper involvement in the war) that was the subject of considerable debate.

The interventionist bias of broadcasting was fully appreciated by administration officials. In July 1941, Secretary of the Navy Knox asked Adlai Stevenson, then his assistant, for suggestions on ways in which the administration might more effectively shape public attitudes on the war. Stevenson's recommendations included an evaluation of the existing war of words.[35] Nowhere, according to this survey, was the interventionist propaganda effort more apparent than on radio. Stevenson's analysis simply divided all radio material bearing on the current situation into two categories—pro- or anti-administration. Against the administration he could find only the speeches of a handful of isolationists. Under "pro," he listed not only obviously interventionist talks, but also the morale building, defense promoting, and patriotic addresses the networks characterized as "non-controversial." Lumping together all these as "pro-administration" speeches, Stevenson counted 67 in the month of July alone, totaling twenty hours and fifteen minutes. "Against" for the same period he listed 23 speeches for eight hours of airtime.

This disparity in volume was made even greater in effect by the variety of speakers, many of them of star quality, available to the administration cause. Only eighteen different individuals spoke against administration policy. Of these, two-thirds were members of Congress, and only two of the remaining six had names likely to be recognized by more than a handful of Americans. Fifty-seven spoke for the administration. Of these, 10 were members of Congress, and 24 served in the administration or were spokesmen for Great Britain. Another 23 statements were delivered by private citizens unconnected with the government's policy. These included celebrities like scientist Marie Curie, actor Douglas Fairbanks, Jr., Sergeant Alvin York of World War fame, mystery writer Rex Stout, and Republican presidential candidate Wendell Willkie. In addition to speeches, Stevenson set up a category which listed programs of clearly propagandistic intent. Naturally none of these was isolationist or critical of the administration. However, counting only the most blatantly propagandistic—"Defense for America," "British War Relief," "Strikes," "Treasury Star Benefit," "Spirit of 41," "America Preferred," and the like—he found that in July, 45 such programs aired for 21 hours and 45 minutes.

This accounting provided a more accurate picture of the great debate on radio than that supplied by the broadcasters or the FCC, but it was not the full story. A handwritten note at the bottom of the "pro" speeches list says simply: "Plus majority of commentators in [sic] all networks." This, as we will see, was in fact an understatement.

Speech making and other broadcast propaganda was heard and understood against a background of events which could either validate or make them so much irrelevant blather. Events, it was argued at the time and since, determined public attitudes. Most Americans relied on radio news for their understanding of these happenings, and, insofar as they did, they received a consistently and consciously biased construction of reality.

Writing in 1940, the distinguished journalist Quincy Howe observed that the silencing of radio commentator Boake Carter in 1938 left "not a single voice" on national network radio consistently critical of administration policy. Indeed, Howe noted, when it came to foreign policy "all regular radio news broadcasts gently, firmly, and consistently support Roosevelt to the exclusion of any other point of view."[36] This conclusion is substantiated by David Culbert in his recent study of the major radio news commentators of the late thirties and early forties. Culbert analyzed the commentary of six broadcasters: Carter, Fulton Lewis, Jr., H. V. Kaltenborn, Elmer Davis, Raymond Gram Swing, and Edward R. Murrow. He notes that only Carter and Lewis opposed the administration with any consistency and that Lewis had access to a very small audience and had little influence.[37] On the other hand, in June 1938, when General Foods at the instigation of the White House refused to renew his contract, Carter was being heard on 85 stations, five days a week at prime broadcasting time. According to polls, he was the most influential broadcaster of his time and continued to receive this rating a year after he was no longer heard on network radio. His views, according to Culbert, were simple-minded, irresponsible, and extremist, but at bottom they confirmed and represented the attitudes to which most Americans still clung in 1938. In particular, they bolstered the belief that Europeans could care for their own concerns and that the United States could safely allow them to do so. Such views encouraged an understanding of events which impeded public acceptance of a greater role for the United States in international affairs, and those who sought to promote interventionism found them obnoxious.[38]

Carter's fate, as Culbert suggests, may have deterred others considering presenting the news from an isolationist perspective. More certainly, it deprived isolationism of an important source and symbol of legitimacy. Carter alone could not have offset the influence of the interventionist bias which, without him, monopolized radio news commentary. But Carter or some other popular isolationist commentator might have provided isolationists with the properly slanted "news" upon which propaganda largely depends for its success. Carter was the first and, apart from Father Coughlin who suffered a similar fate in 1939, the only broadcaster prior to the McCarthy era of the 1950s to be removed from the air for the political opinions he expressed. The result left the broadcast of news to a handful of commentators distinguishable only by style and nuance.

Elmer Davis, the most widely heard of the group, was a genuinely well-informed and thoughtful observer whose gradual conversion to interventionism during 1939 and 1940 suggested a cautious and considered approach to events. However, once converted, he became an uncritical supporter of the administration, insisting that Americans put aside their doubts and reservations and rally behind the President. The focus of his remarks was not administration policy, which may have been too uncertain to warrant sustained commentary, but the evidence of Germany's threat to western civilization and to American security.[39]

Raymond Gram Swing was the most active propagandist of the group, pursuing his interventionist crusade outside as well as in the radio studio. He was closely allied to the administration, mainly through his friendship with Harry Hopkins, and was a founding member of the interventionist Council for Democracy.[40] In broadcasts to the American people and by shortwave to foreign countries, Swing acted as a semi-official spokesman for United States policy, seeking to explain "the correctness of every move toward greater overseas involvement made by Roosevelt."[41]

Edward R. Murrow's contribution consisted mainly of undermining his listeners' sense of remoteness from the European struggle and their suspicions of the British and their will to fight. Broadcasting from London in the midst of the German air blitz he gave the war a dramatic presentness. Nor did Murrow leave the meaning of events to his audience's imagination. In December 1940, he called for an American declaration of war against Germany and over the next several months repeatedly asserted that America's rightful role in the conflict was alongside England as a "fighting ally."[42] Such declarations by Murrow and the others were essentially superfluous—merely making explicit what their news coverage was intended to indicate. The events they chose to describe and the manner in which they described them implied, without need for explication, a Nazi march of conquest which would not stop short of American shores and therefore necessitated a militant administration response, possibly including war.

Although Murrow and the others played an important part in shaping an interventionist consensus, none was more determined, less restrained in his advocacy, or more closely aligned with the administration propaganda effort than Walter Winchell. Nor indeed could the others match the audiences and, presumably, the influence he commanded.[43] Winchell could hardly be classed as a news commentator—his broadcasts had neither sustained description nor analysis of events. But he was, nevertheless, the most prominent single source of information and opinion bearing on the current world crisis. His programs epitomized propaganda as entertainment. Employing a broadcasting style all his own, he left his listeners with feelings like those induced by commercial advertising. His object was not understanding but sensation. What his audiences heard each Sunday evening was a series of brief "flashes" and "exclusives," delivered at machine gun tempo, dealing with the habits and associations of public figures and cast as fearless exposés divulged without regard to propriety or personal risk. By 1941, as much as 90 percent of these revelations related to politics, focusing largely on the disreputable and subversive character of the bundists, isolationists, and others of what he called the "ratzi" ilk.[44] Accompanying himself on a telegraph key beeped with appropriate ferocity for dramatic effect, Winchell reduced the great foreign policy debate of the early 1940s to a parody of Broadway/Hollywood intrigue. Obviously, such fare was not to everyone's taste, but very likely Winchell's gaudy version of the interventionist gospel reached a great many Americans who would forever have remained untouched by the sober analysis of his more restrained brethren.

Winchell's impressive popularity rested in part on his reputation as the premier inside dopester, his ability to pass on tips supplied him from "behind the scenes." In the 1930s these came mostly from his contacts in cafe society, particularly from entertainment figures who happily exchanged gossip for a favorable mention in Winchell's newspaper or radio columns. These "plugs" could mean fame and fortune to their recipients and were greatly prized. A similar symbiotic relationship served Winchell's interest in politics. The tipsters were now government officials; their payoff, promotion of policies they sponsored.

At first Winchell sought out the powerful. Eventually, they came to him. Early in the New Deal, Winchell cultivated contacts in the Navy Department and the FBI. He also undertook a publicity campaign designed to boost FDR, whom he kept fully informed of his efforts.[45] His motives included not only the obvious personal advantages that accrued to him, but also a sense of patriotism, a personal admiration for Roosevelt, a desire to associate with the powerful, and, ultimately, a strong impulse to fight Nazism. Similar motives had produced contacts between other journalists and government officials, but the Winchell relationship was unique. For, unlike the others, Winchell was not just an occasional vehicle for a government "leak," he was a conscious and persistent agent of administration propaganda. It was a role for which he volunteered. In early December 1939 assistant Secretary of State Adolf Berle reported that the columnist had offered to "put his radio time at our disposition . . . to develop any angle of foreign affairs the administration might deem worthwhile."[46] Over the next two years, officials made frequent use of his services. Most assignments came by way of Ernest Cuneo, counsel to the Democratic National Committee, who served Winchell both as ghost writer and as liaison with the White House and the New York–based British intelligence mission.[47] From these sources, interventionist and anti-isolationist material found its way to the approximately 50 million Americans who read Winchell's columns or listened to him each Sunday evening over NBC's Blue network.

The malicious irresponsibility and obvious bias of Winchell's broadcasts were sources of considerable embarrassment to NBC executives. Chary of excessive controversy of any kind and particularly anxious to avoid offending Senate isolationists, they repeatedly cautioned Winchell. Yet Winchell's Hooper listener ratings of "20" or better made him an exceedingly valuable "property" which NBC was loath to surrender. In July 1940, responding to numerous complaints about Winchell's tactics, one NBC official told President Niles Trammell that he assumed "Winchell's importance on the Blue and his ratings are such that we do the best we can and if he doesn't live up to our policy, we should just let it go."[48]

News Director A. A. Schechter was not inclined to be so tolerant. In March 1941, he learned that Winchell intended to "expose" a trip that Senator Wheeler had made to the Soviet Union in the early 1920s. Presumably, Winchell intended to discredit the isolationist Senator by suggesting some Bolshevik connection. Having failed to get Winchell to remove the item from his script, the exasperated News Director was finally obliged to cut him off the air as he attempted to read the piece. This led Schechter to suggest that the time had come for stronger sanctions. Writing to another NBC executive, he noted that regardless of his popularity "Winchell's material is nothing but blackmail now, and he has gotten into a psychotic state where he is defending all of America. . . . I think the decision must now be made whether Walter Winchell is bigger than the National Broadcasting Company."[49] Winchell remained.

Winchell's ability to survive in spite of the controversy he provoked contrasts sharply with the fate of the isolationist Boake Carter. The explanation appears not to lie totally with Winchell's popularity, as Carter's broadcasts also commanded high ratings. Yet when General Foods, at the instigation of the administration, refused to renew Carter's contract, neither NBC nor the other networks could find a way to keep him on the air. It may be that network executives found Carter's controversial broadcasts expressed ideas whose days were numbered, while Winchell's equally controversial interventionism was in the ascendancy, at least among the nation's political leaders. Their response in each case was dictated by a perception of what was good for the nation and what was good for the industry. Neither good appears to have included a commitment to balanced political programming.

Understandably, when administration officials thought of radio propaganda they included in their balance sheet not only the pro- and anti-interventionist speeches, but the whole range of programming calculated to promote an acceptance of administration policy. This accounting produced a very different result from the image of balance the networks sought to create: on one side, the speeches of a handful of isolationist leaders; on the other, the full effect of the informational propaganda and more. Not only were the isolationists matched speech for speech by interventionist spokesmen, but a whole range of public service broadcasting on various non-controversial aspects of defense preparedness also prepared the public for war. In addition, Fibber McGee, Walter Winchell, and other radio entertainers contributed their endorsements of administration policy while a bevy of news commentators provided an uncontradicted rendering of the administration's view of the foreign policy crisis.

By the fall of 1941 non-interventionists had lost the struggle for parity of access to America's ear. Ironically, as they belatedly came to recognize, it was industry's "fairness" doctrine that served as the rationale for the interventionists' total domination of the air. In November a bitter and dejected Norman Thomas sought to air his anti-war views in a broadcast to be paid for by his supporters. The New York station scheduled to carry his speech refused, citing the NAB code forbidding self-sponsorship of controversial material. Thomas had originally supported the code, but he could now see, as he complained to the NAB and Senator Wheeler, that the industry's loudly proclaimed commitment to objectivity covered a practice of denying him time while it permitted the regular broadcasting of a wide array of (sponsored) interventionists ranging from the President's wife to Walter Winchell.[50]

6

Movies, 1940–1941:
Propaganda as
Entertainment

The vast audiences they commanded, and the ready accessibility of the messages they conveyed, made motion pictures a propaganda source of enormous potential. This was recognized but not easily exploited by government officials. Effective film propaganda depended in large measure on the cooperation of Hollywood—on the professional production techniques the industry virtually monopolized and, even more, on access to the national film distribution network dominated by a handful of studios. Until late 1940, the motion picture industry showed little interest in promoting government causes and FDR had experimented with a program of government produced, high quality, commercially competitive documentaries. But masterpieces like *The River* could not be turned out in volume and in any event inevitably suffered the stigma of "government propaganda." By the end of the 1930s it was clear that successful use of film depended on the administration's ability to secure the cooperation of the privately owned motion picture industry.

Cooperation between government and Hollywood was an exception in the thirties, but it did exist in the mutually beneficial relations established between the White House and the newsreel industry. During the early forties, as FDR turned increasingly to defense and foreign relations, the opportunities for the relationship flowered and film versions of the news would become a significant vehicle for the government's view of world and national affairs.

As instruction on world events, newsreels were at best inadequate and often grossly misleading. Nevertheless, newsreel coverage of such happenings was entertaining and popular and probably constituted a major source of the public's impressions of international affairs, particularly for those citizens whose low level of literacy put them beyond the reach of newspapers and magazines.[1] In 1939, foreign news and items concerning the war in Europe made up almost 30 percent of what the newsreels showed. In 1940 and 1941, while material in these categories fell off somewhat, footage relating to national defense expanded sufficiently to more than make up the decline.[2]

Although pictures of actual events had a special eyewitness credibility, the filmed news was in fact constructed of selected portions of contemporary affairs chosen without regard for their representativeness. The determination of what was shown was made largely on the basis of the availability of film footage and its potential entertainment value. As it happened, these factors tended to make the content of newsreels serve the interventionist cause.

The role of this selection process was apparent in the disproportionate emphasis the newsreels gave to the conflict in Europe. Earlier newsreels had contributed to American impressions of events in China. But during the years 1939–1941, while the struggle for Asia continued, newsreels tended to focus on Hitler's war. The conflict in the West was perhaps more dramatic and probably easier to cover than the protracted hostilities in China and although Japanese aggression would ultimately prove of considerable consequence to the United States, newsreel audiences saw little of it after 1938.[3] Even after Japan attacked the United States and American forces engaged in combat with the Japanese, the newsreels consistently neglected the Pacific theater in favor of the less active American involvement in Europe. This emphasis on events in the West, whatever its source, contributed to the administration's effort to focus public opinion on the menace posed by Hitler.

At the same time, the manner in which the European conflict was depicted, while likely to raise American consciousness of the struggle against Germany, was not so graphic as to frighten those contemplating American involvement. Had the horrors of war been more candidly revealed to the American people through the newsreels of 1940–1941, interventionism might well have proven less popular. In fact, the face of war Americans found in their movie theaters was mechanical, almost benign; a struggle of things rather than of people. Guns fired, bombs dropped, and the landscape erupted—all in a rather impersonal way. No effort was made to follow the soldier, to witness combat up close, to see its effects on the fighting men or on the civilians caught up in the battle. Instead of scenes of violence and death, Americans saw "pictures of troops and material in transport, 'atmosphere' glimpses of the various fronts, political and military leaders addressing their people." All these conveyed a sense of the "urgency of the situation" without suggesting its bloody consequences. Such coverage reflected, in the first instance, the censorship imposed by the governments (mainly British) that permitted cameramen to cover the war.[4] At the same time neither editors nor movie exhibitors were disposed to show the public the terror of war. Conflict and destruction were entertaining, but only to a point.

It was not only censors who helped determine newsreel content. American government officials also played an important role in determining what the public saw. As the government and the nation prepared for war, official spokesmen and government agencies tended to dominate the news. The administration, as in the halcyon days of the New Deal, was now again an active newsmaker—and frequently the news it made was more visually interesting and entertaining than its earlier activities. During the period 1940–1941, the administration did the kinds of things that made good newsreels, and shots of defense preparations which made them seem "glamorous, fun, sporting, a kind of 'national frolic,' " were commonly seen.[5] No signs of confusion or mismanagement here, only a constant stream of "publicity" shots—troops on maneuvers, bombs and tanks rolling down assembly lines, the launching of another great warship. The upbeat message helped develop the nation's confidence in its leadership and ability to deal with the challenge from abroad. Without it, isolationism might well have been the chief beneficiary of news from abroad. The isolationists offered nothing comparable. Public demonstrations might have helped but they were few and not of a pictorial value to match the administration's efforts.

Administration opponents were aware of their disadvantage. The effect was apparent. During the debate on Lend Lease legislation, Senator Wheeler wrote to Paramount News and to Will Hays, head of the motion picture trade association, complaining of the newsreel coverage of his side of the great debate. "Will you kindly inform me when, if at all, you intend to carry my answer to the President's most recent fireside chat? And what, if anything, you are going to do about carrying both sides of the controversy on pending legislation which directly involves the question of war or peace." Hays, speaking for the industry, replied with a snide rejection of Wheeler's complaint, sending a copy of the correspondence along to Roosevelt, probably as an example of the industry's loyalty. On the other hand, in late February, with passage of Lend Lease in the offing, Paramount's Robert Denton wrote to Early asking him to arrange for complete newsreel coverage of the signing of the act and promising that the industry would "go to town on this story." Later the companies, in turn, seeking recognition for their contribution, succeeded in having Early place a paragraph in Roosevelt's radio address to the Academy of Motion Pictures, Arts, and Sciences dinner that year (the Oscar awards) in which FDR called attention to the great national service the newsreels had provided.[6]

The entertainment (and propaganda) value of real events was exploited to their fullest in a series of monthly film documentary dramatizations called the *March of Time*. The series began in 1931 as radio reenactments of historical events. In 1935, while the broadcasts continued, the format was adapted to the screen by Louis de Rochement, who skillfully mixed newsreel footage with staged scenes to produce realistic re-creations of recent events. His productions, most of which were about twenty minutes in length, were entertaining, seemingly authoritative, and laden with political messages. Although typically shown along with standard film features, the episodes themselves were popular movie attractions. By 1937 an average of 22 million people saw the *March of Time* each month.[7]

The series dealt with a wide range of subjects, but from the summer of 1939 through the winter of 1941 all but 5 of 32 films released by de Rochement dealt explicitly with military or political subjects and even the exceptions touched on these topics. Although its producers claimed to be nonpartisan, the series was militantly anti-fascist and interventionist. In 1940, for example, a full-length *March of Time* production, *The Ramparts We Watch*, described the impact of World War I on a typical American town stressing the perils of isolationism then and now.[8] In 1941, *Peace by Adolf Hitler* exposed the Nazi record on international agreements, ridiculed the suggestion that a secure peace with Hitler was possible, and argued that those who supported peace were either naive or Nazi sympathizers. In *Main Street USA*, the *March of Time* returned to the typical small town motif, this time to dramatize the effect of a Nazi victory on the average American.

By combining newsreel footage with staged performances, the producers had wide latitude to instruct without losing the credibility inherent in the documentary. As a result, with no apparent instigation from

Washington, *March of Time* conveyed the interventionist view of international affairs to the American people better than government publicists could have done themselves.

The seemingly authentic depictions of world affairs the moviegoers found in the newsreels and *March of Time* often served as "factual" introductions to the fictionalized versions of the same events and themes they encountered in feature films. Propaganda in films did not begin with the crisis of 1940–1941 nor was it always the result of conscious intent. Much of the interventionist indoctrination of the American people was the incidental by-product of certain popular film settings. This was true of the war story whose entertainment and profit potential had long been apparent. Uniforms provided glamorous costume for Hollywood's leading men, while the military setting—even when it did not involve armed combat—was well suited to action and heroics and readily adaptable to romance and even comedy.[9] The military services, for their part, recognizing that films like *The Singing Marines*, *Submarine D-1*, *Annapolis Salute*, *Wings over Honolulu*, *You're in the Army Now*, and other Army/Navy sagas of the late 1930s promoted public acceptance of the military, made it a practice to supply ships, planes, and other "props" to Hollywood.

Mutuality of interest provided the foundations of a military-movie alliance that was to flourish in the years immediately before American entry into the war. As early as 1938, the non-interventionist historians Charles and Mary Beard, noting the increasing preoccupation of film makers with military themes, linked this development to Roosevelt's announced intention to expand United States naval forces. Citing evidence of the government's hand in Hollywood's operations, the Beards concluded that "for all practical purposes, the picture industry has become a servant of the Roosevelt administration in respect of foreign, naval, and military designs."[10] The Beards and others who shared their concerns were particularly disturbed by the appearance of war films at a time when signals from abroad suggested that Americans might soon find themselves pressured to become involved in another foreign war. Also troubling was the fact that, while earlier in the decade films glorifying the armed services had been offset somewhat by anti-war productions like *All Quiet on the Western Front*, by 1939 such films had virtually disappeared, leaving a one-sided positive image of the military in American film.

The same appetite for vicarious adventure that accounts for the popularity of war films also encouraged American taste for the more explicitly propagandist "imperialist" films like *Gunga Din, Drums, Wee Willie Winkle*, and *Charge of the Light Brigade*. These and others, mostly of British origin, were tales of daring, stoic courage, and heroism set in some glorious moment in the history of the British empire. Although they too were conceived as entertainment and produced for profit, they were nonetheless effective in portraying Britain as the determined defender of civilization, hence subtly arguing the interventionist cause.[11]

Although anticipated audience appeal would continue to dominate studio decisions on the content of films, by the beginning of 1939 the ideological concerns of the film makers, already apparent in the *March of Time* series, began to make themselves felt in feature films. Until the late 1930s, Hollywood's producers had been largely indifferent to political issues and reluctant to use film to promote causes of any kind. The market for motion pictures was worldwide and encompassed a wide range of tastes and beliefs. To be profitable a film had to satisfy this audience without offending the various governmental authorities and private pressure groups which presumed to speak for it. Confronted with the ever-present threat of boycott, censorship, and even government controls, the industry sought security in the production of universally unobjectionable film material. True, the social turmoil of the depression era was not entirely lost on the film makers and a number of films which attempted to deal seriously with reality did appear in the 1930s. But they were relatively few, and, as film critic Lewis Jacobs noted, the movies' "treatment of . . . reality was for the major part, so inadequate as to render it at times meaningless."[12]

Indeed, so preoccupied were the producers with avoiding giving offense that the industry leaders turned to self-censorship. Early in the 1920s, industry leaders had formed the Motion Picture Producers and Distributors Association, commonly known as the Hays office after its President ("czar"), Will H. Hays. By the mid-thirties the Hays office had developed a code of production defining certain categories of objectionable themes and practices. It also provided for the review of film scripts and for sanctions against those in violation.[13] Much of the concern of the Hays office and the code was with "immorality" (sex, profanity, lawlessness), but it also sought to prevent the appearance of other controversial matters. Hays and his associates believed, as the historian of his office put it, that "nothing hurts a picture's chance of success more than the whisper" that it contains "propaganda." This caveat, to which the industry generally subscribed, was supplemented by provisions in the code which called upon members "to avoid willful offense to any nation, race, and creed." In part, the concern here was for the various religious and ethnic groups in America, but it also reflected the importance Hollywood attached to its vast foreign markets. In the early 1930s as much as 35 to 40 percent of American film production costs were paid for by foreign distribution, and maintaining this market was a major concern of Hays and the industry.[14]

The desire to avoid controversy encouraged Hollywood to ignore the rise of the European dictators and the increasing international tensions dominating the news in the late thirties. A combination of circumstances, however, was at work to break down this isolation from reality, and by 1938 the industry had made a few tentative excursions into subjects previously considered untouchable. The change, slow in coming, owed much to the increasing awareness in Hollywood of contemporary world affairs, particularly the emergence of the fascist dictatorship.[15] As early as 1936, the film capital's "personalities" began publicly aligning themselves with groups and ad hoc campaigns fighting various ideological battles. Factions from the left preoccupied with the spread of fascism organized to support the loyalists in the Spanish Civil War and generally to promote anti-Nazi causes. Others more concerned about Communism, and particularly about the Communists in their midst, joined with the American Legion to combat "un-Americanism."[16]

Such concerns gradually made their appearance in films. Warner Brothers led the way. The studio earlier had pioneered in the production of pictures with explicitly political or social themes and had contributed airtime over its radio station to anti-Nazi and anti-Communist programming.[17] In 1938, Jack Warner, the studio's head, undertook production of *Juarez*, the story of the leader of the nineteenth-century Mexican movement for independence. Warner's purposes included a desire to enlighten audiences about contemporary international affairs. To this end he ordered a script which so "far as it is political and ideological, must consist of phrases from today's newspapers; every child must be able to realize that Napoleon and his Mexican intervention, is none other than Mussolini plus Hitler in their Spanish adventure."[18]

By 1939 nationalistic feelings growing out of concern with Communism and Nazism evoked a strong interest in "Americanism" among the film makers. In January even Will Hays, speaking for the more conservative studio executives, modified his earlier commitment to pure entertainment by acknowledging that the industry had a responsibility to enlighten as well as to amuse. Hollywood, he announced, would soon have 63 short subjects under production on themes ranging from the "Bill of Rights" to the "Alamo." In addition, 29 scheduled feature-length films were to deal to some degree with aspects of "Americanism."[19]

In 1939 Warner Brothers produced *Confessions of a Nazi Spy*, a melodramatic exposé of Nazi spying in the United States based on revelations at a recent federal trial. The film made use of newsreel clips, a narrator, and other devices intended to give it documentary character. Its heavy-handed message, which exaggerated the importance of German espionage and the German American Bund, apparently reflected the concerns of those responsible for its production, many of whom, including Warner, were Jewish or recent European political refugees. Their object was to raise the consciousness of Americans to the Nazi menace by showing that it was happening here. This could be done, Warner believed, without sacrificing either entertainment value or profit.[20]

The time was propitious for such an undertaking. A blatantly anti-Nazi film was certain to be banned in Germany and other nations which did not wish to incur German ill will. This, however, was no longer a factor in Warner's thinking or of great significance to the industry as a whole. The Nuremberg Laws of 1935 had, in addition to eliminating all non-Aryan employees from the German movie industry, imposed Nazi supervision over the American film companies operating in Germany and additional fees and duties on the importation and exhibition of American films. American film exports to Germany were immediately cut, and in 1936 Germany permitted only 30 Hollywood productions to enter the country. Various restrictions limited the profit margins on even these few, and only three of the major U.S. studios were willing to continue to compete in the German market under these conditions. As Germany's influence and control spread in Europe after 1938, American film revenue declined. By late 1941, returns from the continent had all but come to an end.[21]

With the fear of losing the once lucrative continental market no longer a consideration, Warner and others considering use of the anti-Nazi motif needed only to be concerned with the prospects for acceptance at home. The risk here was not excessive. A true story of spying in America was topical and exciting, the threat of boycott from special interest groups minimal. The number of pro-Nazi Americans was infinitesmal. Isolationists, while numerous, were overwhelmingly anti-Nazi and not likely to voice serious objection. Although executives at Warner were concerned about the prospects of *Confessions of a Nazi Spy*, it was a modest financial success.[22] Anti-Nazism—like anti-Communism—proved a relatively non-controversial theme easily subsumed under the concept of "Americanism." With a militant few actively pushing Hollywood to do its part and foreign commercial objections no longer a consideration, the way was clear for the production of similar "message" films.

How many there would be depended in large part on the interplay of ideological conviction and commercial concerns. This varied among film executives. The Warner brothers were sufficiently concerned about the Nazi menace to subordinate other considerations. But most producers were less ideological and more cautious than the Warners; their decisions seem to have reflected a conviction that a limited amount of anti-Nazi propaganda would not hurt the industry commercially and might do it some good politically. This was especially important in 1939 in view of the threat of hostile government action that now hung over the industry.

By 1938, one expert has noted, the production, distribution, and exhibition of films in the United States was dominated by a "small coterie of vertically integrated, horizontally coordinated, and monopolistically inclined corporations" exercising "cartel-like powers though common submission to the Hays office."[23] Independent theater owners and producers, believing themselves victimized, protested to the government. This protest was joined by civic, religious, and cultural organizations who attributed the objectionable content they found in motion pictures to the industry's domination by an unresponsive handful.[24]

In July 1938, the Justice Department instituted a suit charging Paramount, Loew's Inc. (owner of Metro-Goldwyn-Mayer), RKO, Warner Brothers, Twentieth Century-Fox, Columbia, Universal, United Artists, and their numerous subsidiaries with violations of the Sherman Antitrust Act. The suit, based on the findings of Thurman Arnold, head of the Department's Anti-trust Division, charged that 80 to 90 percent of America's quality feature films were produced or distributed by the eight major companies and that its finer theaters were dominated by the first five companies named, thus enabling them to exclude independent producers from showing their pictures in prestigious and profitable markets. The government also charged that the major companies had apportioned the theater market into exclusive geographic territories, thereby eliminating competition among them.[25]

Some of the arrangements cited in the government complaint had been instituted in the 1920s to save an overly competitive and faltering industry. Altering or eliminating them would have seriously damaged the major studios even in the best of times, and in recent years the effects of the depression, the competition of radio, and the decline of the foreign market had shaken the industry badly. Profits during fiscal 1938 and 1939 were in decline, and, although most studios would show signs of recovery in 1940, significant across-the-board improvement would not come until the following year.[26]

In these circumstances, Hollywood could ill afford the threatened government action and the industry responded by lobbying the public for support, while privately seeking the intercession of friendlier elements in the administration. Industry leaders apparently believed that the anti-trust action was an aberration produced by the radical Thurman Arnold and that, as Hays put it, some settlement based on "proper business and practical necessities and not solely on legalistic theories" could be devised.[27] They found sympathetic ears at the White House and at the Commerce Department, where the President had recently installed his intimate friend and possible successor, Harry Hopkins. In March 1939, Harry Warner, who, along with his brother Jack, had given Roosevelt strong political support in the past, wrote to Hopkins. He warned that a successful anti-trust suit would adversely affect the industry's declining, but still significant, export trade and in the process hurt the U.S. trade balance.[28] Hopkins, perhaps conscious also of the desirability of helping administration friends in Hollywood, undertook to resolve the issues between the Justice Department and the major studios.[29]

After months of discussion within the administration and between representatives of the government and the movie makers, a "compromise" solution was reached. In mid-August 1940, *Variety* reported that the White House had ordered the Department of Justice to settle its case by consent decree. President Roosevelt, the trade journal said, had acted with an eye toward both the coming presidential election and the growing foreign policy debate. "Films can play an important part in putting over the administration's defense plans," *Variety* noted, and if the litigation were settled to the industry's satisfaction, the major studios were prepared to produce "several pictures . . . which might be helpful in swinging public opinion to Roosevelt."[30]

The Justice Department denied White House pressure, but in November government lawyers entered into a consent decree with five of the eight major studios, producing what amounted to near total victory for them.[31] It is not certain if, as *Variety* alleged, the action had come in response to White House pressure. Nor can we say with assurance that subsequent industry offers of cooperation were related to this episode. Nevertheless, in the summer of 1940, just at the time *Variety* reported the forthcoming consent decree, Hollywood seemed to make a special effort to demonstrate its willingness to serve administration propaganda needs. Motives varied and are not in every case totally clear. Ideological concerns piqued by the fate of France were important, but self-interest, which now pointed to the production of propaganda, seems to have contributed to the new eagerness to cooperate.

As earlier, Jack Warner was among the first to lend his studio to propaganda purposes. In August he offered to produce any film the administration wanted without regard to cost. He was, as one official noted, "ahead of us in wanting to see defense incorporated into pictures."[32] Also in August, another offer of help came from Barney Balaban, President of Paramount, who told Harry Hopkins that he would like to arrange for Hollywood to broadcast entertainment to South America by shortwave. His object, he said, was to promote better understanding of the American way of life and to supplant the European influence in Latin America with Hollywood's version of North American culture. Washington had long been interested in promoting good will in Latin America, particularly in combatting the strong German and Italian influences there. In mid-August, the President established the Office for Coordination of Commercial and Cultural Relations between the American Republics under Nelson Rockefeller. Balaban's offer fit in nicely with this enterprise. It also suited the industry's interest in promoting Hollywood films in Latin America at a time when its other foreign markets were failing.[33]

Self-interest of a more immediate variety may help account for the cooperativeness of Metro-Goldwyn-Mayer. According to Assistant Secretary of State Berle, FDR contacted Nicholas Schenck, President of Loew's Inc. (the parent organization of MGM), in the summer of 1940 concerning production of a motion picture dealing with national defense and foreign policy. Schenck offered to place the entire facilities of his studio at the President's disposal, and appropriate film material was prepared by Early and Berle. In mid-October, a two-reel picture, *Eyes of the Navy*, described by a studio executive as certain to gain the "chief thousands of votes" in the coming election, was ready for distribution.[34]

Relations between Schenck and the White House indicate that his generosity in this instance was neither new nor without practical implications. Nicholas and his brother Joseph (Chairman of the Board of Twentieth Century-Fox) had contributed heavily to FDR's 1936 campaign and Joseph had recently lent the President's son, James, $50,000. Perhaps most importantly, in June 1940 Joseph Schenck had been indicted for federal income tax evasion. In these circumstances, *Eyes of the Navy* appears to have been part of a series of actions aimed at cultivating FDR's good will. In any event, upon Schenck's conviction Roosevelt asked Attorney General Robert Jackson to seek a fine rather than imprisonment for the friendly movie mogul, and Edward Flynn, Chairman of the Democratic National Committee, also intervened in Schenck's behalf, as did James Roosevelt. But the principled and independent Jackson was unmoved, declaring that the loan to young Roosevelt gave the appearance of an attempted bribe, and in the circumstances administration intercession was ill advised. Schenck went to prison for four months.[35]

The cooperative spirit, particularly lively in a few, was apparent in lesser degrees throughout the industry. Leo Rosten, then a consultant to the administration on film matters, noted that the Hollywood community without exception subscribed to the idea that promoting defense was a non-partisan responsibility. This commitment was exhibited by the Hays office, which in July established a Motion Picture Committee Cooperating for National Defense. The Committee was to deal with government requests for assistance and make certain that the studios shared the burden equitably. Under the Committee's aegis the studios supplied government film makers with training, production facilities, and expert advice. Cooperation through the Committee, however, did not involve the production of feature length movies.[36] Activity of this kind remained entirely at the discretion of the individual studios.

Although the industry's willingness to cooperate was significant, on the whole it was neither unlimited nor unconditional. Concern over moviegoers' receptivity to theater programs heavily laced with "messages" and the danger that propaganda activities would expose the industry to potentially destructive controversy led the Hays office to proceed cautiously. Many in the industry apparently believed that co-operation should be limited to those services likely to benefit the studios as well. Thus, industry leaders showed no enthusiasm for satisfying the needs of the various civilian defense agencies, preferring to confine their help principally to those agencies with which they expected to have long-term cooperative relationships. George Schaefer, President of RKO and Chairman of the industry coordinating committee, told a government representative that his group "was going to work with the War, Navy, and State Departments just as we have in the past because they're still going to be in existence" long after the emergency defense people "have finished their work."[37] Schaefer's remark reflected the mutuality of interest that undergirded Army, Navy, and State relations with Hollywood. These departments provided the movie makers with military props or facilitated the overseas production and distribution of films. In turn, the industry was willing to carry the departments' mes-sages. None of the parties to the special relationship wished to sacrifice it to some larger concept of the nation's defense needs. According to Rosten, this attitude, together with the slowness of civilian mobilization executives to recognize the full potential of film, meant that documentary film propaganda tended to place an "inordinate emphasis on the me-chanics and mechanical instruments of defense preparation" without adequately engaging the individual citizen in the spirit of mobilization. Rosten, who was completing a brilliant study of the Hollywood com-munity, knew the industry well and thought that he could improve the situation.

In late 1940, following discussions with officials in Hollywood and Washington, Rosten recommended establishment of a permanent in-dustry-government liaison committee responsible for devising propa-ganda themes and arranging for their incorporation in film. Such a committee would provide the non-military agencies, which had no es-tablished contacts in Hollywood, with a way of getting their propaganda messages translated into film. It would also relieve the studios of the task of choosing among competing government demands on their facilities.[38]

Hays resisted. Backed by Army Chief of Staff General George C. Marshall, he insisted that the current arrangement was adequate and that change might jeopardize the close relationship the industry had established with the Army. This opposition blocked any formal liaison arrangement until after Pearl Harbor, when the task was assumed by the Coordinator of Government Films, an office created in December 1941 for that purpose. Until then, the State Department and the military continued to enjoy their privileged status in Hollywood. Other government agencies seeking help from the movies channeled their requests through Lowell Mellett, who maintained an informal clearing house from his post in the White House.[39] The arrangement produced a number of short films prepared in Hollywood on various aspects of the mobilization effort.[40]

Although the object of such films was primarily educational and their content mostly factual, they tended to validate the administration's interpretation of events and to enlist public support for the defense effort and the commander in chief. In some instances at least, producers recognized the propaganda role they were playing and wanted FDR to know of it too. For example, in June 1941 representatives of Columbia Pictures informed Early that the company, at no little cost and risk, had initiated a series of one-reel films designed to "stimulate the defense program and promote the President's foreign policy."[41]

Such productions did not begin to test the propaganda potential of the film industry. Much more important was the possibility, noted by Rosten, of planting material in films "not necessarily dedicated solely to the dissemination of information about defense." There were, he observed, "innumerable pegs on which to hang what we might call our 'Message,' " and Rosten and others, both in Washington and Hollywood, sought bolder propaganda uses for the medium.[42] One such effort was undertaken late in 1940 by White House confidant Morris Ernst. In discussions with Hays and other industry leaders, Ernst sought expanded production of films dealing with defense themes and, in particular, urged a project favored by Eleanor Roosevelt which called for a series of pictures on various social issues raised by the war. Ernst found Hays, whom he described as incapable of understanding the "great social function of Motion Pictures," evasive and cold to the suggestion.

Rebuffed by the spokesman for the major studios, Ernst took his proposal to one of the leading independent producers. Walter Wanger, a warhawk and President of the Academy of Motion Picture Arts and Sciences, represented a faction in Hollywood that opposed Hays' conservative leadership. Wanger was responsive to Ernst's suggestion but could only propose, somewhat mysteriously, a scheme for incorporating pro-administration propaganda into films in a way that "even the heads of the companies will not be informed as to the details.'' Ernst was not impressed, seeing in the suggestion something that would produce no more than a visit by the movies' popular Hardy family to the Tennessee Valley Authority.[43]

The timidity of an activist like Wanger suggests that when it came to feature films, interventionist sentiment alone was not enough to ensure the introduction of propaganda. Even those producers desiring to help were reluctant to risk large capital investment on the production of a ''message'' film that might flop. Those who wished to utilize the interventionist potential of film might envision hard-hitting screen plays, but as businessmen few were willing to risk financial failure. Nevertheless, there were ways, as Warner Brothers had already demonstrated, of making both propaganda and money with the same film. The minimal adaptation of stock themes and characters (like the Hardy family) to war-related situations offered a means of promoting defense and even intervention without jeopardizing profits. This was, in fact, the very best way of introducing the public to the necessity and acceptability of war. Such propaganda vehicles would be entertaining, their stock characters and settings familiar, their message unobtrusive. The effectiveness of any propaganda depended first on the willingness of the public to be exposed to it. Hollywood's insistence on entertainment and profitability ensure realization of this prerequisite.

A good many such films were in fact made and shown in the United States. There were at least 50 American-made pictures dealing directly with the war appearing between the outbreak of hostilities in September 1939 and American involvement early in December 1941. Thirty-six of these appeared from the fall of 1940 on.[44] There were in addition a great many British-made war films distributed in the United States. Whether they dealt with the war directly or obliquely, such films usually made use of ''gangster,'' 'boy meets girl,'' ''swashbuckling adventure,'' or some other such motif long familiar to American moviegoers. With minor alterations these were made to convey a contemporary political meaning. A different city (Lisbon or London for New York or Chicago), a different setting (a modern destroyer for a pirate's galleon), and a different set of uniforms and stock characters (FBI men and spys for cops and robbers, Nazis for gangsters), plus a few lines of appropriate dialogue usually sufficed to effect the transition.

The themes fell into five general categories. Films were: (1) chauvinistic or patriotic, (2) lauded the character of the English and their war effort, (3) reviled the Nazis and Germany, (4) projected a glamorous or at least benign image for the American military, or (5) urged the need to take up arms in defense of the nation. During the first half of 1940, films with propaganda content fell mostly into the first category, ranging from the glorification of the World War I exploits of *The Fighting 69th*, to *Andy Hardy Meets Debutante*, in which Judge Hardy gives Andy lessons in democracy. But in mid-July, *The Man I Married*, described as the strongest American-made anti-Nazi film to date, appeared, and over the next year this theme, together with a number of pro-British pictures (many in both categories were made in Great Britain) came to dominate the political content of movies shown in the United States. Prominent among the anti-Nazi pictures was *Pastor Hill*, made in England and released by a company headed by James Roosevelt; *The Great Dictator*, produced by Charles Chaplin, who also directed himself in the title role;[45] *So Ends My Night, Man Hunt*, and *Underground*. British films in praise of that nation and its fighting qualities included *Blackout, Night Train*, and *Convoy*.[46]

Hollywood's production of films of this kind may have been encouraged by the expectation that they would do well in England. As the export of films to the continent declined in the late thirties and finally disappeared altogether, the importance of Great Britain to American film makers increased. The market was by no means free. The British, like other governments, restricted the import of American films and limited the revenues that American companies could remove from the nation. The British market, though not ideal, was promising, and as the major studios abandoned the continent, the Hays office redoubled its efforts to improve the industry's position in Great Britain. The passage of the Lend Lease Act in March 1941 was particularly welcome in this regard in that it greatly increased Britain's ability to pay for American films and resulted in the immediate release of half the industry's funds frozen in that country. The possibility that the studios might be able to compensate for losses elsewhere by increasing exports to Britain no doubt encouraged Hollywood to make films likely to find ready acceptance there.[47]

At the end of 1940, Hollywood found a fertile source of material closer to home in America's own preparations for war, and during 1941 films dealing with this subject took their place alongside those depicting America's enemies and friends. *Flight Command*, released in December 1940, made explicit the nation's need for military fliers.[48] This was followed by *Buck Private*, *I Wanted Wings*, *Dive Bomber*, *Navy Blues*, *You'll Never Get Rich*, and *Tanks a Million*, each touching on an aspect of rearmament. Most of these were dramatic action films, but even slapstick comedies like the Abbott and Costello farces, *Caught in the Draft* and *In the Navy*, while hardly glorifying the military, did tend to humanize and trivialize the experience, easing the anxieties of the men facing the draft. Such films served a similar function for parents who were likely to conclude that military service resembled nothing so much as a vacation at summer camp.

By mid-1941, American pictures had become quite pointed in their propaganda messages. Films no longer merely presented the circumstances confronting the American people, they clearly indicated what had to be done. *A Yank in the R.A.F.* and *International Squadron* told of Americans so aroused by the plight of Britain that they joined the Royal Air Force and the common struggle against Nazism. The most effective plea for taking up arms in defense of the nation's honor and interests was *Sergeant York*, released by Warner Brothers in late September 1941. The film was based on the experiences of Alvin York, a young naive Tennessean of pacifist convictions, who, faced with the call to duty during World War I, came to see his overriding obligation to country. York goes to France, performs a series of heroic feats, and returns to the United States much decorated and nationally acclaimed. The skillful telling of this story and its obvious parallels to the decisions confronting Americans in 1941 made it the single greatest piece of American film propaganda to appear in the months before U.S. involvement in the war.[49]

Propaganda was extensive but not excessively intrusive. Rather, it blended into the film fare to which Americans had become accustomed and as a result was generally accepted (and presumably absorbed) even by audiences suspicious of propaganda. Administration officials had reason for satisfaction. As early as March 1941 Lowell Mellett, the White House's expert on motion pictures, could report to the President that the industry was "pretty well living up to its offers of cooperation." He noted that "practically everything being shown on the screen from newsreel to fiction that touches on our national purpose is of the right sort." Moreover, there was "a lot of it, perhaps almost as much as the picture patrons can take [and] nothing antagonistic to the national purpose is being shown, except in a few German houses in German communities." More than patriotism accounted for this gratifying state of affairs. "The fact that the picture industry is conscious of the Justice Department just as the radio industry was of the FCC," Mellett noted, probably helped account for its cooperation.[50]

Isolationists witnessed the same conditions that Mellett joyfully reported and they did not like what they saw. Their exasperation was apparent in an account by Margaret Frakes of what it was like to visit a movie theater in the late summer of 1941.[51] The program usually began, she wrote, with a newsreel "likely to be filled with British visitors lauding our support and urging more assistance . . . followed by the Dutchess of Kent reviewing her women's corps, and items showing the marvelous progress of our own defense effort," all without any indication that these activities did not enjoy universal approbation. If a *March of Time* segment appeared, as it usually did, viewers were exposed to a skillfully constructed montage of real and staged scenes over which the authoritative voice of Westbrook Van Voorhies entoned a message of American globalism and damnation for those who opposed it. The propaganda-as-news represented by these "documentaries" would likely be followed by a "defense short" extolling military service or congratulating industry for "going 'all out' in the war effort."

Such messages sometimes served only as a prelude to a main feature echoing the same themes. This might be an anti-Nazi melodrama, ranging from "restrained" and "honest" to bitter caricature, but in any case designed to arouse hatred and fear. Other features made combat appear glorious while, according to Frakes, "realistic films showing the horrors of war" were not to be found. Even when a movie did not blatantly glorify the military, denounce Nazism, or call for intervention, it might still contain "casual, but not-so-subtle bits of propaganda." A "flyweight comedy" had the hero sneer at a weak-kneed rival who refuses his challenge to fight: "Oh, isolationist, eh?"

Evidence of Hollywood's participation in the interventionist effort did not stop with the content of films. As Frakes noted, it was also apparent in the glamour which Hollywood lent to the military build-up. As evidence, she cited the widely publicized visits of "stars" to military training camps, their acceptance of military commissions, and appearances on government-sponsored radio broadcasts. She also noted the "presence of a regular Army recruiting station and poster in the lobby of a theater showing a feature film with a training camp background."

A frustrated bitterness at the nation's seemingly inexorable march toward interventionism led some isolationist leaders to an almost hysterical search for the source of the apostasy. The desirability and possibility of staying out of war was to them a common sense conclusion and the public's passive resignation in the face of deepening involvement suggested not the logic of events but the manipulative power of the administration and the mass media. Just as the interventionists saw isolationism as the handiwork of a handful, the isolationists found an explanation for interventionism in the machinations of small but powerful interest groups within American society.

Isolationists were in fact partial to the conspiratorial explanation. Discussions of United States intervention in 1917 focused on the alleged role of bankers and munitions makers and the supposed effect of British propaganda. It took little imagination to revive the idea, recasting the conspirators to fit and explain the current situation. Instead of munitions makers and foreign propagandists, the isolationists identified a new set of warmongers: a President lusting for power, big businesses grubbing for profits, and the Jews and British in America venting their ethnic loyalties. Those disposed to this outlook found Hollywood a microcosm of the wider interventionist conspiracy. Here was a large community of British actors and directors, significant numbers of producers and writers of Jewish origin, and a large (monopolistic) corporate enterprise with close ties to both the administration and Great Britain.[52]

As early as January 1941, Senator Burton K. Wheeler warned of the treasonous attempts of the movies to "incite the public" to war, citing in particular their "passion-rousing" propaganda in favor of convoys. Hays emphatically denied that films were warmongering, arguing that only a small percentage of film material had any relation to European politics or the war. He reaffirmed the industry's unswerving dedication to pure entertainment which, he said, was "more important than ever in a period of great stress and strain," and constituted the industry's "primary service to our nation."[53]

Understandably, such declarations did not prove entirely convincing, and, in August, Republican Senator Gerald P. Nye of North Dakota charged that Hollywood's "racial prejudices" and economic interests had produced a distorted image of foreign policy issues in American films. Labeling the motion picture industry the "most gigantic engine of propaganda in existence to rouse the war fever in America," Nye co-authored a resolution with D. Worth Clark, Democrat of Idaho, calling for an investigation of Hollywood, its propaganda, and monopolistic practices. The isolationist bloc in the Senate succeeded in having the matter referred to the Interstate Commerce Committee where Chairman Wheeler appointed a subcommittee packed with non-interventionists to conduct the inquiry.[54]

The issue of how best to respond to such charges divided the movie community along familiar lines. Hays and the producers who followed his lead had long been concerned by the possibility that Hollywood's involvement in controversial issues would bring unfavorable publicity and unwanted regulations. He was prepared to go before the Committee and deny, as he had done in the past, that pictures were promoting government policies. Hollywood's more politically active film makers, led by Twentieth Century-Fox Vice President Darryl F. Zanuck,[55] rejected this tactic, believing that it was time for the producers to ''proclaim [that] they are doing everything they know how to make America conscious of the national peril.''[56] Although the industry would not adopt this particular line, it did assume an aggressive stance. Wendell Willkie, a skilled advocate and putative leader of the Republican Party, would present the industry's case.

Although the Committee was determined to make a show trial of the proceedings, it quickly found itself on the defensive. Willkie charged that the investigation was aimed at preventing the public from receiving a true picture of Hitler and world events. He claimed that to the extent that movies dealt with controversial matters, they mirrored reality. It was unfair, indeed somewhat suspect, he said, for the Committee to single out one medium for depicting a situation that was part of the daily intellectual diet of the American people. To illustrate the point, Willkie traced the origins of one of the 38 films the isolationists had labeled propagandistic. *Escape* was based on a novel which had been serialized in the *Saturday Evening Post* in 1939. The story was then published by Little, Brown, and Co., and adopted as a Book-of-the-Month Club selection. Why, Willkie asked, was this story, which had received wide acceptance and distribution in its printed form without incurring charges of propaganda, now the subject of attack as a motion picture?[57]

The Committee was unable to answer such questions. Indeed, its members seemed ill prepared to discuss intelligently many of the films they alleged to be propagandistic. Nor were the isolationists able to counter Willkie's suggestion that in singling out the alleged alien and Jewish influence in films they were deliberately stirring up racial hatred. The charge of anti-Semitism leveled against the isolationists was given ıdded credibility by the enormous blunder committed by Charles Lindbergh in remarks to an America First rally in Des Moines during the movie hearings. Lindbergh charged that the nation was being pushed toward war chiefly by the British, the Jews, and the Roosevelt administration. The Jews, he said, were a particularly dangerous influence because of ''their large ownership and influence in our motion pictures, our press, our radio, and our government.'' The remark was repudiated by many isolationists and widely denounced, but it threw the isolationist camp into disarray and near despair.[58] The issue had much the same effect on the Hollywood hearings, which soon disappeared amidst a welter of ridicule and criticism.

Seen as a contest between congressional isolationists and the movie industry, the latter clearly emerged as the winner.[59] But, as often in such clashes, the hearings shed little light on the issues involved. Neither Willkie's claim that others had discussed war issues with impunity nor his suggestion that the filmmakers were just telling it like it was adequately addressed the charge that the movies were promoting war. It was somewhat beside the point to say that books did it too. What appeared in film was far more important as mass propaganda than similar or even identical material appearing in books. The large audiences commanded by pictures, their unique ability to influence, and the relatively small group who determined their content justified special concern with the propaganda content of film.[60] Nor did it suffice to argue that films were accurate representations. Even if true, this hardly meant that they were for that reason any less propagandistic. Paul Lazarsfeld and Robert K. Merton have defined propaganda as any set of symbols, true or false, which influences opinions on issues regarded by the community as controversial.[61] From this perspective, the same facts or ideas may be educational or propagandistic depending on whether the issue they address is a matter of accepted orthodoxy or the subject of debate. While it is true, as the movie people suggested, that the evils of Nazism and the dangerous nature of the times were universally accepted, the meaning of these circumstances for the United States was still very much a matter of contention. In the same way, while each of Hollywood's politically oriented productions might individually be fairly described as ''educational,'' the sum of these one-sided depictions of reality constituted, as both isolationists and interventionists recognized, powerful propaganda for interventionism. Nor could the producers justifiably claim that their motive was to entertain and not to propagandize.

The two were not mutually exclusive and the evidence suggests that the propaganda appearing in films reflected the maker's intent.

The movies could not help but influence the foreign policy debate. Total neutrality was impossible. Even the stock entertainment themes and subjects of the early thirties had implications for national policy. A continued film diet consisting of *Thin Man* mysteries, Fred Astaire dancing extravaganzas, and the like would have immersed viewers in a fantasy world indifferent to national affairs. Escapism of this kind encouraged or at least helped preserve the illusion that an isolated national existence was possible.

Hollywood treatment of international realities was a foregone conclusion. Contemporary events were too dramatic to be totally neglected, and, when it appeared possible to deal with them profitably, the blackout on such matters was bound to end. This did not, however, dictate the simplistic one-sidedly interventionist propaganda that emerged.[62] Film makers might well have chosen a more balanced presentation on the issues of war and peace. Alongside those films which spoke of America's obligation to respond aggressively, others might have argued the futility of war, the misfortune of those caught up in it, and the valor of those who struggled to avoid it. The producers rejected these themes not because they were any more unrealistic or unpopular than those they produced, but for reasons that reflected their prejudices and interests.

There was little the White House could do to affect the political ideology of the Hollywood's leaders, but it was not without influence in regard to their interests. The influence, however, could not be exerted directly. Excessive pressure from the White House would have provoked a reaction inside the industry and among the general public as well that would have destroyed the propaganda potential of film. Instead, Roosevelt wisely left the initiative to industry leaders, well aware that their sympathies and concerns would lead them to the cooperation he sought.

Movie makers, like the broadcasters, regardless of political outlook, were conscious of the value of cultivating administration good will. Both industries faced a number of problems that might be ameliorated or favorably resolved through White House intercession. The still unsettled threat of anti-trust action was for each only the most obvious of these.[63] Whatever their motives, those who dictated the content of the nation's radio broadcasts and films contributed enormously to the administration's preparation of the public for war. Not only did they provide a vehicle for the informational propaganda supplied by government public relations officers, they went a good deal further to incorporate the substance and thrust of these messages, and even more pointed ones, in the entertainment features the public found when they went to their radio set or movie theater seeking diversion. Hope that "responsible" industry behavior in regard to the national crisis would earn favorable government consideration in the disposition of these matters could not have been far from the thoughts of industry leaders. For the more timid among them, the political value of cooperation may well have been decisive.

Conclusion

Neither the gravity of the various crises confronting the Roosevelt administration nor the actions it took in response were in themselves sufficient to guarantee popular support. The value of Roosevelt's efforts had to be kept constantly before the public, and this required more than the occasional presidential address or even the efforts of a prolific public relations operation. Effective propaganda meant above all continuous, convincing access to the public through the existing mass media, and securing this was the President-as-propagandist's chief task.

White House power in this, as in other matters, was considerable but not unlimited. At its most basic, Roosevelt's ability to shape his public image rested on his understanding of the media and the friendly relations he and his staff cultivated with its representatives. These were supplemented (and sometimes inadvertently offset) by presidential appeals, admonitions, and remonstrances. Most importantly, White House influence grew out of FDR's success in encouraging the cooperation of those who ultimately controlled access to the public mind. Results were not always as he wished, particularly in regard to the press. When circumstances made the media relatively indifferent to administration policies or good will, as was largely the case during the late thirties, cooperation was minimal. When they encouraged it, as they did from the summer of 1940 on, cooperation was close and propaganda formidable.

Writing at the crest of the administration's pre-war success, White House media advisor Lowell Mellett sought to describe the strategy which the White House had employed. Answering critics who either accused the administration of carrying out a vast centralized propaganda effort or lamented the fact that it had not, Mellett declared that there was no American Goebbels and no need for one. Propaganda American-style, he suggested, required only that the administration tell the truth. Its dissemination to the public, he said, had been left to citizen morale groups and to the spontaneous activities of the "three avenues to the public eye and ear." What more could the government do, he asked, even "if it were the kind of government that wanted to try?"[1]

The Roosevelt method, Mellett made clear, was unlike that commonly associated with the totalitarian regimes. So it was, but the conscious decision not to emulate Goebbels cost the administration nothing. Americans were not asked to overcome their natural suspicion of official pronouncements, but only to form their own judgements based on "facts" supplied them in the most palatable forms from the most credible sources.

At its most successful, during the international crisis of 1940–1941, the administration's efforts produced a propaganda din so pervasive and so diverse in its sources that by the end of 1941 it had become an unexceptional element of daily life.[2] Its effect, much to the disappoint-ment of militants, was not to shock or enrage, but to numb the resistance to war. Americans were not compelled by the logic of events or driven by emotion to demand involvement. Indeed, on the very eve of the Pearl Harbor attack only a minority wished the government to initiate hostilities. Nevertheless, by the time war was forced on the United States most Americans had probably come to accept it as a necessity or were at least resigned to it as an inevitability.[3]

Credit for this went in part to the private citizens who, as leaders of the interventionist organizations, editors, broadcasters, or film makers, brought home to the public the interventionist view of world affairs. But the effort was never simply theirs alone. Each facet of their work reflected the hand of government—here providing information, there withholding it, everywhere encouraging, coordinating, facilitating, and discretely shaping what was by design a collaborative effort.

Notes

CHAPTER 1

1. The account follows Robert Hilderbrand, *Power and the People: Executive Management of Public Opinion in Foreign Affairs, 1897-1921* (Chapel Hill: University of North Carolina Press, 1981). For a discussion of the effect of public relations on news gathering see Michael Schudson, *Discovering the News: A Social History of American Newspapers* (New York: Basic Books., Inc. 1978), pp. 140-144. A general account focussing on Washington correspondents is F. B. Marbut, *News from the Capital: The Story of Washington Reporters* (Carbondale: Southern Illinois University Press, 1971).

2. FDR's interest in public opinion in Grace Tully, *F.D.R.: My Boss* (New York: Charles Scribner's Sons, 1949), p. 76; Samuel I. Rosenman, *Working with Roosevelt* (London: Rupert Hart-Davis, 1952), p. 50; Elmer E. Cornwell, Jr., *Presidential Leadership of Public Opinion* (Bloomington: Indiana University Press, 1965), pp. 224-225. His uncanny knowledge of the American mind is described by Stanley High, *Roosevelt—And Then?* (New York: Harper & Brothers, 1937), pp. 13-15. See also Stephen Early's description in letter to Allen L. Appleton, March 14, 1935, Official File (OF) 340, Franklin D. Roosevelt Library (FDRL). Remarks to the editors quoted in Stephen E. Schoenherr, "Selling the New Deal: Stephen T. Early's Role as Press Secretary to Franklin D. Roosevelt," (Ph.D. dissertation, University of Delaware, 1976), p. 92.

3. Graham J. White, *FDR and the Press* (Chicago: University of Chicago Press, 1979), p. ix.

4. Richard W. Steele, "The Pulse of the People: Franklin D. Roosevelt and the Gauging of American Public Opinion," *Journal of Contemporary History*, 9 (October 1974): 195-216.

5. See meeting of January 9, 1934, in "Proceedings of the National Emergency Council" (NEC), Records of the Office of Government Reports, Record Group (RG) 44, National Archives (NA).

6. Perkins also suggests the need for public education as the basis of a permanent reform movement. Ibid. The unprecedented closeness of FDR's new and unique relationship with the public is described by Paul Mallon, "Roosevelt Gets His Story Over," *New York Times Magazine* (November 19, 1933): 1.

7. Delivered March 12, 1933, in Samuel I. Rosenman, comp., *The Public Papers and Addresses of Franklin D. Roosevelt* (13 vols. New York: Random House, 1938-1950), vol. 2, p. 65.

8. Remarks at meeting December 19, 1933, in "Proceedings of NEC."

9. Ibid., December 17, 1935.

10. See Alfred B. Rollins, Jr., *Roosevelt and Howe* (New York: Alfred A. Knopf, 1962), especially pp. 450-455.

11. Paul William Ward, "Roosevelt Keeps His Vow," *Nation* (September 25, 1935): 347-349.

12. The best description of Early's activities as Press Secretary is the laudatory account by Schoenherr, "Selling the New Deal." A brief summary of his life and public service is in Richard W. Steele, "Stephen T. Early," in *Dictionary of American Biography*, supplement 5, 1951-1955, John A. Garraty, ed. (New York: Charles Scribner's Sons, 1977), pp. 196-197.

13. In addition to Schoenherr's account of Early's character, his relations with the press are reflected in a large body of contemporary journal and newspaper accounts, most of which can be found in his "Scrapbook" included among his papers at the Franklin D. Roosevelt Library, Hyde Park. Also useful are Delbert Clark, " 'Steve' Takes Care of It," *New York Times Magazine* (July 27, 1941): 11. Jack Gravelee, "Stephen T. Early: The 'Advance Man,' " *Speech Monographs*, 30 (March 19, 1963): 41-49.

14. This account is based on press conferences, Early papers, FDRL, and William E. Berchtold, "Press Agents of the New Deal," *New Outlook*, 164 (July 1934): 23-31; "Stephen Early," *Current Biography* (1941): 250-252; Schoenherr, "Selling the New Deal," pp. 41-50.

15. Richard L. Strout, "Raw Deal," *Columbia Journalism Review* (July/August 1979): 68-69; Schoenherr, "Selling the New Deal," pp. 85-102.

16. Carl Byoir, a public relations consultant who advised the Democratic National Committee, wrote to Marvin McIntyre on October 7, 1936, congratulating the White House on its success in getting editors to run administration stories without editing. In Byoir folder, Early papers, FDRL. The White House command of the press is also indicated in David Lawrence, "The Battle for the Headlines," *United States News* (June 21, 1937), in the "Scrapbook," Early papers, FDRL; and in Quincy Howe, *The News and How to Understand It* (New York: Simon and Schuster, 1940), p. 205.

17. For fairness in coverage of speeches and press conferences see White,

FDR and the Press, pp. 101-109. For relations with business journalists, see President's Personal File (PPF) 5329, particularly FDR to E. H. Ahrens, April 28, 1938, FDRL. The public apparently believed press coverage was fair. Asked to characterize news reports in their papers, 82 percent of a sampling answered "fair." "Public Finds Press is Fair to Roosevelt," *New York Times* (October 5, 1938): 3:3.

18. Marbut, *News from the Capital*, p. 196.

19. See Clark, " 'Steve' Takes Care of It," and Cornwell, *Presidential Leadership of Public Opinion*, p. 222. For a statistical analysis of Roosevelt's success in having White House press releases run in the *New York Times* and a comparison of press release use in the succeeding three administrations see Cornwell, *Presidential Leadership*, pp. 234-235. Early estimated the number of releases at 1,000 per month. He also notes that a check with the four national press associations on November 11, 1933, revealed that in every instance they had carried the administration's releases. In a quick survey, the administration found that 60 percent of the newspapers in the Middle West were printing government handouts. See "Memo for Colonel Howe," November 14, 1933, OF 340, FDRL.

20. The work of the State Directors is discussed in meeting of December 19, 1933, in "Proceedings of NEC." Memo, Executive Director NEC (Frank Walker) to FDR, October 24, 1935, and "Chart and Summary Reaction by State," December 17, 1936, both in OF 788, FDRL. See also FDR's description at meeting November 7, 1933, in "Minutes of the Executive Council," RG 44, NA.

21. The efforts to place material in the local press are described in "Memorandum for Colonel Howe," November 14, 1933, OF 340, FDRL.

22. For a description of the Bureau of Intelligence and its clipping services see K. C. Blackburn to Howe, August 28, 1933, and Howe to Blackburn, August 29, 1933, in "Secretary to the President" files, Howe papers, FDRL. OF 1275 ("Division of Press Intelligence") contains numerous reports on editorial opinion on various issues and in response to speeches and actions by the President. Howe's role is discussed in Rollins, *Roosevelt and Howe*, pp. 242, 260. See also Cornwell, *Presidential Leadership*, pp. 224-225.

23. Publicity committee is discussed in "Memorandum for Colonel Howe." See also "Michelson: Rise of a Cynic," *Newsweek* (August 7, 1937): 16, and Schoenherr, "Selling the New Deal," pp. 64, 66, 69.

24. The New Deal's use of "handouts" is discussed sympathetically in Leo C. Rosten, *The Washington Correspondents* (New York: Harcourt, Brace and Company, 1937), pp. 71-76; Bruce Catton, "Handouts" in Cabell Phillips, et al., eds., *Dateline: Washington—The Story of National Affairs Journalism in the Life and Times of the National Press Club* (Garden City, N.Y.: Doubleday & Company, 1949), pp. 156-170; critically in Stanley High, "You Can't Beat the Government," *Saturday Evening Post* (November 20, 1937): 7ff. and in

George Michael, *Handout* (New York: G. P. Putnam's Sons, 1935). For a recent brief scholarly account of FDR's "publicity trust" see Betty Houchin Winfield, "The New Deal Publicity Operation: Foundation for the Modern Presidency," *Journalism Quarterly*, 61 (Spring 1984): 40-48ff.

25. The origins of government use of press releases and the implications for news coverage are discussed in Schudson, *Discovering the News*, pp. 139-142, in Rosten, *Washington Correspondents*, pp. 68-70, and in Phillips, *Dateline*, pp. 156-170.

26. For Early's insistence that government releases be purely factual, see his letter to David Barbee, May 21, 1935, OF 340, FDRL, and Clark, " 'Steve' Takes Care of It," p. 11. FDR comments on government publicity in a note attached to his first press conference in Rosenman, *Public Papers of FDR*, 2:38-40.

27. This discussion profited from the analysis of informational propaganda in Jacques Ellul, *Propaganda: The Formation of Men's Attitudes*, trans. Konrad Kellen and Jean Lerner (New York: Alfred A. Knopf, 1965), particularly pp. 85-116.

28. For government power over broadcasting see Minna F. Kassner, "Radio Censorship," James Rorty, "Order on the Air," Louis G. Caldwell, "Freedom of Speech and Radio Broadcasting," all in Harrison B. Summers, comp., *The Reference Shelf*, vol. 12, *Radio Censorship* (New York: H. W. Wilson Company, 1939), pp. 44-45, 80-81. Quotes are from David Sarnoff (NBC) in an address before Town Hall luncheon, April 28, 1938, and Henry Bellows (CBS) "Is Radio Censored?" in *Harper's*, November 1935. Both in ibid., pp. 101-102.

29. See Edward W. Chester, *Radio, Television and American Politics* (New York: Sheed and Ward, 1969), p. 235.

30. Howe to Frank Walker, July 25, 1933, and Thad Brown (acting Chairman, Radio Commission) to Howe, July 28, 1933, both in "Secretary to the President" file, Howe papers, FDRL.

31. Chester, *Radio, Television, and American Politics*, p. 235.

32. This appears to have been the case in regard to the New England "Yankee Network," which, after hearing from Pettey, changed its tone so that henceforth it provided the administration with "a lot of support." See Pettey for Early, October 5, 1934, Early for Howe, October 9, 1934, and Howe to Early, October 12, 1934, all in OF 136 miscellaneous (mis.), FDRL.

33. On Curley see "Summary of Personal and Confidential Memorandum for Hon. Anning Prall, Chairman, Federal Communications Commission, 10-10-36," and telegram Early to James Roosevelt, October 14, 1936; both in PPF 3, FDRL. On the Chicago labor station case, Prall assured the White House the application would be granted. See FDR for James Farley, May 6, 1936, PPF 3189; FDR for MacIntyre, February 19, 1937, and MacIntyre for President February 20, 1937, OF 136 misc., both FDRL. Another instance of White

House intervention with the FCC involved an application of Senator Homer Bone. See Early for FDR, September 25, 1935, FDR for Early, September 26, 1935, both in OF 1789, FDRL.

34. See FDR for Early, October 16, 1936 ("Get busy at once with Prall and tell him that Machold is the Power Trust"), Walter T. Brown to Marguerite Le Hand, October 3, 1936, and Early for Le Hand, October 20, 1936, all in PSF "Executive Office—Early," FDRL. FDR for Early, April 30, 1938, PSF subject file "Executive Office—Early," ("Will you get in touch confidentially with McNinch and ask him if there is something we can do to keep the Wichita Falls papers, who are opposing Congressman McFarlane, from getting control of the radio?") Also see McFarlane to President, November 30, 1936, MacIntyre for Prall, October 10, 1938, FDR for MacIntyre, July 22, 1937, Donley Saddath to Roosevelt, October 31, 1938 (noting that the President's son Elliott was supporting the hostile radio group), all in OF 136 misc., FDRL.

35. Bellows to Early, March 6, 1933; for a similar less effusive pledge from NBC, see Russell to Early, March 6, 1933, both OF 136, FDRL. See also Steven Schoenherr, "Selling the New Deal," p. 128; Harvard connection in Frank M. Russell to Early, May 18, 1934; mild complaint about CBS–White House connection in note Frank Russell to Early (received December 4, 1935), both in OF 228, FDRL.

36. Offer by Alfred McCosker (Mutual network) of a summer job for Franklin, Jr., in Early for Mrs. E. Roosevelt, April 30, 1935, in Eleanor Roosevelt folder, "Correspondence" files, Early papers, FDRL. Offers to Early of radio job as commentator and support for radio czar post in Harry Butcher to Early June 26, 1935, OF 256; Early to Joseph Davies, July 9, 1937, in Davies folder, "Correspondence" files, Early papers, both FDRL.

37. Russell's remarks to the FCC in "Radio 'Education Use' by Government Cited," *New York Times* (October 21, 1943): 29:3.

38. FDR told the Society of Newspaper Editors that he had advised his son-in-law John Boettiger, who had recently become editor of the Seattle *Post-Intelligencer*, to eliminate editorials and cover controversial stories from two perspectives "in parallel columns on the front page, and do not make them too long, so that the reading public will get both sides at the same time." Rosenman, *Public Papers of FDR*, 7:294-295.

39. Growing popularity of radio information vis-à-vis newspapers in *Fortune* survey, "The Press and the People," cited in "Heinl Radio Business Letter," August 1, 1939, in OF 1059, FDRL. *Fortune* found that "nearly two-fifths of the nation has found it can get most of its news without turning to newspapers; and that one-fourth relies most heavily on radio." These figures were to increase dramatically over the next two years. The *New York Times* claimed that FDR's favoritism toward radio began in 1936. See editorial (August 23, 1940): 14:4.

40. See Richard Roper, Executive Secretary DNC, to Daniel Roper (Secretary of Commerce), May 3, 1934, in "Secretary's" file, box 72, Howe papers, FDRL.

41. See Cornwell, *Presidential Leadership*, pp. 257-264; and Schoenherr, "Selling the New Deal," pp. 105-107.

42. See Herbert Pettey for Howe, August 14, 1933. Early agreed to the arrangement only on condition that the White House did not appear to be involved in arranging it. See Early for Pettey, August 16, 1933. Both in OF 136, FDRL.

43. FDR's speech writing is best described by his chief writer, Rosenman, *Working with Roosevelt*, especially pp. 49-59. Scheduling and other broadcasting devices discussed in Schoenherr, "Selling the New Deal," pp. 109-114.

44. Chester, *Radio, Television, and American Politics*, p. 33. Chester also notes (p. 41) that in 1937, NBC alone carried 22 presidential broadcasts, 29 by Secretary of Agriculture Henry Wallace, 18 by Postmaster General James Farley, and 203 by an assortment of other federal officials.

45. See Rollins, *Roosevelt and Howe*, pp. 422-425; and Broadcasts—1933, in "Personal" file, Howe papers, FDRL.

46. "Of the People," discussed in press release "New Deal's Two Years to Be Reviewed by Administration Officers in Two-Hour Programs," January 29, 1935, in OF 256. NBC program in Richberg to Early, December 17, 1934, OF 788. Both FDRL.

47. Early recommended that no action be taken on coordination of radio requests until after the 1936 election lest it be misconstrued by the opposition, Early, "Memorandum for the Honorable Lyle T. Alverson," March 12, 1936, OF 788, FDRL. See also Alverson's description of government as the "greatest single user" of radio (March 4, 1936) quoted in Schoenherr, "Selling the New Deal," p. 68.

48. Russell to Early, June 1, 1936, Frank M. Russell folder, "Correspondence" files, Early papers, FDRL. William S. Paley (President of CBS) on another occasion also reminded FDR of the responsible and self-regulating character of radio. Acting apparently at FDR's suggestion, Paley announced a "housecleaning" at the network which included the exercise of tighter controls on the types of advertising accepted and imposed limits on the airtime devoted to commercials. A CBS official told Early that the President was partly responsible for the changes which he claimed were to cost the network between $2 and $2.5 million in revenue. See Paley to FDR May 13, 1935, and attachments, in OF 256, FDRL.

49. Chester, *Radio, Television and American Politics*, p. 234.

50. Butcher to MacIntyre, November 4, 1936, OF 256, FDRL. The Butcher–Early relationship is discussed in Schoenherr, "Selling the New Deal," p. 39.

51. Alan Brinkley, *Voices of Protest; Huey Long, Father Coughlin and the Great Depression* (New York: Alfred A. Knopf, 1982), p. 100.

52. Erik Barnouw, *The Golden Web: A History of Broadcasting in the United States, 1933-1953* (New York: Oxford University Press, 1968), pp. 45-46.

53. The size and composition of movie audiences from 1935 on is in Michael Conant, *Antitrust in the Motion Picture Industry, Economic and Legal Analysis* (Berkeley: University of California Press, 1960), pp. 4ff. Much larger attendance figures and an extended discussion of the moviegoer is provided in Margaret Farrand Thorp, *America at the Movies* (New Haven, Conn.: Yale University Press, 1939), pp. 3ff.

54. The influence of movies is discussed in Leo C. Rosten, *Hollywood: The Movie Colony, The Movie Makers* (New York: Harcourt, Brace and Company, 1941), pp. 355-368; and in Franklin Fearing, "Influence of the Movies on Attitudes and Behavior," *Annals of the American Academy of Political and Social Sciences*, 254 (November 1947): 70-79.

55. Lewis Jacobs, *The Rise of the American Film: A Critical History* (New York: Harcourt, Brace and Company, 1939), pp. 513-526. Quote on p. 538.

56. Raymond Fielding, *The American Newsreel, 1911-1967* (Norman: University of Oklahoma Press, 1972), pp. 221ff.

57. Ibid., p. 201.

58. Cooperation between the White House and the newsreel companies is described in Steven E. Schoenherr, "Selling the New Deal," pp. 69, 153-158; and in "Robert Denton" fldr., "Correspondence" files, Early papers; and OF 73, particularly Denton to Early, February 21, 1941, both in FDRL.

59. James L. McCamy, *Government Publicity: Its Practice in Federal Administration* (Chicago: University of Chicago Press, 1939), pp. 85-90. Contemporary documentary film developments in Paul Rotha, *Documentary Film* (London: Faber and Faber Ltd., 1952), pp. 189-210; Douglas W. Churchill, "Hollywood Rediscovers the Short," *New York Times* (July 18, 1937): 3. Government filmmaking in the early 1930s and before is discussed in Richard Dyer MacCann, *The People's Films: A Political History of U.S. Government Motion Pictures* (New York: Hastings House, 1973), pp. 43-55.

60. "WPA: Pathe Wins Film Contract as New Deal 'Goes Hollywood,' " *News-Week* (August 15, 1936): 18; "Educational Newsreels for WPA," *Literary Digest* (August 8, 1936): 32.

61. Robert L. Snyder, *Pare Lorentz and the Documentary Film* (Norman: University of Oklahoma Press, 1968), p. 23.

62. The following account is based on Snyder, *Pare Lorentz*, pp. 21-121; MacCann, *People's Films*, pp. 21-120; and Arch Mercey, "Films by American Governments: The United States," *Films* (Summer 1940): 5-20.

63. Lorentz describes his problems and his sense of accomplishment in a letter to Early asking that *The River* be shown to FDR, September 2, 1937, in OF 73, FDRL

64. MacCann, *People's Films*, p. 87.

65. A federal film service was tried and abandoned as we have seen. A federal newspaper was considered by the White House in late 1934 and rejected on the advice of the White House staff. See correspondence, Donald Richberg

to Howe, October 29, 1934; Early for Howe, November 2, 1934; and FDR for Richberg, November 2, 1934, in OF 788, FDRL. In 1940-1941, FDR would consider the establishment of a centralized propaganda agency on defense-related issues. See chapter 5. In October 1941, with the prospect that the networks might be broken up, FDR spoke privately of the creation of a government information network. See entry for October 11, 1941, in "Cabinet Meetings, 1941," Biddle papers, FDRL.

CHAPTER 2

1. "A healthy proportion of the antagonism to Mr. Roosevelt was over-reaction by reporters who would have preferred that their earlier exaltations of the man might be removed from the record. They could not . . . but they intensified their efforts to compensate for them." Leo C. Rosten, *The Washington Correspondents* (New York: Harcourt, Brace and Company, 1937), pp. 252-253.

2. Peter Odegard's phrase quoted in Michael Schudson, *Discovering the News: A Social History of American Newspapers* (New York: Basic Books, Inc., 1978), p. 144.

3. Turner Catledge, "Federal Bureau for Press Urged," *New York Times* (December 29, 1936): 1.

4. FDR's remarks to Joint Meeting of Executive Council and National Emergency Council, June 26, 1934, in "Proceedings of the National Emergency Council" (NEC), Record Group (RG) 44, National Archives (NA).

5. Wheelchair picture policy discussed in Early for Ross McIntyre, August 11, 1937 (complaining of violations and indicating steps to prevent repetition), in McIntyre folder, "Correspondence" files, Early papers, Franklin D. Roosevelt Library (FDRL). Censorship of newsreel filming in Early for James Roosevelt, September 13, 1937, FDRL. See also Steven E. Schoenherr, "Selling the New Deal: Stephen T. Early's Role as Press Secretary to Franklin D. Roosevelt" (Ph.D. dissertation, University of Delaware, 1976), pp. 147-148. The importance of this policy is suggested by Early's use of the Secret Service on one occasion to intimidate a crank alleged to have been spreading rumors concerning FDR's infirmity. See Early for Joe Murphy (Secret Service) in Article, "Below the Belt," Material Not Used fldr., "Subject" file, Early papers, FDRL.

6. Memo, Frank Walker for Louis Howe, November 1, 1933, Official File (OF) 570, FDRL. See also meeting of December 17, 1935, in "Proceedings of the NEC," and Elmer E. Cornwell, Jr., *Presidential Leadership of Public Opinion* (Bloomington: Indiana University Press, 1965), p. 222.

7. See meeting of January 28, 1936, in "Proceedings of the NEC," and Early for Lyle T. Alverson, February 24, 1936, OF 788, FDRL.

8. Joint meeting of the Executive Council and the National Emergency

Council, June 26, 1934, in "Proceedings of the NEC." Director Alverson undertook "to strike out everything that as a matter of policy should not be made public."

9. Rosten, *Washington Correspondents*, p. 265.

10. For two such invitations, see the complaints of columnists Franklin K. Waltman and Raymond Clapper in James E. Pollard, *The Presidents and the Press* (New York: Macmillan Company, 1947), pp. 800, 816. See also Rosten, *Washington Correspondents*, pp. 55-56.

11. The control aspects of the conferences are discussed in Paul W. Ward, "Roosevelt Keeps His Vow," *Nation* (September 25, 1935): 348; Bascom N. Timmons, "This Is How It Used to Be," in Cabel Phillips et al., *Dateline: Washington—The Story of National Affairs Journalism in the Life and Times of the National Press Club* (Garden City, N.Y.: Doubleday & Company, 1949), p. 53; Richard L. Strout, "Raw Deal," *Columbia Journalism Review* (July/August, 1979): 68-69; radio address by Arthur Krock, January 26, 1935; and other comments by critics in "Scrapbook," Early papers, FDRL. FDR's use of "trial balloons" is mentioned in William L. Chenery, *So It Seemed* (New York: Harcourt Brace, 1952), p. 258.

12. FDR to Helen Reid (publisher, New York *Herald-Tribune*), August 26, 1942, President's Personal File (PPF) 897, FDRL. FDR's sensitivity to press criticism is discussed in Graham J. White, *FDR and the Press* (Chicago: University of Chicago Press, 1979), especially pp. 135, 140.

13. In a radio interview (July 6, 1934) Early described what he called FDR's "passion for getting things straight." Interview in Addresses, NBC, July 6, 1934, fldr., "Subject" file, Early papers, FDRL.

14. See, for example, the "inspired letter" discussion in Early for Charles Michelson, September 21, 1936, Charles Michelson fldr.; press conference planted question in Early for McIntyre and FDR, August 24, 1938, McIntyre fldr.; "inspired speech" in "Memorandum for Mr. Early and Mr. Mellett from the President dictated over the telephone to Mr. Corcoran," August 20, 1938, Mellett fldr.; all in "Correspondence" files, Early papers, FDRL. FDR order to Early in memo August 16, 1940, PPF 675, FDRL.

15. Raymond Clapper, writing in November 1939, noted that "never in any 20 years here have newspaper reporters received as much advice as to how to do their work, and as much warning against light-fingered handling of important news situations, as in this administration." Quote in Pollard, *Presidents and the Press*, p. 813.

16. FDR for Early, April 30, 1942, Pres. Roosevelt—1942 folder, "Memos" file, FDRL.

17. See FDR for Early, November 3, 1934, and FDR to Ochs, November 26, 1934, both in PPF 29, FDRL. FDR collected offending *Times* articles and in due course presented them to the newspaper's publisher. See Early memorandum of February 28, 1934, OF 144, and generally PPF 29, both in FDRL.

18. Roosevelt's description of the *Sun* article and his response are in his remarks to a joint meeting of the Executive Council and the National Emergency Council, August 21, 1934. His prediction of opposition is in remarks to the same group on June 26, 1934. Both recorded in "Proceedings of NEC."

19. Reputations of newspapers and news services among journalists in Rosten, *Washington Correspondents*, pp. 120, 122, 195.

20. FDR's collection of evidence against the AP also contains a report to the effect that administration leaders had conferred on a tentative plan for "abolishing child labor, shortening working hours, and raising 'starvation wages.' " The account reflected the substance of administration thinking since a measure incorporating these objectives was passed the following year. Very likely FDR did not welcome this premature revelation of his plans fearing this might compromise their success. On the other hand, the story hardly warranted his declaration that there was "no basis for the story." See "Two-Way Labor Plan Mapped by President," Washington *Post* (January 2, 1937): 1. This and the other examples cited above are in AP News Stories fldr., "Subject" files, Early papers, FDRL. In October 1938, Robert McLean, the President of AP, was invited to the White House for a discussion of AP reporting practices. See McLean to FDR, October 10, 1938, and Early to McLean, October 11, 1938, in OF 171, FDRL. See also memo, "Division of Press Intelligence" to William Hassett, on "Report on Handling of Government News by the Associated Press," January 21, 1939, Flood-Mississippi River fldr., Early papers, FDRL.

21. This discussion follows closely Schudson, *Discovering the News*, pp. 5, 6, 80, 120, 140-147; see also Dan Schiller, *Objectivity and the News: The Public and the Rise of Commercial Journalism* (Philadelphia: University of Pennsylvania Press, 1981), especially p. 194.

22. Rosten, *Washington Correspondents*, p. 121.

23. Stephen T. Early, "Hobgoblins—1935 Model," *Redbook* (April 1935), in "Scrapbook," Early papers, FDRL.

24. On Creel see White, *FDR and the Press*, p. 17, and Chenery, *So It Seemed*, p. 188. Carter's relationship is in "Columnists Pup," *Time* (April 7, 1941): 63; Carter to McIntyre, October 26, 1936, in OF 4514, and President's Secretary's File (PSF) "Subject" file, Carter, FDRL. *Collier's*, which hoped to obtain FDR's services following his retirement from office, seems to have been his favorite magazine outlet. A number of articles and editorials reflecting FDR's influence appeared in its pages. See PPF 5338, FDRL, which contains the *Collier's* White House correspondence.

25. FDR's attitude toward Howard is reflected in correspondence throughout PPF 68, FDRL. See also FDR for Samuel Rosenman, April 29, 1941, PSF, "Rosenman," FDRL. For "breathing spell" see Howard-Early exchange late July and early August 1935, in PPF 68, FDRL. Text of exchange in "Roosevelt Tells Business 'Breathing Spell' Is Here," *New York Times* (September 7, 1935): 1. Delbert Clark suspected White House inspiration but not the extent

of actual collaboration. "Roosevelt Thwarts Republican Thunder," *New York Times* (September 8, 1935): E: 3. The FDR-Howard relationship is also discussed in White, *FDR and the Press*, pp. 55-59.

26. FDR to Joseph Kennedy, July 22, 1939, in PSF, "Subject" file, "K," FDRL. Krock's reputation in Rosten, *Washington Correspondents*, p. 138.

27. The complaint about Krock in FDR for Early, November 3, 1934, and FDR to Ochs November 26, 1934, in PPF 29. Krock's puzzlement in Krock to Early, December 26, 1934, Krock folder, "Correspondence" files. Krock radio address January 26, 1935, in "Scrapbook," Early papers. All in FDRL. White House invitation in Early to Krock, August 11, 1936, PPF 675. Inspired interview in Krock-Early correspondence February 16-26, 1937, in Krock fldr., "Correspondence" files, Early papers. Both FDRL. The Turner Catledge episode in his *My Life and the Times* (New York: Harper & Row, 1971), p. 87, and Arthur Krock, *Memoirs: Sixty Years on the Firing Line* (New York: Funk & Wagnalls, 1968), p. 85. "Inspired News—The Press, the President and the Public," *Christian Science Monitor* (March 3, 1937) in "Scrapbook," Early papers, FDRL. Apology in Rosten, *Washington Correspondents*, p. 51.

28. See Pollard, *Presidents and Press*, p. 788. Favoritism discussed in White, *FDR and the Press*, pp. 17-18.

29. For Early's warnings on the exclusive treatment practice see Early for FDR, November 22, 1937, in Roosevelt 1937 folder, and Early for McIntyre, November 1, 1938, McIntyre fldr., both in "Memos" file, Early papers, FDRL. For "read it and weep" see Albert L. Warner (New York *Herald Tribune*) to Early and attachment, October 18, 1938, PPF 897, FDRL.

30. Moley quoted in Pollard, *Presidents and Press*, p. 799.

31. Howard to Early, August 9, 1935, and reply, August 14, 1935, both in PPF 68, FDRL.

32. Memo, Frank for Tugwell, August 25, 1934, in PPF 1741, FDRL. The result Frank sought in the AP issue would eventually be reached through litigation, but the practical impossibility of obtaining the congressional action required to force government news into the newspapers doomed this aspect of his proposal in advance. For resolution of the AP issue, see Kent Cooper, *Kent Cooper and the Associated Press: An Autobiography* (New York: Random House, 1959), pp. 277-281.

33. Raymond Moley, *After Seven Years* (New York: Harper & Brothers, 1939), pp. 337-339, 341.

34. The speech, delivered October 31, 1936, appears in Samuel I. Rosenman, comp., *The Public Papers and Addresses of Franklin D. Roosevelt* (13 vols. New York: Random House, 1938-1950), vol. 5, pp. 568-569.

35. According to the *Christian Science Monitor*, two-thirds of those newspapers that supported FDR in 1936 opposed him on the Court issue. See George Seldes, *Lords of the Press* (New York: Julian Messner, 1938), p. 340. Reaction of reporters in Rosten, *Washington Correspondents*, p. 55.

36. See Richard Polenberg, *Reorganizing Roosevelt's Government: The Controversy over Executive Reorganization, 1936-1939* (Cambridge: Harvard University Press, 1966), pp. 50-51ff.

37. The resurgence of conservatism is in James T. Patterson, *Congressional Conservatism and the New Deal: The Growth of the Conservative Coalition in Congress, 1933-1939* (Lexington: University of Kentucky Press, 1967), particularly pp. 85-324.

38. The attack on federal publicity is in James L. McCamy, *Government Publicity: Its Practice in Federal Administration* (Chicago: University of Chicago Press, 1939), pp. 10-11.

39. Philadelphia *Inquirer*, May 11, 1936. Attached to memo, William Hassett for Early, April 3, 1936, in OF 340, FDRL. Hassett's note indicates that he anticipated the *Inquirer* exposé and had taken steps to reduce government culpability.

40. McCamy, *Government Publicity*. Volume and cost estimates on pp. 138, 164; WPA spending on p. 29.

41. See, for example, "Federal Press Agents Cost People Millions," Los Angeles *Times* (September 10, 1937) and Stanley High, "You Can't Beat the Government," *Saturday Evening Post* (November 20, 1937). Both in "Scrapbook," Early papers, FDRL. Gordon Carroll, "Dr. Roosevelt's Propaganda Trust," *American Mercury* (September 1937): pp. 1-31. Suggestion of a concerted campaign in Barton to Howard, November 26, 1937, in Roy Howard fldr., Bruce Barton papers, Wisconsin State Historical Society Library, Madison.

42. McCamy, *Government Publicity*, pp. 5-14.

43. See Pollard, *Presidents and Press*, pp. 800, 816-17.

44. Fireside chat, October 12, 1937, in Rosenman, *Public Papers of FDR*, 6:430, and Pollard, *Presidents and Press*, p. 800.

45. "President Charges Most of the Press Is Fostering Fear," *New York Times* (December 22, 1937): 1.

46. Rosenman, *Public Papers of FDR*, 7:39-40.

47. The introduction, dated January 17, 1938, appears in ibid., 5:3.

48. Special press conference, Washington, D.C., April 21, 1938, in ibid., 7:276, 278-283, 293.

49. Conservative press bias is discussed in Seldes, *Lords of the Press*. Election endorsement figures from *Editor and Publisher* quoted in Walter Davenport, "The President and the Press," *Collier's* (January 27, 1945) in "Scrapbook," Early papers, FDRL.

50. On nature of the Hearst and *Tribune* opposition, see Rodney L. Carlisle, *Hearst and the New Deal: The Progressive as Reactionary* (New York: Garland Publishing, Inc., 1979), especially pp. 91-107; and Frank C. Waldrop, *McCormick of Chicago: An Unconventional Portrait of a Controversial Figure* (Englewood Cliffs, N.J.: Prentice-Hall, Inc., 1966). McCormick's hostility was apparent not long after Roosevelt took office. Hearst was slow in coming to this position and was not completely hostile until the beginning of 1935.

51. Memorandum on "Recovery Program—General," in "Secretary to the President" file, Box 74, Howe papers, FDRL.

52. The list included the New York *Daily News*, Denver *Post*, Washington *Star*, Baltimore *Sun*, Miami *Herald*, Atlanta *Constitution*, Chicago *Times*, Louisville *Courier-Journal*, *Christian Science Monitor*, Boston *Globe*, Minneapolis *Star*, St. Louis *Post-Dispatch*, Cincinnati *Enquirer*, Cleveland *Plain Dealer*, Milwaukee *Journal*, Detroit *News*, Philadelphia *Record*, *New York Times*, and, until 1937, the Scripps-Howard chain. The list is attached to Early for FDR, in OF 144, FDRL. A year later, most of the papers on this list opposed FDR's reelection. This may reflect accumulated disappointment or grievances but more likely the discrepancy between election endorsements and the general editorial policy. See list attached to Carl Byoir to Marvin McIntyre, October 7, 1936, in Byoir fldr., Early papers, FDRL.

53. White limited his analysis to papers Roosevelt read regularly. See White, *FDR and the Press*, pp. 73-77. White's account focusses on why Roosevelt persisted in making the charge that "85 percent" of the press opposed him in spite of evidence to the contrary.

54. The press conferences White selected were those occurring in the three months before the 1936 and 1940 elections. Ibid., pp. 102-109.

55. See Robert Dallek, *Franklin D. Roosevelt and American Foreign Policy, 1932-1945* (New York: Oxford University Press, 1979), pp. 171-268, particularly pp. 221-267.

56. FDR to Helen Reid, June 6, 1940, PPF 897, FDRL.

57. FDR to Barton, May 19, 1941, in F. D. Roosevelt fldr., Barton papers, Wisconsin State Historical Society, Madison.

58. The episode is discussed in William L. Langer and S. Everett Gleason, *The Challenge to Isolation, 1937-1940* (New York: Harper & Brothers, 1952), pp. 49-50. See also White, *FDR and the Press*, pp. 40-41. My account is based on a transcript of the press conference and Stephen Early's comments on the episode contained in his letter to Joseph Davies, February 9, 1939, in Davies, 1938-1941 folder, "Correspondence" files, Early papers, FDRL.

59. R. J. C. Butow, "The FDR Tapes," *American Heritage* 33 (February/March 1982): 13-15.

60. "Statement by the President," July 13, 1939, and response by United Press chief, July 17, 1939, both in PPF 68, FDRL.

61. See press conference 575 (September 1, 1939) in *The Complete Presidential Press Conferences of Franklin D. Roosevelt*, with an introduction by Jonathan Daniels (25 vols. New York: Da Capo Press, 1972), vol. 14, p. 456. Hereinafter referred to as *PPC*, conference number, date, volume, and page. "Fireside Chat on the War in Europe," September 3, 1939, in Rosenman, *Public Papers of FDR*, 8:462. See also Pollard, *Presidents and the Press*, pp. 821-822.

62. Issue of press freedom and responsibilities discussed in Quincy Howe,

The News and How to Understand It (New York: Simon and Schuster, 1940); Rosten, *Washington Correspondents*; Seldes, *Lords of the Press*; Harold L. Ickes, *America's House of Lords* (New York: Harcourt, Brace and Co., 1939).

63. *PPC*, 623 (February 13, 1940), 15:158.

64. Beatrice Bishop Berle and Travis Beal Jacobs, eds., *Navigating the Rapids 1918-1971: From the Papers of Adolf A. Berle* (New York: Harcourt Brace Jovanovich, Inc., 1973), pp. 264-265. Arthur Krock, "The Tendency to Cover Up Legitimate News," *New York Times* (October 13, 1939): 22:5.

65. See, for example, Early press conference March 28, 1940, and critical press clippings dated March 30 and 31, 1940, in "Scrapbook," Early papers, FDRL.

66. Bertram D. Hulen, "Relations of U.S. and Italy on Mend," *New York Times* (May 1, 1940): 5:1.

67. FDR to Sulzberger, May 9, 1940, PPF 675, FDRL; Langer and Gleason, *Challenge to Isolation*, p. 442.

68. See R. R. McCormick to L. W. Cook, Jr., November 8, 1938, in "Correspondence" files, Thurman Arnold papers, University of Wyoming Library, Laramie.

69. Jerome E. Edwards, *The Foreign Policy of Col. McCormick's Tribune, 1929-1941* (Reno: University of Nevada Press, 1971), chapters 4-7.

70. Early press conference, June 13, 1940, and Chicago *Tribune* clipping in "Scrapbook," Early papers; letter, Trohan to Early, June 13, 1940, in Trohan, Walter, folder, "Correspondence" files, Early papers, FDRL.

71. FDR's comments on these columns are in his letter to Harold Ickes, June 16, 1941, PSF, "Interior—Ickes," FDRL. The note was probably intended, at least in part, as a rebuke to Ickes, whom FDR suspected of collaborating with the columnists in at least one of these cases.

72. Mallon episode is described in New York *Sun* November 9, 1940, in "Scrapbook," Early papers, FDRL; and in Delbert Clark, *Washington Dateline* (New York: Frederick A. Stokes Co., 1941), p. 74. FDR's intentions toward other columnists in Ickes manuscript (MS) diary entry for November 23, 1940, in Miscellaneous Excerpts, Missy Le Hand fldr., Harold Ickes papers, Library of Congress. For a discussion of columnists and Roosevelt see White, *FDR and the Press*, pp. 27-31.

73. FDR to Lowell Mellett, December 28, 1944, PSF, "Mellett," FDRL.

74. One of the better biographies of Winchell, written by one of his ghost writers, is Herman Klurfeld, *Winchell: His Life and Times* (New York: Praeger Publishers, 1976).

75. Alice Fox Pitts, "Washington Now Says: 'No News' Instead of Old 'Off the Record,' " *P. M.* (July 16, 1940); and "President Cancels Press Talk: Trend Disturbs Reporters," *Christian Science Monitor* (November 12, 1940). Both in "Scrapbook," Early papers, FDRL.

76. See Richard Neustadt, *Presidential Power* (New York: John Wiley & Sons, 1960), p. 63.

77. James A. Farley, *Behind the Ballots* (New York: Harcourt, Brace and Company, 1938), p. 323. See also several boxes of "straw votes" in OF 857, FDRL.

78. See John F. Carter, *Power and Persuasion* (New York: Duell, Sloan & Pearce, 1960), pp. 179-180. For the *Literary Digest* defense, see letter, Eugene Thwing to General A. F. Lorenzen, January 10, 1936, in OF 136 misc., FDRL.

79. The following discussion relies on Richard Jensen, "Public Opinion Polls; Early Problems of Method and Philosophy," a paper presented to the Oxford Conference on the History and Theory of the Social Sciences, July 23, 1977, Oxford, England; and on Richard W. Steele, "The Pulse of the People: Franklin D. Roosevelt and the Gauging of American Public Opinion," *Journal of Contemporary History* 9 (October 1974): 195-216.

80. Jensen, "Public Opinion Polls," pp. 2-3.

81. Ibid., pp. 4-5; Steele, "Pulse of the People," p. 206.

82. Hadley Cantril, *The Human Dimension: Experiences in Policy Research* (New Brunswick, N.J.: Rutgers University Press, 1967), pp. 22-26. See especially letter, Cantril to FDR, March 7, 1941, in OF 857, FDRL.

83. On this point, see also Steele, "Pulse of the People," pp. 207-209.

CHAPTER 3

1. This account based on Manfred Jonas, *Isolationism in America, 1935-1941* (Ithaca, N.Y.: Cornell University Press, 1966). For a perceptive study of some of the isolationists see Ronald Radosh, *Prophets on the Right: Profiles of Conservative Critics of American Globalism* (New York: Simon and Schuster, 1975).

2. Entry for September 29, 1939, in Beatrice Bishop Berle and Travis Beal Jacobs, eds., *Navigating the Rapids 1918-1971: From the Papers of Adolf A. Berle* (New York: Harcourt Brace Jovanovich, 1973), p. 258.

3. Early's no-propaganda pledge given at his press conference September 5, 1939, and reported in clippings in "Scrapbook," Early papers, FDR Library (FDRL). Leaking of Berlin instructions, September 30, 1939, diary entry in Berle and Jacobs, *Navigating the Rapids*, p. 259.

4. Samuel I. Rosenman, comp., *The Public Papers and Addresses of Franklin D. Roosevelt* (13 vols. New York: Macmillian Company, 1941), vol. 10, p. 9.

5. See diary entry for September 30, 1939, in Berle and Jacobs, *Navigating the Rapids*, p. 259. On conservatism of one group of interventionists, see Mark L. Chadwin, *The Hawks of World War II* (Chapel Hill: University of North Carolina Press, 1968), p. 66.

6. This account of the fifth column is based on Louis De Jong, *The German Fifth Column in the Second World War*, trans. C. M. Geyl (Chicago: University of Chicago Press, 1956), especially pp. 62-65, 77, 96, 295-297.

7. Rosenman, *Public Papers of FDR*, 9:198.

8. See Lindbergh's speech of May 19, 1940, in *Vital Speeches of the Day* (June 1, 1940): 484-485. FDR's "Lindbergh Is a Nazi" remark is in Wayne S. Cole, *Charles A. Lindbergh and the Battle against American Intervention in World War II* (New York: Harcourt Brace Jovanovich, 1974), p. 128.

9. Fireside chat on national defense, May 26, 1940, in Rosenman, *Public Papers of FDR*, 9:231, 238-239.

10. Cedric Larson, "Publicity for National Defense—How It Works," *Journalism Quarterly*, 18 (September 1941): 245.

11. For Division of Information activities, see *The United States at War: Development and Administration of the War Program by the Federal Government* (Washington, D.C.: U.S. Government Printing Office, 1946), pp. 22, 211-214; George E. McMillan, "Government Publicity and the Impact of War," *Public Opinion Quarterly*, 5 (Fall 1941): 392-394; Larson, "Publicity for National Defense," pp. 245-255. The description of *Defense* is in Richard Hollander to Mellett, September 19, 1940, in Richard Hollander folder, "Correspondence" files, Mellett papers, FDRL.

12. See Mellett's description of these services in his letter to Francis Perkins, September 19, 1941, in Sec. Francis Perkins fldr., "Correspondence" file, Mellett papers, FDRL. OGR activities in general are described in Lowell Mellett, "The Office of Government Reports," *Public Administration Review*, 1 (Winter 1941): 126-131. Eventually, Horton's Division of Information would also produce a weekly column aimed at the nation's rural newspapers. It was designed to tie the defense effort to local concerns rather than (as Mellett intended) to broaden the outlook of the rural population by bringing them strictly national defense news. The two productions were in conflict and threatened to overburden the rural reader with defense propaganda. See Mellett for Wayne Coy, April 20, 1942, and Coy to William L. Daley, May 1, 1942, both in Coy fldr., "Correspondence" file, Mellett papers, FDRL.

13. Max G. Johl, *The United States Commemorative Stamps of the Twentieth Century* (New York: H. L. Lindquist, 1947), vol. 2, pp. 189-196.

14. Army propaganda concerns are discussed generally in James R. Mock and Cedric Larson, "Public Relations of the U.S. Army," *Public Opinion Quarterly*, 5 (June 1941): 275-282. See also Richard W. Steele, " 'The Greatest Gangster Movie Ever Filmed': *Prelude to War*," *Prologue*, 11 (Winter 1979): 222-226.

15. Memo, Julius H. Amberg (Special Assistant to the Secretary of War) for General Robert C. Richardson, Jr. (Chief, Public Relations Branch), June 27, 1941, transmitting excerpt from minutes of the Council of OPM meeting of June 24. In Adjutant General's Office, Bureau of Public Relations (BPR) file 381-1, in Records of the War Department General and Special Staffs, Record Group (RG) 165, National Archives (NA).

16. McGrady for Patterson, on "Labor Morale," August 16, 1941, in "Labor Morale" file, Patterson papers, Library of Congress (LC).

17. This account is from Lt. Col. Robert Ginsburgh (BPR) for Patterson, on "Cleveland Visit," September 17, 1941, "Labor Morale" file, Patterson papers, LC. Ginsburgh judged the effort a great success, a judgement shared by one of the OPM representatives who often accompanied him on these trips. Letter, Andrew J. Biemiller to author, January 13, 1971. The program is also described briefly in "Morale Work," *Business Week* (December 13, 1941): 18-19.

18. Clark to McCloy, May 23, 1941; Henry B. Cabot to McCloy, June 11, 1941. McCloy's opposition in several memos, including McCloy for Patterson August 28, 1941. Relations with the press and tours of munitions plants in McCloy for Secretary of War, August 1, 1941, and Murrows Matthews to McCloy, August 5, 1941. All in Assistant Secretary of War file 014.3 (box 6), RG 107, Office of the Secretary of War, NA.

19. The entire defense information issue is discussed in Bruce Catton, *The War Lords of Washington* (New York: Harcourt, Brace and Company, 1948), particularly pp. 51-55. See also John Morton Blum, *V Was for Victory: Politics and American Culture during World War II* (New York: Harcourt Brace Jovanovich, 1976), pp. 117-131. Eliot Janeway, *The Struggle for Survival*, vol. 53, *The Chronicles of America Series*, Allan Nevins, ed. (New Haven, Conn.: Yale University Press, 1951. Reprint ed. New York: Weybright and Talley, 1968), pp. 115-162.

20. Confusion in defense information discussed in Edward P. Lilly, "OWI History" (draft typescript), chapter 1, pp. 7-14, in item 4, Records of the Office of War Information (OWI), RG 208, NA, Suitland, Md. Also suggestions as to remedies in Mellett for FDR, September 8, 1941, fldr. 3, White House Memos, Samuel I. Rosenman papers, FDRL.

21. Hadley Cantril, "Public Opinion in Flux," *Annals of the American Academy of Political and Social Sciences*, 220 (March 1942): 144.

22. In connection with the President's May 27 "unlimited national emergency" speech, Early wrote, arrangements for follow-up speakers "should be made outside of Washington. . . . I feel that recently there has been a little too much of [Secretary of Navy Frank] Knox and [Secretary of War Henry L.] Stimson. I believe . . . it would be better to have you followed by outsiders rather than by a repetition of Cabinet speakers." Early for FDR, May 24, 1941, President Roosevelt—1941 fldr., "Memos" files, Early papers, FDRL. FDR acknowledged on another occasion that Stimson and Knox were known as warmongers. See FDR for Early, July 23, 1941, "Dr-Du—misc." fldr., "Correspondence" files, Early papers, FDRL.

23. Walter Johnson, *The Battle against Isolation* (Chicago: University of Chicago Press, 1944), pp. 31-64, 208.

24. White's views are discussed in "White Out," in *Uncensored* (January 4, 1941): 1. Bitter condemnation of White for "doing a typical Laval" is found in Fiorello H. LaGuardia to White, December 26, 1940, in "President—1940" fldr., LaGuardia papers, New York City Municipal Archives.

25. Discussion based on Chadwin, *Hawks of World War II*, especially pp. 44, 89-94, 100-107, 172, 178-179, 189.

26. For efforts of the Century Group to counter isolationism among Irish Americans see Ronald H. Bayor, *Neighbors in Conflict: The Irish, Germans, Jews and Italians of New York City, 1929-1941* (Baltimore: Johns Hopkins University Press, 1978), pp. 111-112.

27. See Chadwin, *Hawks of World War II*, pp. 120-121, 126-129.

28. H. Montgomery Hyde, *Room 3603: The Story of the British Intelligence Center in New York during World War II* (New York: Farrar, Straus and Co., 1962), pp. 73, 196. The "pin . . . the image of a Nazi" quote is from Chadwin, *Hawks of World War II*, p. 208.

29. See entry for September 18, 1941, and his letter of September 27, 1941, to Sumner Welles in the Berle Diary manuscript (MS), FDRL.

30. Raymond Swing, *"Good Evening!" A Professional Memoir by Raymond Swing* (New York: Harcourt, Brace & World, 1964), pp. 216-218.

31. James R. Angell, "The Civilian Morale Agency," *Annals of the American Academy of Political and Social Sciences*, 220 (March 1942): 160-167.

32. Johnson, *The Battle against Isolation*, p. 91.

33. Chadwin, *Hawks of World War II*, pp. 201-203.

34. See entire "Council for Democracy" fldr., "Correspondence" files, Mellett papers, FDRL. In particular, see Selma Hirsch to Mellett, September 27, 1941; C. D. Jackson to Mellett July 3, 1941; Mellett for Jackson, July 10, 1941; Angell to Mellett, August 4, 1941; Mellett to Angell, July 31, 1941; all in above.

35. Sherwood to Early, June 16, 1941, and telegram, Early to Sherwood, June 18, 1941. Both in Official File (OF) 4461, FDRL.

36. "M. A. L." for FDR, May 20, 1941, and Early for FDR May 22, 1941, PSF "Executive Office—Early," FDRL.

37. Warburg to Early, January 24, 1941; William Hassett for Early, February 3, 1941; Early to Warburg February 4, 1941; Wam–War—misc. folder, "Correspondence" files, Early papers, FDRL. Poletti to Hopkins, May 14, 1941, in Hopkins (Harry) folder, Charles Poletti papers, Herbert H. Lehman Collection, Columbia University Library.

38. William L. White to Mellett, and Mellett to White, April 4, 1941 in Wm. A. and William L. White fldr., "Correspondence" files, Mellett papers, FDRL.

39. Evidence of interventionist differences and suggestion of possible presidential intercession in J. Franklin Carter, "Memo on Conversation with Ulric Bell, June 24, 1941," in PSF, "Carter," FDRL. Unresolved problems suggested in Archibald MacLeish to Eleanor Roosevelt, November 12, 1941, Eleanor Roosevelt fldr., MacLeish papers, LC.

40. At the end of March, for example, Grenville Clark was circulating a petition among 200 prominent citizens insisting that the President endorse con-

voys without delay. See Clark to Poletti, March 31, 1941, in "Committee to Defend Democracy" file, Poletti papers, Herbert H. Lehman Collection, Columbia University.

41. See Ickes to FDR, September 17, 1941, PSF, "Ickes 1940-1942," FDRL; Samuel I. Rosenman, *Working with Roosevelt* (London: Rupert Hart-Davis, 1952), p. 277. The inadequacy of the President's rhetoric is discussed in D. A. Saunders, "The Failure of Propaganda and What to Do About It," *Harper's Magazine* (November 1941): 648-654.

42. See Diary (MS) entry for July 24, 1941, Stimson papers, Yale University Library, New Haven, Conn.; and Knox for FDR, August 28, 1941, PSF, "Knox," FDRL.

43. Stevenson to Mellett, August 4, 1941, and attachment, "Proposed Organization" dated August 1, 1941, "Commerce—Misc. Correspondence" folder, "Correspondence" files, Mellett papers, FDRL.

44. At an April 25, 1941 press conference, the President likened Lindbergh, and by inference those who shared his view, to the copperheads of Civil War times. See press conference 738 (April 25, 1941) in *The Complete Presidential Press Conferences of Franklin D. Roosevelt* with an introduction by Jonathan Daniels (25 vols. New York: Da Capo Press, 1972), vol. 17, p. 294. For background to the remark, see Cole, *Charles A. Lindbergh*, pp. 130-131. A government analysis noted: "There has been rather unfavorable press reaction to the President's verbal castigation of ex-Colonel Lindbergh. . . . It is argued that presidential indulgence in personalities diminishes national unity." See memo, Alan Barth for Secretary of Treasury Morgenthau (forwarded to FDR), May 2, 1941, "American Morale," in PSF, "Treasury—Morgenthau," FDRL.

45. See Bernard De Voto, "Report on the Summer Quarter," *Harper's Magazine* (November 1941): 670-671.

46. This idea is discussed in Richard W. Steele, *The First Offensive, 1942: Roosevelt, Marshall and the Making of American Strategy* (Bloomington: Indiana University Press, 1973), p. 3-33, especially p. 13.

47. The anti-war literature dealing specifically with propaganda is discussed briefly in Allan M. Winkler, *The Politics of Propaganda: The Office of War Information, 1942-1945* (New Haven, Conn.: Yale University Press, 1978), pp. 2-4. On Creel's activities and post-war reputation see James R. Mock and Cedric Larson, *Words That Won the War: The Story of the Committee on Public Information, 1917-1919* (Princeton, N.J.: Princeton University Press, 1939), pp. 10-18.

48. See Stephen Vaughn, *Holding Fast the Inner Lines: Democracy, Nationalism, and the Committee on Public Information* (Chapel Hill: University of North Carolina Press, 1980), pp. 24-25, 37, 51-52.

49. Mock and Larson, *Words That Won the War*, pp. viii-ix, and Winkler, *Politics of Propaganda*, pp. 148-151. Quote from Harold D. Lasswell, *Propaganda Techniques in the World War* (New York: Alfred A. Knopf, 1927), pp. 14-15.

50. See, for example, William M. Schuyler and Albert Bushnell Hart, eds. *The American Year Book: A Record of Events and Progress, Year 1939* (New York: Thomas Nelson & Sons, 1940), pp. 950-953.

51. Mock and Larson, *Words That Won the War*, pp. 338-340.

52. Adolf Berle and F.B.I. Director J. Edgar Hoover had a long meeting at which they discussed the increasing need to do something about the "millions of volunteers who want to defend the country in some fashion." In Diary (MS), June 25, 1940, Berle papers, FDRL. The dangers of unchanneled militancy are discussed in Diary (MS), July 2, 1940, Henry Wallace papers (microfilm publication), University of Iowa Libraries, Iowa City.

53. MacLeish to Hopkins, June 24, 1940, and Hopkins reply indicating White House had received a number of similar proposals. Both in Book 2, National Defense Program fldr., "Sherwood Collection," Hopkins papers, FDRL.

54. See Berle for FDR, June 26, 1940, in Roosevelt, Memos To folder, and draft letter "My dear Governor," June 26, 1940, in Director of Public Safety folder; draft letter, Robert Jackson to Raymond J. Kelly (National Commander of the American Legion), June 27, 1940, in Jac–Jss folder, "Correspondence" files, Berle papers, FDRL.

55. See, for example, Hugh Chisholm to FDR, forwarded to Lowell Mellett with covering note dated July 8, 1940, in WH—1940 fldr., "Correspondence" files, Mellett papers, FDRL; Stephen Early for Mellett, July 30, 1940, Mellett folder, "Correspondence" files, Early papers, FDRL. Publicist Fulton Ousler offered to work the kind of transformation of public attitudes in regard to foreign and military affairs he had in regard to gangsters and G-Men in the 1930s. See Ousler to FDR August 20, 1940, and Early for Mellett August 26, 1941, Mellett folder, "Correspondence" files; and Early for FDR, July 12, 1940 in Og–Ow-Misc. folder, "Correspondence" files, Early papers, FDRL. Also see correspondence on "FDR Loyalty Legion" in Orville S. McPherson to Early, January 1, 1941, etc., in "Correspondence" files, Early papers, FDRL.

56. See Diary (MS) June 11, 1940, Berle papers, FDRL.

57. Brownlow's recommendations are outlined in "Conference of the Propaganda Committee," November 18, 1940, in Propaganda Committee—1940 folder, Ickes papers, LC.

58. Diary (MS), November 8, 1940, Stimson papers, Yale University Library, New Haven, Conn.

59. Henry L. Stimson and McGeorge Bundy, *On Active Service in Peace and War* (New York: Harper & Brothers, 1947), p. 342. McCloy's views in "Conference of the Propaganda Committee," November 13, 1940, Ickes papers, LC.

60. The assessment of Nazi propaganda in Harold Lavine and James Wechsler, *War Propaganda and the United States*, published for the Institute for Propaganda Analysis (New Haven, Conn.: Yale University Press, 1940), pp. 350-351. For analysis of Nazi Propaganda Organization see Michael Balfour, *Prop-*

aganda in War, 1939-1945: Organizations, Policies and Publics in Britain and Germany (Boston: Routledge & Kegan Paul, 1979), particularly pp. 103-132.

61. Ickes to FDR, November 28, 1940, in OF 1661A (Fifth Column), FDRL.

62. "Conference of the Propaganda Committee," November 13, 1940, in Propaganda Committee—1940 folder, Ickes papers, LC.

63. See correspondence in OF 4249, particularly Kerr to FDR, January 8, 14, 1941 and John M. Carmody to FDR, January 27, 1941, in FDRL. Harold L. Ickes, *The Secret Diary of Harold L. Ickes* (3 vols. New York: Simon and Schuster, 1953-1954), vol. 3, *The Lowering Clouds*, pp. 407-408.

64. Ickes, *Secret Diary*, 3: 426.

65. "Confidential Memorandum from Committee for National Morale," March 4, 1941, in War—National Morale folder, file 2, Ickes papers, LC. Edward Bernays, the famous public relations consultant, described the thinking of psychological warfare experts on the subject of a national morale agency in a letter to Francis Biddle, November 25, 1940, in "Correspondence, A–H," Biddle papers, FDRL.

66. See letter, Ladislas Farago to the author September 7, 1979.

67. On Ickes' despair see Anna Roosevelt Boettiger and John Boettiger for Missy Le Hand, (filed February 6, 1941) in OF 4224, FDRL.

68. "Conference of the Propaganda Committee," November 18, 1940, pp. 16-17, in Propaganda Committee—1940 folder, Ickes papers, LC.

69. Biddle, "Memorandum on the 'Plan for a National Morale Service,' " March 3, 1941, War—National Morale folder, file 2, Ickes papers, LC.

70. The Committee's very extensive propaganda activities are outlined in "The First Year and After," a report by the Committee dated August 25, 1941 in the Personal Correspondence—Committee for National Morale, 1941-42, "General Correspondence" file, box 4, Arthur Upham Pope papers, New York Public Library.

71. "Memorandum on Committee for National Morale," found in Secretary Ickes fldr., "Correspondence" files, Mellett Papers, FDRL. Ickes recorded that Professor Karl Friedrich had been "knocking" the Committee, and he may have been Mellett's informant. See Ickes, *Secret Diary*, 3: 445. Mellett's views on the Committee are in Mellett to Ickes, February 15 and March 13, 1941, in Secretary Ickes folder, "Correspondence" files, Mellett papers, FDRL.

72. Memorandum of conversation between Lowell Mellett and Sidney Hyman, August 8, 1949, Washington, D.C., p. 13 in file IV-A-4, papers of the FDR Memorial Foundation, FDRL; Mellett to Ickes, March 13, 1941, War—National Morale folder, file 2, Ickes papers, LC.

73. Memo, Mellett for FDR, May 5, 1941, W.H.—1941 fldr., "Personal Files, 1938-1944," Mellett papers, FDRL.

74. Diary (MS), March 1, 1941, in Ickes papers, LC, and Ickes, *Secret Diary*, 3: 445.

75. Memo, Coy, Bullitt, and Smith for FDR, April 4, 1941, in Civilian Defense folder, Wayne Coy papers, FDRL.

76. "Notes on Conference with the President," April 4, 1941, in Conferences with the President file, Harold D. Smith papers, FDRL.

77. The continued confusion is evident in accounts of the cabinet meeting of April 17, 1941 in Ickes, *Secret Diary*, 3: 483-484; Diary (MS), Stimson papers, Yale University; and in "Notes on Conference with the President," April 22, 1941, in "Conferences with the President," Harold D. Smith papers, FDRL. Ickes' frustration with these events is suggested in Ickes to Herbert Bayard Swope, August 5, 1941, War—National Morale folder, file 2, Ickes papers, LC.

78. On this point and for other details of the OCD affair see Richard W. Steele, "Preparing the Public for War: Efforts to Establish a National Propaganda Agency, 1940-41," *American Historical Review*, 75 (October, 1970): 1640-1653. On OCD's failure to employ direct or systematic investigations of morale see Edward A. Shils, "A Note on Governmental Research on Attitudes and Morale," *American Journal of Sociology*, 47 (November 1941): 472-480. La Guardia's distain for morale building, which he disparagingly reduced to "community singing, sweater knitting, and basket weaving," is apparent in his letter to FDR, April 25, 1941, in "President 1941-1945" file; and in the comments of Eleanor Roosevelt (who did believe in morale building through community participation) in her letter to La Guardia, February 18, 1942, in President 1942 folder, both in La Guardia papers, New York City Municipal Archives.

79. Ickes to FDR, May 22, 1941, and FDR for Early, May 26, 1941, OF 4422, FDRL; Ickes, *Secret Diary*, 3: 518, 540.

80. See Steele, "Preparing the Public for War," pp. 1651-1652. Harold F. Gosnell, "Report on the Office of Facts and Figures," November 1943, in item 4, Records of the Office of War Information, RG 208, NA, Suitland, Md.

81. Memos, Lasswell for MacLeish May 1 and 2, 1941, in H. Lasswell folder, "Correspondence" files, Oscar Cox papers, FDRL.

82. Opinion-monitoring function in Richard W. Steele, "The Pulse of the People: Franklin D. Roosevelt and the Gauging of American Public Opinion," *Journal of Contemporary History*, 9 (October 1974): 207.

83. Steele, "Preparing the Public for War," p. 1653.

84. The Canadian experience in morale and propaganda provides interesting parallels to the American, and is admirably described in William R. Young, "Academics and Social Scientists versus the Press: The Policies of the Bureau of Public Information and the Wartime Information Board, 1939 to 1945," in *Historical Papers/Communications Historiques: A Selection from the Papers Presented at the Annual Meeting, London, 1978* (Ontario, Canada: Canadian Historical Association, 1978), pp. 297-339.

CHAPTER 4

1. From a letter by Chandler to Clara Burdette (1934) quoted in Robert Gottlieb and Irene Wolt, *Thinking Big: The Story of the Los Angeles Times*,

Notes 195

Its Publishers and Their Influence on Southern California (New York: G. P. Putnam's Sons, 1977), pp. 204-205.

2. Chandler to Jesse Jones, May 11, 1940; Mellett for Early, June 4, 1940; Early to Chandler, June 13, 1940. In Official File (OF) 463C, Franklin D. Roosevelt Library (FDRL).

3. See Mellett to John N. Wheeler, December 27, 1940, in "W" folder (fldr.), "Correspondence" files, Mellett papers, FDRL.

4. The first quarter of 1941 was the best for the newspaper industry since the 1920s. The defense program increased advertising revenues and circulation. See "Press and the War," *Public Opinion Quarterly*, 7 (June 1941): 299. On Crowell-Collier offer, see Mellett to William L. Chenery et al., March 27, 1941, Collier's folder, "Correspondence" files, Mellett papers, FDRL. Also, "Memo of Conversation between Mellett and Sidney Hyman," August 8, 1949, pp. 10-11, in file IV-A-4, box 8, papers of the FDR Memorial Foundation, FDRL. A number of newspapermen approached various administration officials individually seeking to contribute to the defense effort. One group of about twenty met and discussed with Secretary of the Navy Knox "the place of the newspaper in the national defense picture." See Donald J. Sterling (Managing Editor, *Portland* (Ore.) *Journal*) to Early, February 26, 1941, in Ste—miscellaneous (misc.) folder "Correspondence" files, Early papers, FDRL.

5. See Early for FDR, June 3, 1940, OF 463C; "Memorandum on Editorial Reaction toward Aid for the Allies," June 10, 1940, OF 788, FDRL.

6. Chalmers M. Roberts, *The Washington Post: The First One Hundred Years* (Boston: Houghton Mifflin Company, 1977), pp. 206, 231-234. A Morley editorial challenging inconsistencies in administration policy may have led to his removal. See Gerald K. Haines, "American Myopia and the Japanese Monroe Doctrine, 1931-41," *Prologue*, 13 (Summer 1981): 111-112.

7. James S. Twohey, "An Analysis of Newspaper Opinion on War Issues," *Public Opinion Quarterly*, 5 (Fall 1941): 453. Also, Twohey chart in *Time* (August 25, 1941): 16-17.

8. Division of Press Intelligence, memo on "Editorial Reaction toward Aid for the Allies," June 10, 1940, OF 788; Memo from Executive Officer of OGR to Director (Mellett), August 15, 1940, OF 788; "American Morale," May 2, 1941, Alan Barth for Henry Morgenthau, "The Price of Security," May 9, 1941; both in President's Secretary's File (PSF), "Treasury—Morgenthau," all in FDRL.

9. Division of Press Intelligence, "Weekly Summary," July 25, 1941, and August 1, 1941, in PSF, "Mellett," FDRL.

10. The same report noted, however, that considerable dissatisfaction with the President's handling of domestic defense-related matters existed. See Alan Barth (OFF) to Archibald MacLeish (Director, OFF), November 17, 1941, OWI–Mellett–CWI folder, entry 789, Record Group (RG) 44, National Archives (NA), Suitland, Md.

11. Bingham to Mellett, May 28, 1940, "B" folder, "Correspondence" files, Mellett papers, FDRL.

12. See Lauchlin Currie, "Memorandum for the President," January 13, 1941, in PSF Executive Offices of President—Currie, FDRL. Account of Sulzberger meeting with FDR in Diary Manuscript (MS), September 20, 1941, in Ickes papers, Library of Congress (LC).

13. For a general discussion of the *Times'* sense of responsibility and its susceptibility to pressure from on high, see Murray Kempton, "Winners and Losers at the 'Times,' " *New York Review of Books* (September 25, 1980): 30-32.

14. Hopkins for FDR, November 27, 1941, Harry Hopkins folder, "Memos" files, Early papers, FDRL.

15. FDR to Reid, June 6, 1940, President's Personal File (PPF) 897, FDRL; Early press conference, March 4, 1941, in "Scrapbook," Early papers, FDRL.

16. FDR complaint of press conference distortions in note FDR to Mellett, December 28, 1944, PSF, "Mellett," FDRL.

17. Raymond Clapper, "F. D.'s Mouthpiece," Washington *News* (November 3, 1939) and George Morris, "In Washington," Memphis *Commercial Appeal* (November 4, 1939) and other articles on same theme in "Scrapbook," Early papers, FDRL.

18. Louis Brownlow, *The Autobiography of Louis Brownlow* (2 vols. Chicago: University of Chicago Press, 1958), vol. 2, *A Passion for Anonymity*, pp. 439-449; and memo, Brownlow for FDR, June 14, 1940, PPF 7048, FDRL. On an earlier Brownlow plan for government–press relations, see Arthur A. Krock, "Press vs. Government—A Warning," *Public Opinion Quarterly*, 1 (April 1937): 45-49.

19. Brownlow for FDR, June 14, 1940, PPF 7048, FDRL.

20. Early press conference, July 6, 1940, and articles filed for July 7 and 10 in "Scrapbook," Early papers, FDRL. For background of this episode, see Haines, "American Myopia and the Japanese Monroe Doctrine, 1931-41," pp. 112-114.

21. Walter Davenport, "You Can't Say THAT!" *Collier's* (February 15, 1941): 19, 65.

22. Mellett discusses his background in "Memo of Conversation between Mellett and Sidney Hyman," August 8, 1949, in file IV-A-4, box 8, papers of the FDR Memorial Foundation, FDRL; James Rowe for FDR, September 23, 1940, PSF subject file "Executive Office—Rowe," FDRL. See also Delbert Clark, " 'Steve' Takes Care of It," *New York Times Magazine* (July 27, 1941): 11; Lee Carson, "Self-Effacing Mellett Rated 'Dangerous' Man," *Miami Herald* (August 13, 1941) "Scrapbook," Early papers, FDRL; "Presidential Legmen," *Newsweek* (April 26, 1943): 39.

23. The White House rejected censorship in several statements issued by Early and the President in September 1939. These are discussed in James E. Pollard, *The Presidents and the Press* (New York: Macmillan Company, 1947), p. 821. Early repeated the disclaimer in "Washington Correspondents," *Liberty*

(February 1940): 14-16; "There Is No Iron Heel in the United States," Philadelphia *Inquirer* (June 15, 1941) in Article—There Is No Iron Heel folder, "Subject" files; and in his response to a question at his August 18, 1941, press conference, in "Scrapbook," both in Early papers, FDRL.

24. Conference no. 720 (February 21, 1941), in *The Complete Presidential Press Conferences of Franklin D. Roosevelt*, with an introduction by Jonathan Daniels (25 vols. New York: Da Capo Press, 1972), vol. 17, pp. 141-148. Hereinafter cited as *PPC* conference number (date), volume: page.

25. See minutes of "Conference between Representatives of State Department, Military Intelligence Division of War Department, Naval Intelligence, and the Federal Bureau of Investigation on April 3, 1940," in file 9794-186A, in the Military Intelligence Division, Records of War Department General and Special Staffs Record Group (RG) 165, National Archives (NA).

26. See Secretary of War and Secretary of the Navy to FDR, June 10, 1940 and attached "Basic Plan" dated September 2, 1939, in PSF, "War Department—1940;" Stimson and Knox to FDR, February 1, 1941; Mellett for FDR, February 18, 1941; and FDR for Stimson and Knox, February 20, 1941, in PSF, "War Department—Henry L. Stimson," all in FDRL. Instruction to bury it reported in "Memorandum of Conversation between Mellett and Hyman, August 8, 1949," FDR Memorial Foundation papers, FDRL.

27. For a general discussion of government deception, see David Wise, *The Politics of Lying: Government Deception, Secrecy and Power* (New York: Random House, 1973), pp. 1-18.

28. The administration's prior censorship program was modelled on one adopted in 1940 by the Navy. This is described by Commander H. R. Thurber in *Proceedings of the Nineteenth Annual Convention, American Society of Newspaper Editors, April 17, 1941* (N.p., American Society of Newspaper Editors, 1941), pp. 146-150. These guidelines, which asked journalists not to print classified information, were applied to British warship movements. Secretary of the Navy Knox complained of violations of the voluntary censorship in regard to two episodes. He denied both stories, each of which was true, and urged reporters to adopt the rule: "If you can't confirm, don't print." See Delbert Clark, *Washington Dateline* (New York: Frederick A. Stokes Co., 1941), pp. 301-302; and "Knox Curbs News of Navy Actions," *New York Times* (June 12, 1941): 4:1.

29. Mellett for FDR, March 17, 1941, in White House, 1941 fldr., Mellett papers, FDRL.

30. Although the American Newspaper Publishers Association passed a resolution at its July 1940 convention pledging its cooperation to the government, a year later Mellett observed that the organization had failed to implement its resolve. See Mellett to S. E. Thomason, July 18, 1941, in S. E. Thomason folder, "Correspondence" files, Mellett papers, FDRL. The editors, in Mellett's judgement, did no better. See Mellett to Morris Ernst, November 26, 1941, Ernst fldr., ibid.

31. Concern for leaks noted in Berle to FDR, September 22, 1939, and FDR for Early, September 23, 1939 (regarding Alsop-Kintner article on FBI), in Corcoran fldr., "Correspondence" files, Early papers, FDRL. Stimson to FDR, November 25, 1941 (regarding FDR's note of November 2, concerning publication of confidential information) in Knudsen, Wm., folder, ibid. See also Hopkins for FDR, November 27, 1941, Harry Hopkins fldr., "Memos" file, Early papers, FDRL.

32. *Tribune* account described in *New York Times* (December 5, 1941): 3:1. On investigation of Victory Program leak, see W. B. Woodson (Judge Advocate General, Navy Department) for Knox, March 18, 1942; Knox to FDR, March 21, 1942; FDR for Attorney General (Francis Biddle), March 24, 1942; all in OF 144, FDRL. See also Harold L. Ickes, *The Secret Diary of Harold L. Ickes* (3 vols. New York: Simon and Schuster, 1953-1954), vol. 3, *The Lowering Clouds*, pp. 659-660; Frank C. Waldrop, *McCormick of Chicago: An Unconventional Portrait of a Controversial Figure* (1966; reprint ed., Westport, Conn.: Greenwood Press, 1975), pp. 256-257; Albert C. Wedemeyer, *Wedemeyer Reports!* (New York: Henry Holt & Co., 1958), pp. 28-43; Frank C. Waldrop, "A 'Scoop' Gave Axis Our World War II Plans," Washington *Post* (January 6, 1963): pp. E-5. Concern and confusion over the leak are reflected in Biddle's account of December 5, 1941, in "Cabinet Meetings—1941," and in his memo for FDR, December 6, 1941, in "Roosevelt, Franklin D." file. Both in Biddle papers, FDRL.

33. Inconsistencies in government information on defense-related issues are discussed and criticized in an editorial "The Facts about Defense," *New York Times* (February 6, 1941): 20:1. Although newspapers and magazines continued to supply information for German intelligence, much of value also came from official government releases. See David Kahn, *Hitler's Spies: German Military Intelligence In World War II* (New York: Macmillan Publishing Co., 1978) pp. 81-83.

34. For examples, see *PPC* 741 (May 16, 1941), 17:320; *PPC* 742 (May 20, 1941), 17:334; *PPC* 762 (August 19, 1941), 18:94.

35. See *PPC* 771 (September 30, 1941), 18:187-188; and origins of question in Harry Hopkins for Stephen Early, September 25, 1941, Early for Hopkins, September 26, 1941, in Harry Hopkins folder, "Memos" file, Early papers, FDRL.

36. *PPC* 620 (February 2, 1940), 15:115. A few months later FDR also declined comment on implications of Nazi offensive in the West. *PPC* 642 (May 10, 1940), 15:327.

37. *PPC* 677 (September 3, 1940), 11:175, 177.

38. *PPC* 715 (February 4, 1941), 17:105.

39. Diary (MS), April 22, 1941, Stimson papers, Yale University Library, New Haven, Connecticut.

40. Ibid., December 19, 1940.

41. *PPC* 712 (January 21, 1941), 17:86.

42. Thomas A. Bailey and Paul B. Ryan, *Hitler vs. Roosevelt: The Undeclared Naval War* (New York: Free Press, 1979), pp. 42-43. Quote is found in *PPC* 738 (April 25, 1941), 17-287.

43. Samuel Eliot Morison, *History of United States Naval Operations in World War II*, (15 vols. Boston: Little Brown and Company, 1947-1964), vol. 1, *The Battle of the Atlantic, September 1939–May 1943*, pp. 56-62.

44. *PPC* 735 (April 15, 1941), 17:259.

45. See *PPC* 737 (April 22, 1941), 17:282, and *PPC* 738 (April 25, 1941), 17:287.

46. "F. D. Allows Guard for Allies' Munitions Cargos, Is Claim," Washington *Times-Herald* (April 17, 1941) in J. David Stern folder, "Subject" files, Early papers, FDRL.

47. FDR's remark in a letter dated June 7, 1940, quoted in Robert Dallek, *Franklin D. Roosevelt and American Foreign Policy, 1932-1945* (New York: Oxford University Press, 1979), p. 228.

48. Early's "deliberate lie" charge was picked up by the strongly pro-administration Philadelphia *Record* and repeated in an editorial that also charged that O'Donnell was a notorious Naziphile. O'Donnell sued for libel. Administration officials, including Early, testified on behalf of *Record* publisher J. David Stern, but he was found to have libeled the columnist. See J. David Stern folder, "Subject" files, Early papers, FDRL, and "O'Donnell Suit Victory Seen Blow to New Smear Campaign," in Washington *Times-Herald* (January 31, 1943) in "Scrapbook," Early papers, FDRL. FDR's "horse and cow" analogy in *PPC* 738 (April 25, 1941), 17:286-289.

49. *PPC* 741 (May 16, 1941), 17:317.

50. Alan Barth to Secretary [of the Treasury Henry] Morgenthau, May 2, 1941, "American Morale," in PSF, "Treasury—Morgenthau," FDRL. This is one of a series of reports on press and public opinion done for Morgenthau and forwarded to the White House during 1941. The President also learned that in mid-May, 55 percent of those surveyed by Gallup favored convoys. See memo of telephone call from Anna Rosenberg, May 16, 1941, in PPF 8101, FDRL.

51. See Phelps Adams, "Convoy Pleas Fail to Stir Warm Reaction in Country," New York *Sun* (May 8, 1941); Early press conference, May 12, 1941; both in "Scrapbook," Early papers; Ickes to FDR, May 24, 1941, PSF, "Dept. of Interior—Harold Ickes," both in FDRL.

52. Telegram signed by Senators Burton K. Wheeler, Robert La Follette, and Robert Taft and Congressmen John M. Robsion, John O'Connor, Carl Curtis, Frank B. Keefe to FDR, May 27, 1941, in OF 463C, FDRL.

53. Samuel I. Rosenman, comp., *The Public Papers and Addresses of Franklin D. Roosevelt* (13 vols. New York: Harper & Brothers, 1950), vol. 9, p. 191. See also Dallek, *FDR and American Foreign Policy*, pp. 266-267.

54. Adlai Stevenson ascribed FDR's silence to his desire to avoid a distracting "public controversy now on some incidental issue like convoys." In a letter to Ulric Bell, May 5, 1941, in Adlai E. Stevenson, *The Papers of Adlai E. Stevenson*, ed. Walter Johnson and Carol Evans (8 vols. Boston: Little Brown and Company, 1972-1979), vol. 1, *Beginnings of Education, 1900-1941*, p. 547.

55. Clark, *Washington Dateline*, pp. 247-248.

56. Early press conference, May 28, 1941, in "Scrapbook," Early papers, and "President to Clear Up Convoy Issue," newspaper clipping from Albany (Georgia) *Herald* dated May 28, 1941, p. 1, in OF 136 misc., both in FDRL.

57. Roy Roberts, publisher of the Kansas City *Star*, in a note to Early dated June 16, 1941, noted that while the speech was good, the President's press conference "sort of let things down and there was some confusion which continued for days." In Roy Roberts fldr., "Correspondence" files, Early papers, FDRL.

58. *PPC* 745 (May 28, 1941), 17:364, 370.

59. See Bailey and Ryan, *Hitler vs. Roosevelt*, pp. 156-157, and *PPC* 756 (July 18, 1941), 18:38-39.

60. The *Greer* episode is described in Bailey and Ryan, *Hitler vs. Roosevelt*, pp. 168-187.

61. *PPC* 767 (September 5, 1941), 18:140-145; fireside chat, September 11, 1941 in Rosenman, *Public Papers of FDR*, 9: 384-392.

62. Press conferences, September 11 and 12, 1941, in "Scrapbook," Early papers, FDRL.

63. See editorial "More about the U.S.S. *Greer*," in New York *Daily News* (October 29, 1941). This is attached to a draft letter which FDR suggested that Secretary of the Navy Frank Knox send to publisher Joseph Patterson concerning this editorial. Also see memo, FDR for Harry Hopkins, November 3, 1941, all in PPF 245, FDRL.

64. *PPC* 770 (September 23, 1941), 18:174-178.

65. *PPC* 771 (September 30, 1941), 18:183-185. For background material on *Pink Star* and its cargo, see Robert E. Kintner to Early, October 3, 1941, in Kintner fldr., "Correspondence" files, Early papers, FDRL.

66. American policy and public attitudes toward Japan are discussed in William L. Langer and S. Everett Gleason, *The Challenge to Isolation, 1937-1940* (New York: Harper & Brothers, 1952), pp. 42, 147-159.

67. R. J. C. Butow, "The FDR Tapes," *American Heritage*, 33 (February/ March 1982): 8-24.

68. The indexes to the President's public papers for 1940-1941 list under "Japan" only a few formal statements accompanying the issuance of Executive Orders, in addition to one brief comment in his "Extemporaneous Remarks to Volunteer Participation Committee of the Office of Civilian Defense," July 24, 1941. See Rosenman, *Public Papers of FDR*, 10:280.

69. Public attitudes on U.S.–Japanese relations are in Office of Public Opinion Research polls found in: James Rowe for FDR, October 14, 1940, in PSF

subject file "Executive Office—Rowe," and in Hadley Cantril to Anna Rosenberg, September 13, 1941, in PSF, "Public Opinion," both FDRL. See also Dallek, *FDR and American Foreign Policy*, pp. 272ff.

70. Editorial opinion on Japanese-American relations in James S. Twohey, "An Analysis of Newspaper Opinion on War Issues," *Public Opinion Quarterly*, 5 (Fall 1941): 448-455; Division of Press Intelligence, "Weekly Summary," August 1, 1941, p. 2, in OF 1413, FDRL; Alan Barth to Ferdinand Kuhn, "Editorial Opinion on Foreign Affairs: The Crucial Test," October 17, 1941, in PSF, "Treasury—Morgenthau," FDRL.

71. The President's handling of Japanese relations at his press conferences is suggested by his refusal to comment on the status of relations with Japan on the expiration of U.S.-Japanese commercial treaty in *PPC* 618 (January 26, 1940), 15:101 and 619 (January 31,1941), 15:111; to discuss implications of British closure of Burma road, *PPC* 661 (July 16, 1940), 16:49; to comment on effect of possible involvement in Asia on aid to Britain in *PPC* 717 (February 11, 1941), 17:120; to comment on Lauchlin Currie mission to China in *PPC* 731 (April 1, 1941), 17:217-218; and in his noncommital answer to a question on aid to China in *PPC* 736 (April 18, 1941), 17:264-265.

72. *PPC* 651 (June 11, 1940), 15:558.

73. See Paul W. Schroeder, *The Axis Alliance and Japanese-American Relations, 1941* (Ithaca, N.Y.: Cornell University Press, 1958), pp. 24-25.

74. *PPC* 683 (September 27, 1940), 16:228. See also President's comment in response to reporter's request for comment on the "ominous picture or rumor arising as if from the horizon." *PPC* 718 (February 14, 1941), 17:126-127.

75. *PPC* 758 (July 25, 1941), 18:52-56. The episode is discussed in Charles A. Beard, *President Roosevelt and the Coming of the War, 1941: A Study in Appearances and Realities* (New Haven, Conn.: Yale University Press, 1948), pp. 180-182. See also Dallek, *FDR and American Foreign Policy*, p. 274.

76. *PPC* 759 (July 29, 1941), 18:64-65. David Reynolds notes that FDR sought to preserve his flexibility in dealing with Japanese not to sever trade. See *Creation of Anglo-American Alliance 1937-1941*, (Chapel Hill: University of North Carolina Press, 1982), p. 234.

77. *PPC* 783 (November 14, 1941), 18:304.

78. Entry for November 7, 1941, "Cabinet Meetings—1941," Biddle papers, FDRL.

79. *PPC* 787 (November 28, 1941), 18:326-328.

80. Reynolds, *Creation of the Anglo-American Alliance*, particularly pp. 195-247.

CHAPTER 5

1. On the rise of radio news see David H. Culbert, *News for Everyman: Radio and Foreign Affairs in Thirties America* (Westport, Conn.: Greenwood Press, 1976).

2. Memo dictated by Early, October 13, 1937, Frank M. Russell folder (fldr.), "Correspondence" files, Early papers, FDR Library (FDRL). Replacement by J. Franklin in Edward W. Chester, *Radio, Television and American Politics* (New York: Sheed and Ward, 1969), p. 174.

3. Carter's unique popularity is discussed in Culbert, *News for Everyman*, pp. 5, 47, 53, 203. Pettey information on Carter in Pettey for Early, September 7, 1934, in Official File (OF) 1059, FDRL.

4. See Butcher to MacIntyre, November 4, 1936, in OF 256, FDRL. On Court issue, see Culbert, *News for Everyman*, p. 48; on *Panay*, see Chester, *Radio, Television and American Politics*, p. 174. The characterization and interest in deportation is in Harold L. Ickes, *The Secret Diary of Harold L. Ickes* (3 vols. New York: Simon and Schuster, 1954), vol. 2, *The Inside Struggle, 1936-1939*, p. 313. Jerre Mangione, who dined with the President in May 1939, notes the President was still pursuing his effort to silence Carter: "The President made no bones of the fact that he was having Carter 'thoroughly investigated,' apparently by the FBI. He was quite certain that Carter—'or whatever his real name is'—had a nefarious background which, when brought to light would put an end to his career." See *An Ethnic at Large: A Memoir of America in the Thirties and Forties* (New York: G. P. Putnam's Sons, 1978), p. 248.

5. Culbert, *News for Everyman*, pp. 47-48, 53, 203.

6. McIntyre for Early, November 27, 1937, and memo, Joseph Davies for Early, February 8, 1938, attached to the Carter agreement in Davies, 34-37 fldr., "Correspondence" files, Early papers, FDRL.

7. Chester, *Radio, Television and American Politics*, p. 174. Chester attributes Carter's pulling his punches to a warning from the FCC to networks that he should be impartial.

8. Quincy Howe, *The News and How to Understand It* (New York: Simon and Schuster, 1940), pp. 187, 205.

9. Llewellyn White, *American Radio: A Report on the Broadcasting Industry* (Chicago: University of Chicago Press, 1947), pp. 68-71. "Broadcasters Air Their Woes," *Business Week* (June 19, 1937): 44-45.

10. Relations among the broadcasters, Congress, and the FCC are suggested in C. K. Friedrich and E. Sternberg, "Congress and the Control of Radio Broadcasting," *American Political Science Review*, 37 (October 1943): 797-818; Thomas Porter Robinson, *Radio Networks and the Federal Government* (New York: Columbia University Press, 1943), pp. 64-65; and Senator Burton K. Wheeler interview, September 30, 1964, and Neville Miller interview, September 25, 1973, in Broadcast Pioneers Collection, National Association of Broadcasters Library, Washington, D.C.

11. See Harry Butcher "Memorandum for Mr. Early," March 13, 1941, in Radio fldr., Mellett papers, FDRL.

12. See Robinson, *Radio Networks and Government*, p. 65; Freidrich and Sternberg, "Congress and the Control of Radio Broadcasting," pp. 797-818.

13. *Variety* editorial, March 8, 1939, in OF 136 miscellaneous (misc.), FDRL.

14. Early to Joseph Davies, July 9, 1937, in Davies fldr., "Correspondence" files, Early papers, FDRL; "Radio Reorganizes: Plans a Czar," *Business Week* (February 19, 1938): 46-47. File memo by "PLS," March 10, 1938, OF 228; Mark Ethridge to Early, March 6, 1939, OF 136 misc., FDRL.

15. "Radio Reorganizes; Plans a Czar," pp. 46-47; "Radio Czar Pro-Tem," *Business Week* (April 9, 1938): 53; "FCC Head Warns Stations against Monopoly, Indecency, and Equivocal Ads," *Newsweek* (February 28, 1938): 30.

16. "Chains Get Headache," *Business Week* (June 22, 1940): 40; "Battle Joined," *Time* (October 20, 1941): 57-58; Friedrich and Sternberg, "Congress and the Control of Radio Broadcasting," pp. 797-818.

17. White, *American Radio*, p. 73. "Industry Upset by Possible Meaning of FCC's Latest Flank Maneuvers," *Variety* (March 8, 1939) and "Radio Censorship Issue Flares Anew in Controversy," *Advertising Age* (March 6, 1939), both in Harrison B. Summers, comp., *The Reference Shelf* (New York: H. W. Wilson Company, 1939), vol. 12, *Radio Censorship*, pp. 110, 112.

18. Ethridge to Early, March 6, 1939, "Memorandum for General Watson," by "K," April 12, 1939; FDR to Marvin Watson, April 17 and James Rowe for FDR, April 20, 1939; Early to Neville Miller, April 26, 1939; all in OF 136 misc., FDRL.

19. "Address on 'Radio and Its Relation to Government' to be delivered before the convention of the National Association of Broadcasting at Atlantic City, N.J., July 11, 1939," and memo, William Hassett for Early (enclosing draft and explaining genesis), July 8, 1939 in Address—National Association of Broadcasters, July 11, 1939, fldr., "Subject" file, Early papers, FDRL.

20. "1939 'Standards of Practice' " in White, *American Radio*, pp. 242-246.

21. See Minna F. Kassner, "Radio Censorship," *Air Law Review* (April 1937): 99-111, reprinted in Summers, *Radio Censorship*, p. 81.

22. Newspaper comment singled out Early's phrase "for the present." See Early press conference, September 6, 1939, and associated clippings in "Scrapbook," Early papers, FDRL.

23. See clippings from the *Christian Science Monitor* and *New York Times* for September 8, 1939; and Early press conference, September 12, 1939, both in "Scrapbook," Early papers, FDRL. FCC Chairman James L. Fly also spoke of self-regulation as an alternative to government controls. See "Remarks in National Defense Series interview," September 29, 1940, in Some Comments on Current Radio Problems fldr., and "Address over CBS," October 26, 1939, in Extracts on Government Controls fldr., both in Fly papers, Columbia University Library, New York.

24. See Ed Kirby (Secretary, Code Compliance Committee) to Board of Directors and the Code Committee of the NAB, "Re: Father Coughlin's Broad-

casts," September 24, 1940, in NAB fldr., National Broadcasting System (NBC) papers, Wisconsin State Historical Society, Madison. Also "Code to Be Enforced," October 1, 1939, p. 10; "Restrictions Made on Radio Programs," October 4, 1939, p. 15, both in the *New York Times*.

25. Results of surveys summarized in H. M. Neville, Jr., for Ken R. Dyke, "Roper Survey on Radio Programs," May 5, 1941, in Elmo Roper Survey, 1941, fldr., NBC papers, Wisconsin State Historical Society, Madison.

26. See Early press conferences September 6 and 12, 1939, in "Scrapbook," Early papers, FDRL.

27. See National Emergency Council script, in Secretary Cordell Hull fldr., Mellett papers, FDRL. FDR's views on the radio as an alternative to the press are in FDR to Helen Reid, June 6, 1940, President's Personal File (PPF) 897, FDRL. The series is described in Mellett to Samuel I. Rosenman, December 16, 1940, Rosenman fldr., Mellett papers, FDRL.

28. A poll taken at the National Association of Broadcasters convention in mid-May 1941 (members were mostly owners and operators of independent local broadcasting outlets rather than network executives) found that 80 percent favored sending half of American military production to England, while 45 percent favored convoying. George Storer to Early, May 22, 1941, in OF 857, FDRL. For isolationist suspicions, see Michele Flynn Stenehjem, *An American First: John T. Flynn and the America First Committee* (New Rochelle, N.Y.: Arlington House, 1976), pp. 152-153. NBC President Niles Trammell, it might be noted, was a member of the Council for Democracy. Protests against broadcaster bias in America First Committee—1941 fldr., "General Correspondence" files, NBC papers, Wisconsin State Historical Society, Madison.

29. FCC form letter and questionnaire to stations attached to Early to FDR, July 3, 1941, Radio—misc. official correspondence fldr., "Subject" files, Early papers, FDRL. Results in Fly for FDR, October 31, 1941, in OF 1059, FDRL. Network figures for NBC covering January 1–August 18, 1941: interventionists, 15 hours, 6 minutes; isolationists, 20 hours, 20 minutes. Found in America First Committee—1941 fldr., "General Correspondence" files, NBC papers. On lend lease bill, NBC lists 26 speeches (9 hours, 41 minutes) "for" and 26 speeches (8 hours, 22 minutes) "against." On convoy issue, 35 minutes "for" and 50 minutes "against." These surveys found in Lend Lease Bill (Wm. B. Miller's) 1941 fldr. and Talks on Convoy fldr., all in "General Correspondence" files, NBC papers. A public statement on lend lease debate differed slightly. See Jeanette Sayre, "Radio: Congress Has an Inning," *Public Opinion Quarterly*, 5 (June 1941): 303. CBS statistics covering both networks for the period January 1 through October list 73 hours of interventionist speeches and 63.5 by the isolationists. See "Memorandum for Mr. William Hassett from Paul Porter CBS," in OF 3575, FDRL. Wheeler charged bias and threatened NBC in a telephone conversation with W. B. Miller on October 28, 1941. See America First Committee—1941 fldr., "General Correspondence" files, NBC papers.

Also "NBC Head Denies Curb on Isolationist View," October 28, 1941, p. 12:4 and "Broadcasters Deny Prejudice Charges," October 31, 1941, p. 3:4, both in the *New York Times*. CBS President William S. Paley, in *As It Happened: A Memoir* (Garden City, N.Y.: Doubleday and Company, Inc., 1979), describes the network's rigid insistence on "objectivity," pp. 139-140.

30. White, *American Radio*, p. 190. Figures supplied by CBS for the three major networks show a total of about 136 hours of debate through the end of October. Other figures show that the Mutual network scheduled an additional 20 percent of the total number of such presentations. Increasing the figure of 136 by 20 percent gives a total of 163 hours over a period of about 300 days.

31. Mark R. Show to Norman Thomas, September 9, 1941, "General Correspondence" files, box 31, Norman Thomas papers, New York Public Library.

32. This material appears in "In Defense of America, a Nation Listens," in Defense Programs—1941 fldr., "General Correspondence" files, NBC papers, Wisconsin State Historical Society, Madison.

33. C. D. Jackson to Mellett, June 6, 1941, in Council for Democracy fldr., Mellett papers, FDRL.

34. See Early correspondence with Leonard Levinson in Le—misc. fldr., "Correspondence" file, Mellett papers, FDRL.

35. Adlai Stevenson to Mellett, August 4, 1941, in Commerce, misc. fldr., "Correspondence" file, Mellett papers, FDRL.

36. Howe, *The News and How to Understand It*, pp. 205-206.

37. Culbert, *News for Everyman*, pp. 47-58.

38. Ibid., p. 7.

39. Alfred Haworth Jones, "The Making of an Interventionist on the Air: Elmer Davis and CBS News, 1939-1941," *Pacific Historical Review*, 42 (February 1973): 74-93; Culbert, *News for Everyman*, pp. 141-142, 205.

40. See Raymond Swing, *"Good Evening!" A Professional Memoir by Raymond Swing* (New York: Harcourt, Brace & World, 1964), especially pp. 216-217; Robert E. Sherwood, *Roosevelt and Hopkins: An Intimate History* (New York, Harper & Brothers, 1948), p. 835 mentions Hopkins' friendship with Swing and Walter Winchell.

41. Culbert, *News for Everyman*, pp. 104, 115, 206.

42. Ibid., p. 207.

43. Good accounts of Winchell's activities, including material on his relations with the administration, are found in Bob Thomas, *Winchell* (Garden City, N.Y.: Doubleday & Company, Inc., 1971); Herman Klurfeld, *Winchell: His Life and Times* (New York: Praeger Publishers, 1976); and in Ernest Cuneo's introduction to Walter Winchell, *Winchell Exclusive* (Englewood Cliffs, N.J.: Prentice-Hall 1975).

44. Klurfeld, *Winchell*, p. 86.

45. Contacts with Navy and FBI in Klurfeld, *Winchell*, p. 70, and in Winchell, *Exclusive*, pp. 95, 99. Plugging and keeping FDR informed reflected in correspondence found in OF 5547, FDRL.

46. See Diary Manuscript (MS) entry for December 8, 1939, in Berle Papers, FDRL.

47. See Klurfeld, *Winchell*, pp. 97, 98, 102, and H. Montgomery Hyde, *Room 3603: The Story of the British Intelligence Center in New York during World War II* (New York: Farrar, Straus and Co., 1962), p. 27; Winchell, *Exclusive*, p. vi.

48. J. F. Royal to Niles Trammell, July 3, 1940, in Winchell—1940 fldr., "General Correspondence" files, NBC papers, Wisconsin State Historical Society, Madison.

49. A. A. Schecter to Sidney Strotz, "Winchell," May 19, 1941, in Walter Winchell—1941 fldr., ibid.

50. See Thomas to Wheeler, November 17, 1941, Thomas to Russell Place (NAB), November 19, 1941. Both in "General Correspondence" files, box 21, Norman Thomas papers, New York Public Library.

CHAPTER 6

1. See Raymond Fielding, *The March of Time, 1935-1951* (New York: Oxford University Press, 1978), p. 4.

2. Newsreel topical content from a chart adapted from Leo A. Handel, *Hollywood Looks at Its Audience* (Urbana: University of Illinois Press, 1950), in Raymond Fielding, *The American Newsreel 1911-1967* (Norman: University of Oklahoma Press, 1972), p. 290.

3. Ibid.

4. See Lewis Jacobs, "World War II and the American Film," *Cinema Journal*, 7 (Winter 1967-1968): 1-21, quotes on p. 3.

5. Ibid.

6. Wheeler to Paramount and Hays, January 13, 1941; Hays to Wheeler, January 14, 1941, forwarded to FDR on January 17, 1941, all in President's Personal File (PPF) 1945, Franklin D. Roosevelt Library (FDRL).

7. This account is based entirely on Fielding's *March of Time*, pp. 1-77, 169-185, 241-278.

8. A detailed critique of the film from a non-interventionist perspective (*"Ramparts . . . is, as a whole, a lie."*) may be found in *Uncensored* (September 21, 1940): 1-4.

9. Margaret Farrand Thorp, *America at the Movies* (New Haven, Conn.: Yale University Press, 1939), p. 279, discusses the popularity of military films.

10. Charles A. Beard and Mary R. Beard, *The Rise of American Civilization* (3 vols. New York: Macmillan Company, 1939), vol. 3, *America in Midpassage*, pp. 596-600.

11. The empire theme is discussed in Harold Lavine and James Wechsler, *War Propaganda and the United States* (New Haven, Conn.: Yale University Press, 1940), p. 276, and in Thorp, *America at the Movies*, pp. 294-295.

12. Lewis Jacobs, *Rise of American Film: A Critical History*, (New York: Harcourt, Brace and Company, 1939), p. 538.

13. Will H. Hays, *The Memoirs of Will H. Hays* (Garden City, N.Y.: Doubleday & Company, Inc., 1955), pp. 427-454, 483-486ff.

14. The industry's attitude toward controversy and self-regulation is discussed in Raymond Moley, *The Hays Office* (Indianapolis: Bobbs-Merrill Company, 1945), pp. 25-120; and Thorp, *America at the Movies*, pp. 1-25.

15. Hollywood's developing social conscience is discussed in Leo C. Rosten, *Hollywood: The Movie Colony, the Movie Makers* (New York: Harcourt, Brace and Co., 1941), pp. 153-157; Thorp, *America at the Movies*, pp. 275-278; and Jacobs, *Rise of American Film*, pp. 527-528. The demand for more realism is discussed in Walter Selden, "Movies and Propaganda," *Forum* (April 1940): 209-213. The few pictures of social content that appeared in the thirties are discussed in Charles C. Alexander, *Nationalism in American Thought, 1930-1945* (Chicago: Rand McNally & Company, 1969), pp. 90-93.

16. Hollywood had become politically involved in 1934 in a direct effort to defeat the "radical" Upton Sinclair in his bid to become governor of California. Hollywood's political involvement is discussed in Larry Ceplair and Steven Englund, *The Inquisition in Hollywood: Politics in the Film Community, 1930-1960* (Garden City, N.Y.: Anchor Press/Doubleday, 1980), pp. 1-199. See also Rosten, *Hollywood*, pp. 133-155.

17. Warner's story (poorly told) is in Jack L. Warner with Dean Jennings, *My First Hundred Years in Hollywood* (New York: Random House, 1965).

18. Quoted in Paul Vanderwood, ed., *Juarez* (1983). A volume in *Wisconsin/Warner Brothers Screenplay Series*, Tino Balio, ed. (Madison: University of Wisconsin Press, 1979-   ), pp. 19-20.

19. "Americanism" is discussed in Thorp, *America at the Movies*, pp. 188-191, 296-298; Jacobs, *Rise of American Film*, pp. 531-532.

20. Eric J. Sandeen, "*Confessions of a Nazi Spy* and the German American Bund," *American Studies*, 20 (Fall 1979): 69-81.

21. Industry's problems in Germany discussed in Moley, *Hays Office*, pp. 172-173.

22. Thorp, *America at the Movies*, p. 298, points out that though the picture did well at the box office overall, it drew little interest in small towns and cities. Rosten, *Hollywood*, p. 327, notes that surveys by Gallup indicate that only New York audiences seemed to want pictures involving Hitler and the Nazis.

23. Robert A. Brady, "The Problem of Monopoly," *Annals of the American Academy of Political and Social Sciences*, 254 (November 1947): 125–136, particularly p. 131.

24. The complaints of independents and civic groups in "Pass the Neely Bill!" *Christian Century* (February 21, 1940): 240-241. See also "Motion Pictures" file, Hopkins (Secretary Commerce) papers, FDRL, particularly J. Hazen to Tupper, April 2, 1940.

25. Government's suit described in Arnold for FDR, June 24, 1938, President's Secretary's File (PSF), "Justice Department—Homer Cummings," and Cummings (Attorney General) to FDR, July 22, 1938, Official File (OF) 10, both FDRL; and "Wide Scope of U.S. Anti-monopoly Suit against Movie Moguls Jolts Hollywood," *Newsweek* (August 1, 1938): 18.

26. Figures for profitability of various studios found in Floyd B. Odlum, "Financial Organization of the Motion Picture Industry," *Annals of the American Academy of Political and Social Sciences*, 254 (November 1947): 18-25, particularly p. 23. Interesting discussion of the industry's business practices in Morris Ernst, "Super Colossal: The Movies," *Atlantic Monthly* (July 1940): 17-28.

27. See Hays to FDR (November 1939?), PPF 1945, FDRL.

28. Harry Warner to Hopkins, March 6, 1939, in Motion Picture fldr., Hopkins papers, FDRL.

29. FDR's role in securing agreement is suggested in his undated pencilled note to Hopkins in PSF "Will Hays," FDRL. The White House did not want its role publicized. See diary manuscript (MS) entry for March 13, 1939, in Wendell Berge papers, Library of Congress (LC). Eventually, Arnold's enthusiasm for anti-trust actions against industries whose cooperation the administration needed would pose a problem for both Arnold and the President. See James Rowe for FDR, August 15, 1940, in PSF, "Executive Office—Rowe," FDRL. Arnold's reluctance to settle and his negotiation with the film makers is described in "Arnold Scorns Movie Code," *Business Week* (August 26, 1939): 43.

30. Excerpts from the *Variety* story dated August 13, 1940, attached to Leo Rosten for Robert Horton, August 17, 1940, in Rosten fldr., entry 78, Records of the Office of Government Reports (OGR), Record Group (RG) 44, National Archives (NA), Suitland, Md.

31. Justice Department denial in diary (MS) March 13, 1939, Berge papers, LC. Outline of consent decree in "Movies Arbitrate," *Business Week* (November 2, 1940): 15; followup material in "Antitrust Scenario," ibid., September 6, 1941, p. 32; final resolution of the matter in Simon N. Whitney, "The Impact of Antitrust Laws: Vertical Disintegration in the Motion Picture Industry," *American Economic Review*, 45 (May 1955): 491-498.

32. Warner's offer in Rosten to Horton, August 17, 1940, Rosten fldr., entry 78, RG 44, NA, Suitland, Md.

33. Balaban to Hopkins, August 8, 1940, ibid.

34. Diary (MS) August 27, 1940, Berle papers; Berle for FDR, August 28, 1940; and W. S. Van Dyke to Early, October 17, 1940, both in OF 73, all FDRL.

35. On Schenck's contributions see Rosten, *Hollywood*, p. 160. On efforts to intercede with the Justice Department see Diary (MS), March 8, 1941, Ickes papers, LC. Joseph Schenck was indicted for federal income tax evasion and

perjury in June 1940. His trial was postponed in October. See *New York Times* (June 4, 1940): 1:4; (October 3, 1940): 30:1. He went to prison in June 1942 and was paroled in October. See *New York Times* (June 24, 1942): 15:4; (October 24, 1942): 17:5.

36. See Rosten to Horton, August 17, 1940, Rosten fldr., entry 78, RG 44, NA, Suitland, Md.; "Hollywood in Uniform," *Fortune* (April 1942): 92-95ff.

37. Hollywood's lively concern for self-interest in cooperating with the government was suggested by the Truman Senate Special Committee to Investigate the National Defense Program and by the comments of officials who dealt with the studio movie makers. See Ceplair and Englund, *The Inquisition in Hollywood*, p. 178. Quote from George Schaefer is in "Report from Leo C. Rosten," attached to Rosten to Mellet, October 23, 1940, Rosten fldr., entry 78, RG 44, NA, Suitland, Md.

38. Rosten for Horton (and Mellett), September 5, 1940, Rosten fldr., entry 78, RG 44, NA, Suitland, Md. Rosten's background and efforts are mentioned in John Devine, "Washington Contact," *Public Opinion Quarterly*, 4 (December 1940): 686.

39. Rosten's thinking on government-Hollywood liaison is in his memo for Mellett, May 29, 1941. Hays' rejection of the idea and the suspicions he and other Hollywood leaders harbored concerning government propaganda designs and the New Deal slant thereto are discussed in "Report from Leo C. Rosten," October 23, 1940, both in Rosten fldr., entry 78, RG 44, NA, Suitland, Md. Marshall's support for Hays is in Marshall for Mellett, February 24, 1941, Walter Wanger fldr., entry 264, Records of the Office of War Information (OWI), RG 208, NA, Suitland, Md.

40. See "Hollywood in Uniform," pp. 92-95. Mellett's role as coordinator of government films is described in Mellett to Archibald MacLeish, December 12, 1941, Rosten fldr., entry 78, RG 44, NA, Suitland, Md.

41. Early for Missy (LeHand) (filed June 25, 1941), OF 73, FDRL. Douglas Fairbanks, Jr., told Early of his determination to make a film that was "quite frankly anti-Nazi and pro-Allies," and asked for some sort of White House endorsement. Early refused. See Fairbanks to Early, May 27, 1940, and reply June 1, 1940, both OF 73, FDRL.

42. Rosten to Horton, August 17, 1940, Rosten fldr., entry 78, RG 44, NA, Suitland, Md.

43. Ernst's efforts are described in correspondence among Ernst, Allen Rivken, and Eleanor Roosevelt, December 31, 1940, January 2, 7, 8, 13, February 6, 24, and March 25, 1941, in file "100," 1941-E fldr., Eleanor Roosevelt papers, FDRL. See also Ernst for FDR, December 18, 1940, and January 30, 1941, in PSF "Ernst," FDRL; and Mellett for FDR, December 23, 1940, White House—1940 fldr., Mellett papers, FDRL.

44. Ken D. Jones and Arthur F. McClure, *Hollywood at War: The American Motion Picture and World War II* (New York: Castle Books, 1973) provides

the essential facts on each of these films. Additional material is provided in an interesting introductory essay. For a similar discussion see Charles Higham and Joel Greenberg, *Hollywood in the Forties* (New York: A. S. Barnes & Co., 1968), pp. 86-103.

45. For a discussion of the *Great Dictator* and some of the other films mentioned here see Jacobs, "World War II and the American Film," pp. 5-9.

46. This discussion is based on film reviews by Phillip T. Hartung appearing in *Commonweal* from the fall of 1939 through the end of 1941.

47. Hollywood's difficulties with the British government and its efforts to improve its position in the British market are discussed in Moley, *Hays Office*, pp. 178-184. FDR's role in helping the industry secure release of a greater percentage of its frozen assets, and the attempts of rival factions within the industry to claim credit for the action are described in Zanuck to Early, November 28, 1941, Z—miscellaneous (misc.) fldr., "Correspondence" files, Early papers, FDRL.

48. *Flight Command* and other war-related movies are described in Philip T. Hartung, "Men Must Work, and Women Must Weep—and Work," *Commonweal* (January 24, 1941): 352.

49. The new militancy in films and *Sergeant York* are described in Jacobs, "World War II and American Film," pp. 10-11.

50. Mellett for FDR, March 17, 1941, White House—1941 fldr., Mellett papers, FDRL.

51. Margaret Frakes, "Why the Movie Investigation?" *Christian Century* (September 24, 1941): 1172-1174.

52. The large English contingent in Hollywood and its activities are described in Lavine and Wechsler, *War Propaganda and the US*, pp. 230-231; and Eric Cleugh (British Consul in Los Angeles), *Without Let or Hindrance: Reminiscences of a British Foreign Service Officer* (London: Cassell & Company Ltd., 1960), pp. 105-138.

53. Episode is discussed in Hays, *Memoirs*, pp. 538-539. Hays reiterated the industry's rejection of the propagandist's role in July. See "Film Propaganda Is Barred by Hays," *New York Times* (July 21, 1941): 17:4.

54. The Senate inquiry is discussed in Michele Flynn Stenehjem, *An American First: John T. Flynn and the America First Committee*, (New Rochelle, N.Y.: Arlington House, 1976), pp. 145-149. Flynn, an important isolationist spokesman, seems to have inspired the investigation. Ceplair and Englund, *The Inquisition in Hollywood*, pp. 159-161 describe the united stand taken by the Hollywood community and contrast it with its divided response to other political investigations.

55. Zanuck, along with the Warner brothers, and Wanger were contributors to the Fight for Freedom. See Mark L. Chadwin, *The Hawks of World War II* (Chapel Hill: University of North Carolina Press, 1968) pp. 64-65, 177-178, 216-218.

56. See Mellett for FDR, August 27, 1941, and Zanuck to Early, November 28, 1941, OF 73, FDRL.

57. See the extensive and hostile coverage given the Committee's efforts by the Luce publications: "Senate Isolationists Run Afoul of Willkie in Movie 'Warmonger' Hearings," *Life* (September 22, 1941): 21, 25; "Hollywood in Washington," *Time* (September 22, 1941): 13-14. Luce was both an interventionist and a supporter of the industry's attorney, Wendell Willkie.

58. For the reaction to the Lindbergh speech see Wayne S. Cole, *Charles A. Lindbergh and the Battle against American Intervention in World War II* (New York: Harcourt Brace Jovanovich, 1974), pp. 171-184.

59. One commentator saw the outcome of the hearings as a significant victory for Hollywood interventionists. "Indications are," she wrote, "that film producers will take heart from the general reaction to the congressional comedy and begin with renewed energies to deal with the realities of the world about. The recent purchase . . . of the anti-Nazi thriller *Above Suspicion*, and lively bidding for William Shirer's *Berlin Diary* lend support to this contention." Hermione Rich Isaacs, "Fact Is Stranger Than Fiction," *Theatre Arts* (December 1941): 881-885.

60. Various theories of movie influence are discussed in Franklin Fearing, "Influence of the Movies on Attitudes and Behavior," *Annals of the American Academy of Political and Social Sciences*, 254 (November 1947): 70-79.

61. "Studies in Radio and Film Propaganda," *Transactions of the New York Academy of Sciences*, series 2, vol. 6 (November 1943): 58-79. An alternative definition which insists on conscious motive as a necessary ingredient of propaganda is Leo C. Rosten, "Movies and Propaganda," *Annals of the American Academy of Political and Social Sciences*, 254 (November 1947): 116-124.

62. "Seldom did war films clarify any of the fundamental issues of the war or display our basic differences from the enemy in terms of ideals and philosophy. References to issues usually were generalities such as 'the fight for freedom' or a 'free world.' " Jones and McClure, *Hollywood at War*, p. 22.

63. Court proceedings in New York revealed that the heads of the International Alliance of Theatrical Stage Employees, Willie Bioff and George E. Browne, had received more than half a million dollars in bribes from major studio heads. Other movie problems included the scandalous conditions in labor relations, the attempts of the studios to secure release of their frozen assets in Great Britain, and, ultimately, the industry's access to film and other vital supplies under conditions of intensifying shortage of strategic materials.

CONCLUSION

1. "Government Propaganda," *Atlantic Monthly* (September 1941): 313-314.

2. See Jacques Ellul, *The Technological Society*, trans. John Wilkinson (New York: Alfred A. Knopf, 1964), p. 366.

3. A mid-November 1941 Cantril survey asked if Americans favored sending a large American army to Europe should this become necessary to defeat Germany: 47 percent said yes; 44 percent, no; the rest were undecided. Asked if they favored a congressional resolution declaring a state of war with Germany, 61 percent opposed such a move. See Cantril to Rosenberg, November 17, 1941, in Official File 3618, FDR Library. This result was probably low. Negative responses during 1941 ranged between 75 and 80 percent according to William Langer and S. Everett Gleason, *The Undeclared War, 1940-1941* (New York: Harper & Brothers, 1953), p. 732. The overwhelming approval of measures that risked war and the refusal to approve a declaration of war may be reconciled by a widespread faith in British survival without the need for American military assistance. On the eve of Pearl Harbor, polling revealed that 72.5 percent expected Great Britain to win the war, while only 7 percent expected Germany to win. See results of *Fortune* poll in *Time* (December 1, 1941): 17-18. For a summary of the foreign policy debate see Richard W. Steele, "The Great Debate: Roosevelt, the Media, and the Coming of the War, 1940-1941," *Journal of American History* 71 (June 1984): 69-92.

Bibliography

MANUSCRIPT COLLECTIONS

Broadcast Pioneers Library, National Association of Broadcasters, Washington, D.C.
  Miller, Neville (interview)
  Wheeler, Burton, K. (interview)
Columbia University Library
  Fly, James Lawrence
  Poletti, Charles (Herbert Lehman Collection)
Library of Congress
  Berge, Wendell
  Ickes, Harold
  MacLeish, Archibald
  Patterson, Robert
Mass Communications History Center, State Historical Society of Wisconsin, Madison
  Barton, Bruce
  National Broadcasting Company
Franklin D. Roosevelt Library, Hyde Park, New York
  Berle, Adolf
  Biddle, Francis
  Cox, Oscar
  Coy, Wayne
  Early, Stephen T.
  Franklin D. Roosevelt Memorial Foundation
  Hopkins, Harry

Howe, Louis
Mellett, Lowell
Morgenthau, Henry, Jr.
Roosevelt, Eleanor
Roosevelt, Franklin D.
Rosenman, Samuel I.
Smith, Harold D.
New York City Municipal Archive
  La Guardia, Fiorello H.
New York Public Library
  Pope, Arthur U.
  Thomas, Norman
  Uncensored
University of Iowa, Iowa City
  Wallace, Henry A.
University of Wyoming, Laramie
  Arnold, Thurman
  Munson, Edward L.
Yale University Library, New Haven, Connecticut
  Stimson, Henry L.

GOVERNMENT DOCUMENTS

Office of Government Reports, Record Group 44, National Archives, Suitland, Maryland
Office of War Information, Record Group 208, National Archives, Suitland, Maryland
War Department, General and Special Staffs, Record Group 165, National Archives, Washington, D.C.
War Department, Office of the Secretary of War, Record Group 107, National Archives, Washington, D.C.

PUBLISHED DOCUMENTS AND PAPERS

Berle, Adolf A. *Navigating the Rapids 1918-1971: From the Papers of Adolf A. Berle.* Ed. Beatrice Bishop Berle and Travis Beal Jacobs. New York: Harcourt Brace Jovanovich, 1973.
Congress, United States. *Hearings of the Joint Committee on the Investigation of the Pearl Harbor Attack*, 79th Congress, 1st and 2nd sessions. 39 volumes. Washington, D.C.: U.S. Government Printing Office, 1946.
Ickes, Harold L. *The Secret Diary of Harold L. Ickes.* 3 volumes. New York: Simon and Schuster, 1953-1954.

Roosevelt, Franklin D. *The Complete Presidential Press Conferences of Franklin D. Roosevelt*, with an introduction by Jonathan Daniels. 25 volumes
in 12. New York: Da Capo Press, 1972.
Rosenman, Samuel I., comp. *The Public Papers and Addresses of Franklin D.
Roosevelt*. 13 vols. New York: Random House, Macmillan Company,
Harper & Brothers, 1938-1950.
Stevenson, Adlai E. *The Papers of Adlai E. Stevenson*, Ed. Walter Johnson
and Carol Evans. 8 volumes. Boston: Little Brown and Company, 1972-
1978.

ARTICLES

Angell, James R. "The Civilian Morale Agency." *Annals of the American
Academy of Political and Social Sciences*, 220 (March 1942): 160-167.
"Antitrust Scenario." *Business Week* (September 6, 1941): 32.
"Arnold Scorns Movie Code." *Business Week* (August 26, 1939): 43.
Berchtold, William E. "Press Agents of the New Deal." *New Outlook*, 164
(July 1934): 23-31.
Brady, Robert A. "The Problem of Monopoly." *Annals of the American Acad-
emy of Political and Social Sciences*, 254 (November 1947): 125-136.
Broughton, Philip S. "Government Agencies and Civilian Morale." *Annals of
the American Academy of Political and Social Sciences*, 220 (March
1942): 168-177.
Butow, Robert J. C. "The FDR Tapes." *American Heritage*, 33 (February/
March 1982): 8-24.
Cantril, Hadley. "Public Opinion in Flux." *Annals of the American Academy
of Political and Social Sciences*, 220 (March 1942): 136-152.
Carlisle, R. "W. R. Hearst and the International Crisis 1936-41." *Journal of
Contemporary History*, 9 (July 1974): 217-277.
Catledge, Turner. "Federal Bureau for Press Urged." *New York Times* (De-
cember 29, 1936): 1, 4.
Clapper, Raymond, "Why Reporters Like Roosevelt." *Review of Reviews* (June
1934): 14-17.
Clark, Delbert, " 'Steve' Takes Care of It." *New York Times Magazine* (July
27, 1941): 11ff.
Creel, George. "Propaganda and Morale." *American Journal of Sociology*,
vol. 47, no. 3 (November 1941): 340-351.
Davenport, Walter. "The President and the Press." *Collier's* (January 27,
1945): 12, 46.
———. "You Can't Say That!" *Collier's* (February 15, 1941): 19, 65.
Doenecke, Justus. "Non-Interventionism of the Left: The Keep America Out
of War Congress, 1938-41." *Journal of Contemporary History*, 12
(1977): 221-236.

Doob, Leonard W. "Some Attitudes Underlying American Participation in War." *Journal of Social Psychology*, 13 (May 1941): 475-87.

De Voto, Bernard. "Report on the Summer Quarter." *Harper's Magazine* (November 1941): 669-672.

Ernst, Morris. "Super Colossal: The Movies." *Atlantic Monthly* (July 1940): 17-28.

Fearing, Franklin. "Influence of the Movies on Attitudes and Behavior." *Annals of the American Academy of Political and Social Sciences*, 254 (November 1947): 70-79.

Frakes, Margaret. "Why the Movie Investigation?" *Christian Century* (September 24, 1941): 1172-1174.

Friedrich, C. K., and E. Sternberg. "Congress and the Control of Radio Broadcasting." *American Political Science Review*, 37 (October 1943): 797-818.

Gravelee, Jack. "Stephen T. Early: The 'Advance Man.' " *Speech Monographs*, 30 (March 19, 1963): 41-49.

Haines, Gerald K. "American Myopia and the Japanese Monroe Doctrine, 1931-41." *Prologue*, 13 (Summer 1981): 101-114.

Hartung, Philip T. "Men Must Work, and Women Must Weep—And Work." *Commonweal* (January 1941): 352-353.

High, Stanley. "You Can't Beat the Government." *Saturday Evening Post* (November 20, 1937): 5-7ff.

"Hollywood in Uniform." *Fortune* (April 1942): 92-95ff.

"Hollywood in Washington." *Time* (September 22, 1941): p. 13.

Isaacs, Hermione R. "Fact Is Stranger Than Fiction." *Theatre Arts Monthly* (December 1941): 881-885.

Jacobs, Lewis. "World War II and the American Film." *Cinema Journal*, 7 (Winter 1967-1968): 1-21.

Jensen, Richard. "Public Opinion Polls: Early Problems of Method and Philosophy." Paper read at Oxford Conference on the History and Theory of the Social Sciences, July 23, 1977, Oxford, England.

Jones, Alfred Haworth. "The Making of an Interventionist on the Air: Elmer Davis and CBS News, 1939-1941." *Pacific Historical Review*, 42 (February 1973): 74-93.

Kempton, Murray. "Winners and Losers at the 'Times.' " *New York Review of Books* (September 25, 1980): 30-32.

Krock, Arthur A. "Press vs. Government—A Warning." *Public Opinion Quarterly*, 1 (April 1937): 45-49.

———. "The Tendency to Cover Up Legitimate News." *New York Times* (October 13, 1939): 22.

Landis, James M. "Morale and Civilian Defense." *The American Journal of Sociology*, vol. 47, no. 3 (November 1941): 331-339.

Larson, Cedric. "Publicity for National Defense—How It Works." *Journalism Quarterly*, 18 (September 1941): 245-255.

Lazarsfeld, Paul F., and Robert K. Merton. "Studies in Radio and Film Propaganda." *Transactions of the New York Academy of Sciences*, series 2, vol. 6 (November 1943): 58-79.

McMillan, George E. "Government Publicity and the Impact of War." *Public Opinion Quarterly*, 5 (Fall 1941): 383-398.

Mellett, Lowell. "Government Propaganda." *Atlantic Monthly* (September 1941): 313-314.

————. "The Office of Government Reports." *Public Administration Review*, 1 (Winter 1941): 126-131.

Mercey, Arch. "Films by American Governments: The United States." *Films* (Summer 1940): 5-20.

————. "Modernizing Federal Publicity." *Public Opinion Quarterly*, 1 (July 1937): 87-94.

Mock, James R., and Cedric Larson. "Public Relations of the U.S. Army." *Public Opinion Quarterly*, 5 (June 1941): 275-282.

"Movies Arbitrate." *Business Week* (November 2, 1940): 15.

Odegard, Peter H., and Alan Barth. "Millions for Defense." *Public Opinion Quarterly*, 5 (Fall 1941): 399-411.

Odlum, Floyd B. "Financial Organization of the Motion Picture Industry." *Annals of the American Academy of Political and Social Sciences*, 254 (November 1947): 18-25.

Park, Robert E. "Morale and the News." *The American Journal of Sociology*, 42 (November 1941): 360-377.

"Pass the Neely Bill!" *Christian Century* (February 21, 1940): 240.

Rogers, Lindsay. "Do the Gallup Polls Measure Opinion?" *Harper's Magazine* (November 1941): 623-632.

Rosten, Leo C. "Movies and Propaganda." *Annals of the American Academy of Political and Social Sciences*, 254 (November 1947): 116-124.

Ruetten, Richard T. "Burton K. Wheeler and the Montana Experience." *Montana: The Magazine of Western History*, 27 (Summer 1977): 2-19.

Sandeen, Eric J. "Anti-Nazi Sentiment in the Film: *Confessions of a Nazi Spy* and the German American Bund." *American Studies*, 20 (Fall 1979): 69-81.

Saunders, D. A. "The Failure of Propaganda and What to Do About It." *Harper's Magazine* (November 1941): 648-654.

Sayre, Jeanette. "Radio: Congress Has an Inning." *Public Opinion Quarterly*, 5 (June 1941): 303.

Selden, Walter. "Movies and Propaganda." *Forum* (April 1940): 209-213.

"Senate Isolationists Run Afoul of Willkie in Movie 'Warmonger' Hearings." *Life* (September 22, 1941): 21-25.

Shils, Edward A. "A Note on Governmental Research on Attitudes and Morale." *American Journal of Sociology*, 47 (November 1941): 472-480.

Sondren, Frederic Jr., with C. Nelson Schrader. "Hollywood Handles Dynamite." *Commonweal* (December 12, 1941): 195-197.

Steele, Richard W. "American Popular Opinion and the War against Germany: The Issue of Negotiated Peace, 1942." *The Journal of American History*, 65 (December 1978): 704-723.

————. "Franklin D. Roosevelt and His Foreign Policy Critics." *Political Science Quarterly*, 94 (Spring 1979): 15-32.

————. "Preparing the Public for War: Efforts to Establish a National Propaganda Agency, 1940-41." *American Historical Review*, 75 (October 1970): 1640-1653.

————. "The Great Debate: Roosevelt, the Media, and the Coming of the War, 1940-1941," *Journal of American History*, 71 (June 1984): 69-92.

————. "The Pulse of the People: Franklin D. Roosevelt and the Gauging of American Public Opinion." *Journal of Contemporary History*, 9 (October 1974): 195-216.

————. "Stephen T. Early," in *Dictionary of American Biography*, supplement 5, 1951-1955, John A. Garraty, ed. (New York: Charles Scribner's Sons, 1977), pp. 196-197.

Strout, Richard L. " 'Raw Deal': A Review of Graham J. White, *FDR and the Press.*" *Columbia Journalism Review* (July/August 1979): 68-69.

Twohey, James S. "An Analysis of Newspaper Opinion on War Issues." *Public Opinion Quarterly*, 5 (Fall 1941): 448-455.

Ward, Paul W. "Scandal in the Air." *Nation* (April 24, 1937): 455-456.

Whitney, Simon N. "The Impact of Antitrust Laws: Vertical Disintegration in the Motion Picture Industry." *American Economic Review*, 45 (May 1955): 491-498.

"Wide Scope of U.S. Anti-monopoly Suit against Movie Moguls Jolts Hollywood." *Newsweek* (August 1, 1938): 18.

Winfield, Betty Houchin. "The New Deal Publicity Operation: Foundation for the Modern Presidency." *Journalism Quarterly*, 61 (Spring 1984): 40-48ff.

Young, William R. "Academics and Social Scientists versus the Press: The Policies of the Bureau of Public Information and the Wartime Information Board, 1939 to 1945." In *Historical Papers/Communications Historiques: A Selection from the Papers Presented at the Annual Meeting, London, 1978*. Ontario, Canada: Canadian Historical Association, 1978.

BOOKS

Alexander, Charles C. *Nationalism in American Thought, 1930-1945*. Chicago: Rand McNally & Company, 1969.

American Society of Newspaper Editors. *Proceedings of the Nineteenth Annual Convention, American Society of Newspaper Editors*. N.p., 1941.

Bailey, Thomas A., and Paul B. Ryan. *Hitler vs. Roosevelt: The Undeclared Naval War*. New York: Free Press, 1979.

Balfour, Michael. *Propaganda in War, 1939-1945: Organizations, Policies and Publics in Britain and Germany*. Boston: Routledge & Kegan Paul, 1979.

Barnouw, Erik. *A History of Broadcasting in the United States*. Vol. 2, *The Golden Web 1933-1953*. New York: Oxford University Press, 1968.

Bayor, Ronald H. *Neighbors in Conflict: The Irish, Germans, Jews and Italians of New York City, 1929-1941*. Baltimore: Johns Hopkins University Press, 1978.

Beard, Charles A. *President Roosevelt and the Coming of the War, 1941: A Study in Appearances and Realities*. New Haven, Conn.: Yale University Press, 1948.

Beard, Charles A., and Mary R. Beard. *The Rise of American Civilization*. 3 vols; New York: Macmillan Company, 1939. Vol. 3, *America in Midpassage*.

Blum, John Morton. *V Was for Victory: Politics and American Culture during World War II*. New York: Harcourt Brace Jovanovich, 1976.

Brownlow, Louis. *The Autobiography of Louis Brownlow*. 2 vols; Chicago: University of Chicago Press, 1958. Vol. 2, *A Passion for Anonymity*.

Butler, J. R. M. *Lord Lothian (Philip Kerr), 1882-1940*. London: Macmillan & Co. Ltd., 1960.

Cantril, Hadley. *The Human Dimension: Experiences in Policy Research*. New Brunswick, N.J.: Rutgers University Press, 1967.

Carter, John F. *Power and Persuasion*. New York: Duell, Sloan & Pearce, 1960.

Catledge, Turner. *My Life and the Times*. New York: Harper & Row, 1971.

Catton, Bruce. *The War Lords of Washington*. New York: Harcourt, Brace and Company, 1948.

Ceplair, Larry, and Steven Englund. *The Inquisition in Hollywood: Politics in the Film Community, 1930-1960*. Garden City, N.Y.: Anchor Press/ Doubleday, 1980.

Chadwin, Mark Lincoln. *The Hawks of World War II*. Chapel Hill: University of North Carolina Press, 1968.

deChambrun, Rene. *I Saw France Fall: Will She Rise Again?* New York: William Morrow and Company, 1940.

Chenery, William L. *So It Seemed*. New York: Harcourt, Brace, 1952.

Chester, Edward W. *Radio, Television and American Politics*. New York: Sheed and Ward, 1969.

Clark, Delbert. *Washington Dateline*. New York: Frederick A. Stokes Co., 1941.

Cleugh, Eric. *Without Let or Hindrance: Reminiscences of a British Foreign Service Officer*. London: Cassell & Company Ltd., 1960.

Cole, Wayne S. *Charles A. Lindbergh and the Battle against American Intervention in World War II*. New York: Harcourt Brace Jovanovich, 1974.

Conant, Michael. *Antitrust in Motion Picture Industry: Economic and Legal Analysis*. Berkeley: University of California Press, 1960.

220   Bibliography

Cooper, Kent. *Kent Cooper and the Associated Press: An Autobiography*. New York: Random House, 1959.

Cornwell, Elmer E., Jr. *Presidential Leadership of Public Opinion*. Bloomington: Indiana University Press, 1965.

Culbert, David Holbrook. *News for Everyman: Radio and Foreign Affairs in Thirties America*. Westport, Conn.: Greenwood Press, 1976.

Dallek, Robert. *Franklin D. Roosevelt and American Foreign Policy, 1932-1945*. New York: Oxford University Press, 1979.

Davis, Kenneth S. *FDR: The Beckoning of Destiny, 1882-1928*. New York: Putnam, 1971.

De Jong, Louis. *The German Fifth Column in the Second World War*. Trans. C. M. Geyl. Chicago: University of Chicago Press, 1956.

Diamond, Sander T. *The Nazi Movement in the United States, 1924-1941*. Ithaca, N.Y.: Cornell University Press, 1974.

Edwards, Jerome E. *The Foreign Policy of Col. McCormick's Tribune, 1929-1941*. Reno: University of Nevada Press, 1971.

Ellul, Jacques. *Propaganda: The Formation of Men's Attitudes*. Trans. Konrad Kellen and Jean Lerner. New York: Alfred A. Knopf, 1965.

———. *The Technological Society*. Trans. John Wilkinson. New York: Alfred A. Knopf, 1964.

Elson, Robert T. *The World of Time Inc.: The Intimate History of a Publishing Enterprise 1941-1960*. New York: Atheneum, 1973.

Farley, James A. *Behind the Ballots*. New York: Harcourt, Brace and Company, 1938.

Farrago, Ladislas. *The Game of the Foxes: The Untold Story of German Espionage in the United States and Great Britain During World War II*. New York: David McKay and Company, 1971.

Fielding, Raymond. *The American Newsreel, 1911-1967*. Norman: University of Oklahoma Press, 1972.

———. *The March of Time, 1935-1951*. New York: Oxford University Press, 1978.

Fisher, Charles. *The Columnists*. New York: Howell, Soskin, 1944.

Gottlieb, Robert, and Irene Wolt. *Thinking Big: The Story of the Los Angeles Times, Its Publishers and Their Influence on Southern California*. New York: G. P. Putnam's Sons, 1977.

Hays, Will H. *The Memoirs of Will H. Hays*. Garden City, N.Y.: Doubleday & Company, Inc., 1955.

High, Stanley. *Roosevelt—And Then?* New York: Harper & Brothers, 1937.

Higham, Charles, and Joel Greenberg. *Hollywood in the Forties*. New York: A. S. Barnes & Co., 1968.

Hilderbrand, Robert C. *Power and the People: Executive Management of Public Opinion in Foreign Affairs, 1897-1921*. Chapel Hill: University of North Carolina Press, 1981.

Howe, Quincy. *The News and How to Understand It*. New York: Simon and Schuster, 1940.

Hyde, H. Montgomery. *Room 3603: The Story of the British Intelligence Center in New York during World War II*. New York: Farrar, Straus and Co., 1962.

Ickes, Harold L. *America's House of Lords: An Inquiry into the Freedom of the Press*. New York: Harcourt, Brace and Co., 1939.

Jacobs, Lewis. *The Rise of the American Film: A Critical History*. New York: Harcourt, Brace and Company, 1939.

Janeway, Eliot. *The Struggle for Survival*. Vol. 53, *The Chronicles of America Series*. Allan Nevins, ed. New Haven, Conn.: Yale University Press, 1951; Reprint ed. New York: Weybright and Talley, 1968.

Johl, Max G. *The United States Commemorative Stamps of the Twentieth Century*. 2 vols. New York: H. L. Lindquist, 1947. Vol. 2, 1935-1947.

Johnson, Walter. *The Battle against Isolation*. Chicago: University of Chicago Press, 1944. New York: Da Capo Press, Inc., 1973.

Jonas, Manfred. *Isolationism in America, 1935-1941*. Ithaca, N.Y.: Cornell University Press, 1966.

Jones, Ken D., and Arthur F. McClure. *Hollywood at War: The American Motion Picture and World War II*. New York: Castle Books, 1973.

Kahn, David. *Hitler's Spies: German Military Intelligence in World War II*. New York: Macmillan Publishing Co., 1978.

Kennedy, David M. *Over Here: The First World War and American Society*. New York: Oxford University Press, 1980.

Klurfeld, Herman. *Winchell: His Life and Times*. New York: Praeger Publishers, 1976.

Krock, Arthur. *Memoirs: Sixty Years on the Firing Line*. New York: Funk & Wagnalls, 1968.

Lambert, Gerard B. *All Out of Step*. Garden City, N.Y.: Doubleday and Co., 1956.

Langer, William L., and S. Everett Gleason. *The Challenge to Isolation, 1937–1940*. New York: Harper & Brothers, 1952.

――――. *The Undeclared War, 1940-1941*. New York: Harper & Brothers, 1953.

Lash, Joseph P. *Roosevelt and Churchill, 1939-1941: The Partnership That Saved the West*. New York: W. W. Norton & Company, 1976.

Lasswell, Harold D. *Propaganda Techniques in the World War*. New York: Alfred A. Knopf, 1927.

Lavine, Harold, and James Wechsler. *War Propaganda and the United States*. Published for the Institute of Propaganda Analysis. New Haven, Conn.: Yale University Press, 1940.

McCamy, James L. *Government Publicity: Its Practice in Federal Administration*. Chicago: University of Chicago Press, 1939.

MacCann, Richard Dyer. *The People's Films: A Political History of U.S. Government Motion Pictures*. New York: Hastings House, 1973.

Mangione, Jerre G. *An Ethnic at Large: A Memoir of America in the Thirties and Forties*. New York: G. P. Putnam's Sons, 1978.

Marbut, F. B. *News from the Capital: The Story of Washington Reporting*. Carbondale: Southern Illinois University Press, 1971.

Michael, George. *Handout*. New York: G. P. Putnam's Sons, 1935.

Michelson, Charles. *The Ghost Talks*. G. P. Putnam's Sons, 1944.

Mock, James R., and Cedric Larson. *Words That Won the War: The Story of the Committee on Public Information, 1917-1919*. Princeton, N.J.: Princeton University Press, 1939.

Moley, Raymond. *After Seven Years*. New York: Harper & Brothers, 1939.

———. *The Hays Office*. Indianapolis: Bobbs-Merrill Company, 1945.

Morison, Samuel Eliot. *History of United States Naval Operations in World War II*. 15 vols. Boston: Little Brown and Company, 1947-1964. Vol. 1, *The Battle of the Atlantic, September 1939–May 1943*.

Neustadt, Richard. *Presidential Power*. New York: John Wiley & Sons, 1960.

Patterson, James T. *Congressional Conservatism and the New Deal: The Growth of the Conservative Coalition Congress, 1933-1939*. Lexington: University of Kentucky Press, 1967.

Phillips, Cabell, et al. *Dateline: Washington—The Story of National Affairs Journalism in the Life and Times of the National Press Club*. Garden City, N.Y.: Doubleday & Company, 1949.

Pollard, James E. *The Presidents and the Press*. New York: Macmillan Company, 1947.

Radosh, Ronald. *Prophets on the Right: Profiles of Conservative Critics of American Globalism*. New York: Simon and Schuster, 1975.

Reynolds, David. *The Creation of the Anglo-American Alliance 1937-1941: A Study in Competitive Cooperation*. Chapel Hill: University of North Carolina Press, 1982.

Roberts, Chalmers M. *The Washington Post: The First 100 Years*. Boston: Houghton Mifflin Company, 1977.

Robinson, Thomas Porter. *Radio Networks and the Federal Government*. New York: Columbia University Press, 1943.

Rollins, Alfred B., Jr. *Roosevelt and Howe*. New York: Alfred A. Knopf, 1962.

Rosenman, Samuel I. *Working with Roosevelt*. London: Rupert Hart-Davis, 1952.

Rosten, Leo C. *Hollywood: The Movie Colony, the Movie Makers*. New York: Harcourt, Brace, and Company, 1941.

———. *The Washington Correspondents*. New York: Harcourt, Brace and Company, 1937.

Rotha, Paul. *Documentary Film*. London: Faber and Faber Ltd., 1952.

Rupp, Leila J. *Mobilizing Women for War, German and American Propaganda, 1939-1945*. Princeton, N.J.: Princeton University Press, 1978.

Schoenherr, Steven E. "Selling the New Deal: Stephen T. Early's Role as Press Secretary to Franklin D. Roosevelt." Ph.D. dissertation, University of Delaware, 1976.

Schroeder, Paul W. *The Axis Alliance and Japanese-American Relations, 1941*, Ithaca, N.Y.: Cornell University Press, 1958.

Schudson, Michael. *Discovering the News: A Social History of American Newspapers*. New York: Basic Books Inc., 1978.

Seldes, George. *Lords of the Press*. New York: Julian Messner, 1938.

Sherwood, Robert E. *Roosevelt and Hopkins: An Intimate History*. New York: Harper & Brothers, 1948.

Smith, Geoffrey S. *To Save A Nation: American Counter-subversives, the New Deal, and the Coming of World War II*. New York: Basic Books, 1972.

Snyder, Robert L. *Pare Lorentz and the Documentary Film*. Norman: University of Oklahoma Press, 1968.

Steele, Richard W. *The First Offensive, 1942: Roosevelt, Marshall and the Making of American Strategy*. Bloomington: Indiana University Press, 1973.

Stenehjem, Michele Flynn. *An American First: John T. Flynn and the America First Committee*. New Rochelle, N.Y.: Arlington House, 1976.

Stern, J. David. *Memoirs of a Maverick Publisher*. New York: Simon and Schuster, 1962.

Stimson, Henry L., and McGeorge Bundy. *On Active Service in Peace and War*. New York: Harper & Brothers, 1947.

Summers, Harrison B., comp. *The Reference Shelf*. Vol. 12, *Radio Censorship*. New York: H. W. Wilson Company, 1939.

Swing, Raymond. *"Good Evening!" A Professional Memoir by Raymond Swing*. New York: Harcourt, Brace & World, 1964.

Thomas, Bob. *Winchell*. Garden City, N.Y.: Doubleday & Company, 1971.

Thorpe, Margaret Farrand. *America at the Movies*. New Haven, Conn.: Yale University Press, 1939.

Tully, Grace. *F. D. R.: My Boss*. New York: Charles Scribner's Sons, 1949.

The United States at War: Development and Administration of the War Program by the Federal Government. Washington, D.C.: U.S. Government Printing Office, 1946.

Vanderwood, Paul J., ed. *Juarez* (1983). In *Wisconsin/Warner Brothers Screenplay Series*. Ed. Tino Balio. Madison: University of Wisconsin Press, 1979-

Vaughn, Stephen. *Holding Fast the Inner Lines: Democracy, Nationalism, and the Committee on Public Information*. Chapel Hill: University of North Carolina Press, 1980.

Waldrop, Frank C. *McCormick of Chicago: An Unconventional Portrait of a Controversial Figure*. Englewood Cliffs, N.J.: Prentice-Hall, 1966. Reprint ed., Westport, Conn.: Greenwood Press, 1975.

Warner, Jack L., with Dean Jennings. *My First Hundred Years in Hollywood.* New York: Random House, 1965.

Wedemeyer, Albert C. *Wedemeyer Reports!* New York: Henry Holt & Co., 1958.

Wheeler, Burton K., with Paul F. Healy. *Yankee from the West.* Garden City, N.Y.: Doubleday & Co., 1962.

White, Graham J. *FDR and the Press.* Chicago: University of Chicago Press, 1979.

White, Llewellyn. *The American Radio: A Report on the Broadcasting Industry in the United States from the Commission on Freedom of the Press.* Chicago: University of Chicago Press, 1947.

Winchell, Walter, with an introduction by Ernest Cuneo. *Winchell Exclusive.* Englewood Cliffs, N.J.: Prentice-Hall, 1975.

Winkler, Allan M. *The Politics of Propaganda: The Office of War Information, 1942-1945.* New Haven, Conn.: Yale University Press, 1978.

Wise, David. *The Politics of Lying: Government Deception, Secrecy and Power.* New York: Random House, 1973.

Index

About the Author

RICHARD W. STEELE is Professor of History at San Diego State University. He is the author of *The First Offensive, 1942: Roosevelt, Marshall and the Making of American Strategy* as well as numerous articles in the *Journal of American History*, the *American Historical Review*, and *Political Science Quarterly*.